High-Technology Entrepreneurship

With the global economy in a precarious position, nurturing new entre-preneurial high-technology firms is likely to comprise a key component of any policy to encourage economic growth, in both developed and developing countries. Recent high-technology ventures – such as retailing in the music industry – have shown how entrepreneurs can radically change, or even replace, existing industries.

High-Technology Entrepreneurship introduces and analyses all the major aspects of high-technology small-firm formation and growth. Locational and functional aspects of the process, as well as how contexts for develop-ment may vary between developed and developing economies, are also discussed. Other key topics that are addressed include:

- How high-technology firms originate in theory and practice
- Entrepreneurship theory
- Incubators, science parks and clustering
- Entrepreneurial strategy and finance.

Students taking undergraduate and Master's-level courses in entre-preneurship, technology, innovation, academic enterprise and industrial development will find this an essential textbook for completing their studies.

Ray Oakey is Professor of Business Development at the University of Manchester, UK. His research interests include the problems of innovation and growth in high-technology industry in general, and high-technology small firms in particular, at both UK national and international levels. He is the author of *High-Technology Small Firms* (Frances Pinter Publishing, 1984) and *High-Technology New Firms: Variable Barriers to Growth* (Paul Chapman Publishing, 1995).

High-Technology Entrepreneurship

Ray Oakey

Routledge
Taylor & Francis Group

LONDON AND NEW YORK

First published 2012
by Routledge
2 Park Square, Milton Park, Abingdon, Oxon, OX14 4RN

Simultaneously published in the USA and Canada
by Routledge
711 Third Avenue, New York, NY 10017

Routledge is an imprint of the Taylor & Francis Group, an informa business

British Library Cataloguing in Publication Data
A catalogue record for this book is available from the British Library.

Library of Congress Cataloging in Publication Data
Oakey, R. P. (Raymond P.)
    High-technology entrepreneurship/Ray Oakey.
    p. cm.
    Includes bibliographical references and index.
    1. High technology industries.   2. Small business.   3. Technological
    innovations – Economic aspects.   4. Entrepreneurship.   I. Title.
    HC79.H53O148 2012
    338'.04 – dc23   2011043841

ISBN: 978-0-415-59392-2 (hbk)
ISBN: 978-0-415-59393-9 (pbk)
ISBN: 978-0-203-12075-0 (ebk)

Typeset in Times New Roman
by Florence Production Ltd, Stoodleigh, Devon

MIX
Paper from
responsible sources
FSC
www.fsc.org   FSC® C018575

Printed and bound in Great Britain by MPG Printgroup

Contents

List of figures

1 Introduction

1.1 The rise of the high-technology small firm

Although the high-technology small firm (HTSF) has become a key part of the contemporary industrial scene throughout the developed world, the origins of this size and type of industrial enterprise are difficult to fix. However, it is clear that much of the stimulus for the emergence of this technologically sophisticated small firm must partly stem from the spontaneous development, in the United States, of the high-technology industrial clusters in Silicon Valley south of San Francisco in California, and around the Massachusetts Institute of Technology (MIT) on Route 128 in the suburbs of Boston. Worldwide interest in these developments occurred suddenly during the late 1970s and early 1980s and, although this was a frenetic period when the industrial growth potential of such focussed developments began to become clear, in both these cluster cases, growth had not been achieved overnight, but had been a gradual process over several decades.

The growth of these clusters was nurtured after the Second World War by the huge Keynesian-type public sector defence spending of the United States government in the 1950s and 1960s that funded the development of a series of progressively smaller semiconductor-based technical inventions, initially for military purposes. This was followed in the 1970s by extensive civil commercial applications of this technology based on the silicon chip (Saxenien 1985; Roberts 1991; Cardullo 1999). However, during the almost hysterical rush to *replicate* these high-technology clusters in Europe, the long development periods involved in the growth of such high-technology clusters were overlooked; and rather simplistically, many industrial planners throughout the developed and developing world assumed that, because they had become aware of these developments 'overnight', the clusters had suddenly emerged overnight, and, perhaps more seriously damaging for subsequent development planning, could be replicated virtually overnight. This was a misconception that has bedevilled

HTSF development policy outside the United States since the 1980s, a topic discussed in greater detail below in this chapter, and in other parts of this book.

The extent to which both academics and politicians in Europe were unaware of high-technology industrial developments in the United States was brought into sharp focus by a television programme. In 1978, the BBC's *Horizon* documentary series produced perhaps one of its most effective investigations, entitled 'Now the chips are down', in which the growing threat posed by the new silicon chip technology to many traditional industries was foreshadowed. This programme began a debate in the United Kingdom on how the growth achieved in the United States in Silicon Valley and elsewhere might be emulated by British industry. The discussion was heavily influenced by consideration of the role of entrepreneurial HTSFs in inventing, developing and finding markets for key new products (e.g. desktop computers, word processors), and of the venture capitalists who were funding such enterprises (Cooper 1970; Roberts 1991). This rise of interest in HTSFs was assisted by related work on small and medium-sized enterprises (SMEs) that was also emerging in the late 1970s. In particular, work by David Birch (1979) in the United States and by Fothergill and Gudgin (1979) and David Storey (1982) in the United Kingdom emphasized the role played by small firms, both in terms of the individual growth that could be achieved by fast-growing 'winner' small firms that individually grow large, and through the longer-term impressive growth that new and existing small firms can achieve in aggregate within local, regional and national economies. This enthusiasm for small firms in general, and HTSFs in particular, by politicians was partly caused by a realization that well-established large firms located in developed countries had become largely multinational in scope, and consequently operated beyond the control of national governments. However, in addition, Western developed economies were coming under increasing pressure from emerging industrial nations in South East Asia (especially Japan) in sectors such as motor vehicles, machine tools and consumer electronics (Oakey 1991). HTSFs were seen as particularly attractive vehicles for both aggregate and individual strong employment growth to replace these declining traditional manufacturing sectors, a view largely based on impressive but limited evidence of employment growth from United States high-technology clusters (Cooper 1970; Morse 1976).

1.1.1 Positive aspects of HTSF development

However, from the outset, thinking on the attributes of HTSFs was based on a mixture of myths and realities, as previously noted by other authors

(Massey *et al.* 1992). One problem with assessing the growth potential of entrepreneurially led HTSFs was a difficulty shared with assessing the impact of entrepreneurship in general, in that spectacular and rare successes that are, in fact, exceptions, often become accepted as 'the rule' by media journalists and politicians. Probably the best example of this phenomenon was that of Steve Jobs and Steve Wozniak – founders of Apple Computers. While it remains possible for new entrepreneurs to begin a garage-based business in a high-technology sector and grow it into a world-class company, substantial evidence on the extent to which new HTSFs fail, sell out, or are acquired by large multinational firms indicates that, in general, the Apple Computers 'story' is atypical (Oakey 1993). Nonetheless, despite over-optimism in the early days of the HTSF boom in the late 1970s and early 1980s regarding the potential for spectacular entrepreneurial growth of the 'Apple' type, it remains clear that, both individually and in aggregate, HTSFs – especially when located in successful clusters – have the potential to grow relatively fast and create substantial employment. Moreover, the jobs created by these firms, whether blue- or white-collar, tend to be skilled, relatively highly paid, and long lasting.

There is also substantial evidence to indicate that HTSFs are highly efficient when it comes to industrial invention and innovation. This 'small-firm' environment, in which there is little spatial or organizational distance between key actors in the invention or innovation process, ensures that specialist teams can work together as a close-knit group to bring new products to the customer. In particular, the links between research and development (R&D), production and marketing in HTSFs are often very close and productive (Rothwell and Zegveld 1982; Oakey 1991). The proof of this assertion lies in the fact that many large firms set up HTSF subsidiaries, or take equity stakes in existing HTSFs, in order to benefit from this highly productive and efficient environment, which, importantly, is largely free from the constraints upon R&D workers in large firms, where organizational and physical distances are often large and bureaucracy is obstructive. However, as will be detailed in a number of chapters below, although R&D in HTSFs may be efficient, this does not mean that it is inevitably successful. Research and development in HTSFs remain extremely risky in that success in the development of 'leading-edge' technologies can never be guaranteed, while development costs may be high and of long duration. Thus, put simply, although HTSFs might be the best place to perform leading-edge R&D in many areas of high-technology, such activity remains risky and, as Chapter 7 on HTSF finance will reveal, is difficult to resource, especially in *new* HTSFs.

Nonetheless, by the early 1980s, it was clear that successful HTSFs in the United States tended to be clustered when occurring spontaneously as a result of local agglomeration economies (e.g. skilled labour availability, capital, a rich supply of input materials at competitive prices and local tacit knowledge advantages) (Oakey 1984a, 1985a). This initial local advantage was buttressed by 'spin-off' activity in which early established cluster firms 'incubated' (often involuntarily) further new businesses into their local environment (Mason1979; Rothwell and Zegveld 1982). The success of this phenomenon was then seized upon by government economic planners in other countries as an ideal basis for *artificially replicating* such developments in order to generate or regenerate regional or sub-regional economies, based on high-technology production. However, the rush to replicate what had been achieved in locations such as Silicon Valley led to a number of misconceptions concerning the *rate* at which successful high-technology cluster replication could occur, and what was the *main causal mechanism* of such growth. For example, an early mistake was the assumption, especially in the United Kingdom, that the presence of Stanford University and MIT, respectively located in the centres of the Silicon Valley and Route 128 high-technology agglomerations, were major catalysts for the growth of these clusters.

While there was some beneficial impact on the relevant clusters through entrepreneurial 'spin-off' from these universities (Roberts 1991; Cardullo 1999), the idea, common among European planners of the early 1980s, that universities would act as information hubs of technical expertise that new HTSFs could draw upon when located in science parks or incubators on or near university campuses was proved by empirical investigation to be largely a myth (Oakey 1985b; Westhead and Cowling 1995). Even in the United States, it was noted that links between HTSFs in Silicon Valley and Stanford University were rare (Oakey 1984a), and usually of low technical importance when they occurred. The science park movement in Europe in general, and the United Kingdom in particular, was largely built on a false premise promoted by science park developers (e.g. Trinity College, Cambridge 1983) that firms locating themselves on science parks and incubators, based on university campuses, would develop useful technical links with their local university (see Section 3.5 for a full discussion of science parks and incubators). Nonetheless, although the university-based drive towards HTSF promotion had a number of flaws, and diverted attention away from a much-needed, more comprehensive, government-based development policy for HTSFs, it at least raised the profile of HTSF development in the 1980s and 1990s, and acknowledged the reality that new high-technology industrial production was essential to the prosperity of many Western developed and South East Asian developing economies beyond the year 2000.

Indeed, perhaps the most potent reason why, after intermittent periods of neglect, HTSFs return to the top of the government industrial development agendas of developed industrial nations, is their relevance to the long-term national industrial health. For example, in the United Kingdom, after the initial burst of enthusiasm for HTSFs in the early 1980s noted above, there was a gradual decline in interest in the late 1980s and early 1990s, followed by a resurrection of HTSF interest around the time of the 1997 general election, reflected in a number of public sector and private sector reports of how HTSFs might best be promoted (House of Lords 1997; Confederation of British Industry 1997; Bank of England 2001). It is generally agreed that HTSFs have long-term strategic importance because, in a range of key strategic future industries (e.g. electronics; biotechnology; software; the internet), new HTSFs are a major means by which a future industrial 'foothold' can be established (Office of Technology Assessment 1984). Indeed, for all developed national economies, manufacturing should continue to form a crucial part of national earnings for the foreseeable future (as the recent over-reliance on financial services has reminded us), since it remains the case that it is in the HTSF-inspired 'start of cycle' industries that developed high-wage economies have the best chance of maintaining competitiveness, high profit margins, and high-salaried jobs. For this reason alone, HTSFs will remain of key importance. However, as noted above, to this assertion must be added the also incontrovertible fact that the long-term planning required to put HTSFs at the heart of any economic policy for a developed industrial nation has not been a consistent concern of national governments. A major and intractable problem is that, to be effective, industrial planning horizons should be extended over 20- to 30-year periods, when in fact, politicians are forced by their electoral systems to take a 'short-termist' attitude based on the average of five years they can be sure that they will be in office, after which a different party in power might change the direction of policy. This will be a theme that is returned to at many points subsequently in this book and especially in Chapter 8, which is concerned with 'short termism' regarding HTSF funding.

1.1.2 Negative aspects of HTSF development

It must be acknowledged, as will be discussed in detail in Chapter 7 on finance, that recently, HTSFs have not proven to be very attractive investment vehicles for external providers of capital in general, and venture capital firms in particular (Murray and Lott 1995; Bank of England 2001; Oakey 2003a, 2007a). Put simply, new HTSFs are no different to any other small firms during formation in the sense that they go through all the same stages that most new medium- or low-technology firms experience. However, the major difference for HTSFs is that virtually all these stages are more protracted and more precarious than for their lower-technology counterparts. At formation, many HTSFs do not have a product to sell, and spend a considerable amount of time either on perfecting a new technological 'idea', often 'spun out' from a university in an unproven conceptual state, or in circumstances where the new technology must be developed 'from scratch'. This inevitably means that such firms are what is termed 'front-end loaded' in that they require external financial support for a number of years *prior* to the launch of the initial new product that they are developing, and the hoped-for arrival of subsequent income from product sales. Moreover, this period of 'front-end' development is often so protracted that it sometimes exceeds the R&D development period predicted in an HTSF's business plan when applying for external venture capital funding support (Oakey 1995) and, in the biotechnology sector, can easily last at least ten years. Clearly, in such circumstances, a three-year bank loan would be inappropriate, since it would need to be repaid in the middle of the development period, when such a firm would have accumulated debt and have no means of repayment.

For these reasons, it is frequently the case that venture capital is the best source of investment for HTSFs. Not only can capital be advanced in exchange for equity over longer periods than three years, the purchasing of equity by the venture capital investor (or investors) ensures that a degree of longer-term commitment is assured, because the venture capitalist will be reluctant to see such a firm collapse, since a return on an investment depends on obtaining a successful 'out' for the venture capitalist when the equity held by them is sold. However, while venture capital investment, overall, might be the best form of funding for HTSFs, there are two major problems that inhibit such funding. First, a significant proportion of HTSF founders are reluctant to surrender equity in the firm that they have founded, often in a desire to be independent after previously working for large firms (Oakey 2003b). Second, since the late 1980s, many venture capital firms have progressively seen HTSF investments as too risky, and have tended to shift their investment portfolios away from high-technology sectors to lower-technology activities in general, and management buy-outs, buy-ins and expansions of existing firms in particular (Murray and Lott 1995). These existing entities are seen as less risky because they have track records of performance which can be extrapolated into the future, as compared with a new HTSF with no record of performance and only a business plan that predicts sales volumes that are pure speculation (see Chapter 7 for a full discussion of this problem).

The problem of high-technology cluster replication

The principles that lie behind the cluster formation process are not new. The concepts of clustering and agglomeration are very similar, and agglomeration principles have their roots in the early works of academics writing on industrial location theory. The seminal work of Alfred Weber (1929) argued that industrial firms would migrate from a 'least cost' transport-cost location to urban areas if such sites offered economies associated with 'labour advantages' (Riley 1973). Interestingly, the enduring relevance of this early work is borne out by the fact that a major locational advantage of Silicon Valley, for example, has been observed to be access to a concentrated pool of high-quality blue- and white-collar workers (Oakey 1984a). Indeed, many of the staple industries in the United Kingdom emerging from the industrial revolution (e.g. watches and clock production in Clerkenwell in London; gun and jewellery production near the centre of Birmingham; and cotton textile production in Lancashire) (Wise 1949; Hall 1963; Martin 1966) were all strong examples of clustering, exhibiting many of the strengths of Silicon Valley (e.g. skilled labour; vertically disintegrated input and output local linkage patterns; and especially local entrepreneurship).

However, those practitioners concerned with the post-Second World War period of industrial development in the United Kingdom had tended to downplay such locationally constraining factors, and considered most industrial activities to be 'footloose' by proposing that the relocation from core areas of the country to peripheral development areas could be achieved without damage. Nonetheless, this approach often resulted in substantial harm to the relocated industries involved when they were moved to peripheral regions outside established clusters (e.g. the relocation of the United Kingdom motor vehicle industry from the South East of England and the West Midlands to peripheral areas; see Townroe 1971; Sant 1975; Smith 1979). Overall, there was a general feeling that locationally constrained production was a feature of Victorian industries which had ceased to exist or were in terminal decline. With the rise of interest in high-technology industry in general, and HTSFs in particular in the 1980s, it was a shock to many academics and planners to discover that this new type of highly technologically advanced production was heavily agglomerated in a very similar manner to the Victorian industries of the past (Oakey 1985a). The strong production efficiencies of a cluster, which outweigh other disadvantages of high local costs (e.g. staff wages, property prices), are now well established as a price worth paying to be 'at the heart of things' (Porter 1998). The challenge for politicians wishing to copy this type of highly profitable and forward-looking industry, clearly evident in the

United States, then involved solving the problem of how successful replication of this phenomenon can be achieved in other national contexts (Oakey 2003c).

A number of major problems confronted government policy makers when they attempted to replicate, through planning, phenomena that originally were caused by spontaneous 'natural' economic forces. One major contextual difficulty confronting any form of replication was the problem of time lapse. It is obvious that any attempt to copy phenomena must be hampered by the fact that time will have elapsed between the original occurrence and the replication. While entrepreneurs obviously play a key role in the establishment of any new industry, there is also a strong part played by 'windows of opportunity'. If Silicon Valley is used as an example, the key 'window of opportunity' was approximately between 1965 and 1975. By the time politicians and planners in other countries noticed the existence of Silicon Valley in the 1980s, the window of opportunity for this type of cluster based on semiconductor production and computers had begun to close. First, this was partly because the firms that had grown to dominate these sectors in the Silicon Valley cluster had reached such a large size that they tended to inhibit new HTSFs subsequently founded in Europe and elsewhere from entering this sector (e.g. Intel; Hewlett-Packard); and second, consistent with the maturing semiconductor industry, manufacturing output was becoming more mass production in nature, and was progressively moving 'offshore' to other parts of the United States and Southeast Asia. Moreover, by the early 1980s, much of the high-volume silicon chip production had been captured from the United States by large Japanese producers (Langlois *et al.* 1988). Put simply, the entrepreneurial HTSF phase of the semiconductor industry, and its related downstream sectors (e.g. computers) had ended.

As noted above, the problems associated with the false assumption by European planners seeking to replicate these concentrations that United States universities acted as 'accretion nodes' for the development of high-technology clusters have caused many difficulties. While there has been some limited success with the development of totally new clusters in Europe (e.g. Sophia Antopolis in France), it might be argued that it is illogical to assert that an entity derived from spontaneous economic forces could be replicated using public capital and development planning, since these stimuli are polar opposites of free market economic forces. In the United Kingdom, much cluster development policy towards industry has been focussed on managing the decline of older industrial clusters (e.g. cotton textiles in the North West of England), or allocating cluster status to industrial associations that were not functioning clusters for non-economic regional political reasons (e.g. The North West Aerospace Cluster; see

Oakey 2003c). A major problem in planning regional clusters is that when the leaders of an industry (usually an Association) discover that local or national government is investing capital in a cluster development policy in their region, they apply for cluster status, notwithstanding the fact that, viewed objectively, they often do not qualify as a cluster, and have few cluster attributes. This pattern of behaviour has led to an unwieldy plethora of new 'clusters', which has meant that, in contradiction of a focussed cluster policy, potentially viable clusters are often starved of financial support because the total budget for cluster development is spread too thinly (see Chapter 3 for a further discussion of these issues). Ironically, perhaps the best candidate for a high-technology cluster in the United Kingdom is the area around Cambridge, which, although there are a few planned science parks in the area, is largely a spontaneous development based on labour and infrastructural advantages.

1.2 Defining HTSFs

Clearly, a major early task for academic researchers seeking to investigate the nature of the HTSF as it emerged to become important to national industrial planning in the developed and developing world was to define this subject of study (Markusen *et al.* 1986). Since the term 'high technology' carried with it the promise of new product development, wealth creation and success (as discussed above regarding Silicon Valley and its successful entrepreneurs), identifying and supporting the next technology-based sectors to emerge became a key task for industrial planners in order that HTSF-oriented policies could be tailored towards, and *targeted* at, this size and sophistication of firm. However, this task has always been exacerbated in the case of HTSFs because the term 'high technology', rather akin to 'entrepreneurship', is in popular use in all forms of the media and, indeed, is often misused or overused when discussing new forms of industrial and/or commercial activity. For example, during the 'dot.com bubble' episode of the early 2000s, many of the firms termed 'high technology' were, in fact, low-technology mail-order firms selling their goods by means of the internet. While the internet was high technology, the firms using this method of accessing customers were not. And while it was generally agreed in a number of empirical and conceptual contributions during the 1980s that a common definition would be highly desirable in order that academic work in this area might proceed on an agreed basis (Premus 1982; Breheny *et al.* 1983; Glasmeier 1985; Kelly 1986), arriving at a commonly accepted definition has continued to elude HTSF researchers for the following set of complex reasons.

1.2.1 The input–output problem

An obvious starting point for any academic seeking to define high-technology industry, in general, or HTSFs, in particular, is to search government industrial statistics to find a robust definition of a given high-technology sector. Such a search is often inhibited by the fact that many emerging high-technology sectors are not separately represented in government statistical data, which are, in any case, always slightly out of date regarding the most recently available statistics, and yet more 'outdated' in terms of their sectoral classification. Moreover, many areas of high technology develop on the borders between existing recorded sectors. A good example of this phenomenon is the emerging multimedia industry (e.g. in California). This new sector has developed in an area of technology where computer hardware, software and the media industries (e.g. publishing, film making) functionally and/or physically overlap (Scott 1993). Similarly, the biotechnology industry is an amalgam of parts of other traditional industries (e.g. brewing) and new technologies in the biomedical area (Oakey *et al.* 1990a).

However, in addition to the above problems with government definitions of high-technology activities, most of the measures that academics have developed in the past to identify high-technology sectors have also encountered problems (Markusen *et al.* 1986). Such academic measures tend to be 'data-driven' in that, although the statistics on which the definitions are based are not ideal, they are often the only data available from government. Apart from the above problems of classification of high-technology activities, even in those sectors that do not suffer from definitional problems, available statistics typically include *input measures* such as R&D expenditure and the employment of scientist and engineers. However, there are a number of problems associated with these measures in that, essentially, they are *costs* which might be used to define high-technology status but which, although they are *necessary* to achieve success, are *not sufficient*. Indeed, problems of HTSF formation and growth often stem from the sad reality that the funding of HTSFs, after extensive periods of R&D, often results in failure (see Chapter 7 for a further discussion of this issue). Thus, since the main interest of governments is the economic growth potential of HTSFs, basing any definition of high-technology industries with strong growth potential on speculative costs is likely to be unreliable. To this reservation might also be added the fact that, in both the United States and the United Kingdom, a good deal of HTSF productive activity is defence-related, in circumstances where HTSFs act as sub-contractors to larger high-technology firms in the defence industry. The products produced, although high technology in nature and consuming large amounts of R&D inputs, are often dependent on public expenditure and therefore are not commercially competitive, without potential for civil industrial market exploitation (Oakey *et al.* 1988).

For the above reasons, it would seem sensible to argue that output measures would be far more reliable indicators of the type of HTSF success sought by government planners. However, although accurate measures of, for example, profitability and/or turnover would indicate the degree to which the firm was growing on the basis of successful HTSF product sales, such figures are often unreliable, even when collected by means of face-to-face questionnaire interview surveys, due to problems with tax avoidance and difficulties associated with the misinterpreting of data – for example, on turnover, in cases where high turnover can be recorded in a firm that is about to fail due to the price of its products being less than they cost to produce. Unfortunately, accurate output measures signifying profitability, for similar reasons to those given above, are generally not available from government sources, thus rendering problematic the use of output measures in academic studies.

While at first sight, patents might seem an ideal measure of invention and/or innovation success, there are problems here too, particularly in high-technology industries, where the pace of technological change is extremely fast – product life cycles can be as short as three to five years (Oakey 1984a, 1995). In such circumstances, many firms decide not to patent a new device they have invented, since it would become obsolete before a competitor is in a position to copy it (e.g. advances in silicon chip technology). Thus, in such instances, the inventiveness of high-technology firms in such a sector would be under-recorded. Conversely, other high-technology firms may adopt a 'blanket patent' policy towards their new inventions in which new ideas are patented regardless of their actual worth to the firm. It is certainly true that not all the inventions patented by high-technology firms become successful products in terms of sales (Oakey *et al.* 1980; Pavitt and Soete 1980; Macdonald and Lefang 1998). In the above instances, it is clear that merely counting registered patents would substantially overestimate or underestimate the innovation success of a sector, or an individual HTSF.

Moreover, it might be also argued with some justification that, especially for HTSFs, it would be simplistic to propose that merely registering a patent would secure sole rights to the exploitation of a given technology. Ample evidence has emerged over recent years that, if an HTSF does produce a highly important and lucrative new technology, the chances of such a firm bringing a winning product to market as an independent firm are slim. Larger well-established firms with access to strong legal support are often willing to infringe patents, copy the new technology when it first appears on the market (with slight modifications to confuse the issue of patent breaking) through 'reverse engineering', and pay damages in due course if the inventor HTSF is able to prove that a breach of patent has taken place (Macdonald and Lefang 1998). In such circumstances, it is often the case that HTSFs in possession of a 'world-beating' technology will decide not to patent, since such an act would render this technology available to public scrutiny by larger, more resourceful competitors who would be prepared to infringe such a patent and bear any litigation costs that might ensue. Indeed, a major reason why new HTSFs often agree to be acquired by a larger competitor firm is the realization that they would be unlikely to be able to raise the substantial additional resources with which to produce and launch the new technology onto the market, or to defend the new technology against infringement behaviour by a larger firm (Oakey 2003b). This strategic dilemma for new HTSFs is further discussed in Chapter 5 on strategy.

1.2.2 A caveat regarding the general inapplicability of using input measures to define HTSFs

Measures of expenditure on industrial R&D may represent good intentions rather than proven economic success (as discussed above), and are therefore unreliable indicators of the economic growth that government economic planners might seek to encourage and/or exploit, in order to give an impressive but misleading impression of success. Nonetheless, R&D investment remains important in terms of future invention and innovation in any developed economy (Freeman 1982, 1986). Indeed, part of the curiosity-driven R&D performed in public institutions in general, and universities in particular, while not initially intended to produce saleable products, does often, however, lead to the discovery of key new technologies that have high economic growth potential when eventually brought to the marketplace. Perhaps one of the best examples of this phenomenon was the discovery by Watson and Crick of the 'double helix' in their research on genetics in the early 1950s, both because of the subsequent growth of the new biotechnology industry out of this radical new scientific breakthrough, but also because it shows how long the 'lead time' on the development of new high-technology sectors can be. Indeed, as argued above, those seeking to exploit new technologies are often over-optimistic when anticipating such lead times, which is reflected in the belief during the 1980s that biotechnology, almost seamlessly, would take over from semiconductor technology as the boom industry of the 1990s (Office of Technology Assessment 1984).

When the commercial relevance of a new technology takes many years to emerge in the university sector, there is not really a commercial problem, since the necessary R&D is publicly funded, and often driven by quite appropriate academic curiosity alone (Russell Group 2010). However, while the above criticisms of input R&D measures are valid to a degree in that they do not guarantee success, it is also true that in certain areas of HTSF production, notably biotechnology, product development lead times often extend well beyond ten years (Countopoulos-Ioannidis *et al.* 2008). Thus, for this type of firm, discounting their relevance to industrial growth on the basis that all that can be shown is R&D-driven 'red numbers' on their balance sheets, and the failure of several HTSFs during the development of this new technology, can be mistaken. It may well transpire that, after a long period of 'front-end'-loaded development work, enabled by the support of patient venture capital investors, an HTSF will produce a 'world-beating' product technology that leads to high profitability in a totally new sector of industrial activity. At this point such a firm would qualify for HTSF status on any output definition of high technology, since it would have a credible volume of sales. However, the danger of according such a firm HTSF status when in the product development stage is that many firms in this sector do fail and, after incurring substantial R&D costs, do not move into profitability, and thus have a negative economic impact in terms of wasted investment and job losses. A major reason why venture capital firms have tended to drift away from investment in HTSFs since the early 1980s has been the long lead times that are often associated with HTSF production (Murray and Lott 1995; Oakey 2003a, 2007a) and the subsequent increased risks that these imply, together with a high overall failure rate for new HTSFs when compared with existing management buy-outs, buy-ins and expansions of existing firms, thus rendering an important measure of HTSF status precarious if viewed in terms of short-term development potential (see Chapter 7 on finance).

Nonetheless, the key argument here is that, in an attempt to resolve the tension between input and output definitions of HTSFs, the type of definition applied should depend on the use to which it is put. Those interested parties concerned with the short-term impact of HTSFs, 'picking winners' in order to, for example, encourage regional growth, might use an output definition of HTSFs. In contrast, long-term government planners may have a different view in which R&D input measures are condoned on the basis that technologies being developed in HTSFs with long lead times will be relevant to economic prosperity in ten or 20 years' time. This time span, as noted above, is a perfectly reasonable planning horizon for government economic planners, but one that politicians seeking to win elections are often reluctant to entertain. Interestingly, such long-term (often curiosity-driven) research, which frequently lies on the interface between basic and applied research, is often best performed by speculative new

HTSFs (Cooper 1970; Rothwell and Zegveld 1982; Oakey 1984a; Roberts 1991). When this research is performed in universities, adequate public funds should be provided to support such efforts; and in cases where these activities 'spin out' into, often local, HTSFs, there should be adequate public or private capital provided to ensure that such work is supported. However, as discussed above, the high attrition rate among these types of long-lead-time firms, and the degree to which 'patient' investment is required, suggest that public sector financial support should be combined with private sector financial involvement in order that risk can be reduced and the long-term commercial viability of such investment be made credible (discussed in detail in Chapter 5 on strategy and Chapter 7 on finance).

1.3 The origins of HTSFs

Academics and government industrial policy makers are understandably keen to explore the manner in which HTSFs are founded, for two major reasons. First, economists and economic geographers are concerned with the origins of this type and size of firm for the light that might be shed on theory (e.g. concerning entrepreneurship, agglomeration and regional development planning). Second, government planners need to understand how HTSFs are formed and thrive in order to be better able to replicate, for example, HTSF clusters (as mentioned above and developed further in Chapter 3) in their attempts to maintain and/or regenerate industrial regions. However, the founding of new HTSFs is not a simple process due to the nature of the high and leading-edge technologies on which the products or services of these new firms are based. Unlike many low-technology firms, where the barriers to entry are also low because the basic technology of the newly proposed firm is known to (or can easily be learnt by) any member of the general public (e.g. window cleaning; opening a café), the skills required to develop a product or process suitable for the foundation of a new HTSF are more difficult to acquire.

While there are exceptional examples of school boys forming new high-technology computer games software companies, in the majority of cases, the skills necessary for forming a new HTSF take a number of years to acquire. This means that, typically, HTSF (usually technical) entrepreneurs rarely emerge as independent founders of new firms until they are at least 30 years old. There are two main environments from which these new HTSF entrepreneurs emerge. First, the skills learnt in the physical science departments of universities or other non-commercial research centres (e.g. government defence establishments) may generate new HTSF entre-preneurs. These may be newly qualified PhD students in their late twenties, or slightly older workers who have further developed their expertise (e.g.

a university researcher, lecturer or professor). This expertise may lead, during their research work, to the (often chance) discovery of a new technology with commercial potential that, in turn, prompts the discoverer of this new intellectual property to seek to found a new firm with which to exploit this new discovery, perhaps on an adjacent university incubator or science park. However, in all these cases, a period of *at least* six to eight years will elapse following graduation before an individual of the above type has the technical expertise necessary to begin a new firm.

Second, new entrepreneurs may 'spin off' from an existing (usually large) firm at which, over a number of years, following their initial employment in this 'incubating' firm as a graduate, they gain substantial technical experience (Roberts 1991; Oakey 1995). In common with the academic route to HTSF entrepreneurship, this process is not rapid, since it involves a number of years inside the incubating organization (usually involving promotion) before an individual is in a position to create and/or take advantage of technology worthy of exploitation. Since 'acorns do not fall far from the tree', this type of 'spin-off' usually has implications for local regional development in general, and cluster formation in particular (Oakey *et al*. 2001). Such 'splintering' of expertise into the vicinity of larger, better-established incubator firms is often termed the 'spill-over' effect, although in many cases it should be noted that this is not a benign process in which the 'spin-off' occurs with the blessing of the 'incubating' parent (Oakey 2007b). Indeed, when they establish a new HTSF, 'spin-off' entrepreneurs often seek to obfuscate their act of taking valuable intellectual property with them that is technically the property of their previous employer, by leaving a time gap between leaving their previous employer and the beginning of their new HTSF (Roberts 1991).

Indeed, rather than the 'spinning off' of such technology being seen as a virtuous process in which there are no losers, the reality remains that, in many instances, such behaviour is a subtle form of industrial espionage. This concurs with a subsequent view in this book that clusters are a contradictory blend of collaboration and intense competition, both of which, when combined, prove (perhaps ironically) to be a highly 'fertile' environment for HTSF formation and growth (see Chapter 3; also Oakey 2007b). The proof of the potency of this phenomenon is perhaps best exemplified by the well-documented 'spin-off' link between Shockley Semiconductor, Fairchild Semiconductor and the subsequent host of 'Fairchildren', including Intel, that were 'milestones' in a serial 'spin-off' process that formed much of the industrial core of Silicon Valley (Mason 1979; Rothwell and Zegveld 1982; Cardullo 1999). While it would be difficult to argue that the famous personnel who journeyed from the Shockley Transistor Company, through Fairchild, in a series of 'spin-offs', to Intel did not take any of the corporate knowledge of their incubating firms with them, the *overall* impact of this 'churning' of key staff was beneficial through the jobs and wealth created locally in Silicon Valley during this process.

Moreover, the case of Silicon Valley indicates that industrial 'spin-offs' have produced a cumulative impact in which, for example, local early-established firms (e.g. Hewlett-Packard; Fairchild; Intel) have 'incubated', directly or indirectly, hundreds of subsequent new Silicon Valley HTSFs. Nonetheless, while understanding such a key phenomenon may lead to a better theoretical grasp of how and why high-technology clusters develop, a second goal of using such information to inform the artificial replication of this 'natural' process is a more challenging exercise.

1.3.1 HTSF entrepreneurship – a qualification of the 'third mission' role of universities

The potential of academia in acting as a source of HTSF entrepreneurship has, since the early 1980s (and increasingly since 1997), been seized upon by national governments as a vehicle for urban, regional and national industrial and commercial regeneration, particularly in the United Kingdom (Select Committee on Science and Technology 1993; DTI 1998; Oakey and Mukhtar 1999; Birley 2001; Lambert 2003) and other European nations (Klofsten and Jones 2000; Lockett *et al.* 2005). Moreover, this tendency has been given wider academic credibility by the influential 'triple helix' view of how university, industry and government should interact in order to benefit regional and national economies (Etzkowitz and Leydesdorff 1997). Broadly, this approach argues that academic entre-preneurship provides a key vehicle for such a 'third mission' by transferring ideas into saleable products, through academic enterprise, into the local economy, while university applied-research expertise can be utilized to develop further the product technologies of existing (often large) firms (Goddard and Chatterton 1999; Benworth *et al.* 2009).

However, a major problem with the growing interest of governments in exploiting the potential of university R&D outputs is that, although this focus was partly based on a laudable desire for universities to be socially responsible through using their scientific expertise to contribute to the economic wealth of the local off-campus environment (particularly at regional and sub-regional levels, especially in depressed inner-urban areas), such enthusiasm was also partly driven by a financially motivated desire to reduce the direct central government costs of funding universities. This goal was to be achieved by encouraging universities to exploit the commercial value of their scientific discoveries and consultancy expertise in an attempt to ensure that university R&D funding received increased contributions from the private sector, which would be achieved by moving the emphasis of academic research from basic to applied agendas.

The role of academic entrepreneurial enterprise

The Science Enterprise Challenge (SEC), launched in the United Kingdom in the early 2000s, has been active in the entrepreneurship education of undergraduates, and led to the introduction of various types of Master of Enterprise postgraduate degrees, partly directed at developing new business ideas from student entrepreneurs in universities throughout the United Kingdom. These activities were aimed at creating a climate among students in which an entrepreneurial career would become a popular option. However, although the target number of entrepreneurs expected from attempts to deliver graduate entrepreneurship was not stated by government, it is likely that the actual level of student entrepreneurship achieved thus far will not be significant in local or regional development terms. The types of business ideas proposed by students generally tend to be poorly conceived; when taken together with their lack of business experience and the reality that many of these students are wildly over-optimistic about their likelihood of success, this means that their business plans often become no more than a 'class exercise', rather than a serious attempt to launch a new firm. The tendency to accept students of dubious entrepreneurial potential on such Master's programmes has been exacerbated by the supply-side nature of SEC funding provision in circumstances where capacity is created *in advance* of high-quality student demand. Moreover, the real personal financial dangers of beginning a business with a poor idea that is doomed to fail are often not forcefully enough made clear by those who deliver entrepreneurship courses.

Clearly a greater potential for academic enterprise within universities lies with postdoctoral students and more experienced academic staff from the physical sciences. These are the members of the university who have often accumulated substantial R&D expertise and resultant product ideas on which a new high-technology enterprise realistically might be based. Research and development outputs with commercial exploitation potential range from the type of radical breakthrough inventions (discussed further in Chapter 2) that create, destroy or revolutionize industries, to marginal new discoveries, the potential commercial application (or applications) for which are not clear. Apart from the problem of whether the academic who discovers a new technology with clear commercial potential wishes, or has the personal ability, to become an entrepreneur, the rate at which such discoveries come forward is largely not amenable to direct stimulation. For example, simply spending more money on university R&D, although welcome for purely scientific reasons (i.e. the pursuit of knowledge *per se*), will not necessarily produce the new inventions upon which 'spin-off' academic enterprises might be based. Thus, in a very real sense, there are no reliable means by which governments can raise the rate of university inventiveness, and consequently, spawn more entrepreneurial spin-off firms that would, in turn, better meet the needs of local and regional industrial development. The inventive system of universities is predominantly driven by a *curiosity* rather than a profit ethic, and therefore is not designed directly to meet the needs of industrial development. Universities should not, therefore, be condemned if they fail to fulfil a 'third mission' role, and any attempts to tamper with this delicate system, such as the United Kingdom government setting the research agenda of scientists, or seeking to promote 'applied' over 'basic' R&D, is dangerous and almost certainly in the long term will be counterproductive, since scientific knowledge cannot be applied until it has been invented (Russell Group 2010).

However, beyond the problem of how to increase the flow of new academic inventions that might stimulate academic 'spin-offs', there is a further problem of the suitability of academics to an entrepreneurial career. Although there have been notable exceptions, most academics choose an academic career because they enjoy the academic environment, in which non-financial job satisfaction is gained from the rewards of teaching and research rather than a high salary. Many such individuals are not interested in becoming entrepreneurs, while for others, any attempt to do so might prove a complete disaster due to their unsuitable temperament and lack of relevant business skills. Perhaps the most famous example of an excellent scientist who tried (and failed) to become an entrepreneur was that of William Shockley, who left Bell R&D Laboratories to form the Shockley Transistor Company in 1955. However, this new company was short-lived and many of his original appointments (including Gordon Moore and Robert Noyce) left to establish Fairchild Semiconductors, from which they later moved on to found Intel (Cardullo 1999).

Most of the problems associated with the encouragement of risk concern the balance between risk and reward in general, and between who is encouraging the risk compared with who is taking the risk. One obvious risk-averse conclusion that might be drawn from the above assertions on the attitude of academics with ownership of intellectual property would be that they should *always* sell such assets without beginning a new business that might be used to exploit them (see Chapter 5 for a detailed elaboration of this concept). However, while this would certainly be low-risk, some more enterprising academics with the potential for developing business skills might decide, with the encouragement of entrepreneurship development practitioners, to attempt to develop the technology they have invented into a new product that will form the basis for a new enterprise to build and sell such a product on the open market.

Clearly when entrepreneurs in a free market decide to begin a new firm, the risks that they take are solely attributable to them. However, it is significant that in cases of academic entrepreneurship where government-funded practitioners are attempting to 'tease out' new entrepreneurial ventures on which *their own* success depends, there is a moral hazard issue present in that such a practitioner, who has no personal risk, attempts to encourage an academic to take the major step of founding a new enterprise which may involve him or her *alone* in substantial personal financial risk (e.g. possible loss of savings, pension or property). This problem is exacerbated by the rhetoric surrounding university entrepreneurship, in which, as noted above, the likelihood of success is often over-exaggerated, although failure is far more likely than success (Storey 1994; Cressy 2006). In general, prospective entrepreneurs are encouraged to have over-optimistic views of how easy beginning a business will be, and consequently need to be carefully counselled on how risky and likely to fail most businesses are in reality. Moreover, in terms of the potential of academic institutions for producing high levels of HTSF entrepreneurs, it might be concluded that such potential is real and of value to the local economies in which the universities are located, but that it should not be artificially forced beyond the point at which it appears during the normal course of curiosity-driven basic academic research.

1.4 Chapter summary

Any measured view of the development of HTSFs over the past 30 years must conclude that the overall picture is mixed. While much has been achieved regarding progress with academic theory and policy prescription towards HTSFs, problems of definition, replication, funding and industrial policy remain to confuse and/or frustrate the newcomer to this specialist area of industry. In conclusion to this initial chapter, it is useful to consider a 'balance sheet' of what has been achieved thus far.

1.4.1 Positive factors

Perhaps the foremost point to make about HTSFs is that they are highly inventive and/or innovative and, beyond bringing new ideas to the consumer in the form of high-technology products, they often fulfil the key role in competitive capitalist systems of disrupting monopolistic or oligopolistic technological paradigms that established large firms tend to develop. This phenomenon will be discussed in more detail in Chapter 2. Whether new HTSFs make the rare transition from new small firm to multinational enterprise, or champion a new technology to be acquired by a larger firm that fully exploits this new departure, HTSFs often refresh the technology agenda of existing sectors and sometimes create completely new sectors to the benefit of all concerned, including the governments which collect the taxes that ensue, the workers who are employed in this new industry, and the customers who benefit from its 'ground-breaking' new products.

Part of the reason why HTSFs are particularly inventive and innovative is their ability to perform R&D effectively. The close-knit spatial and organizational distance between all the functions of the firm, from R&D, through production, to sales, enables a high level of teamwork to develop, without the bureaucracy that often inhibits larger firms. The HTSF environment is often one in which job satisfaction is high, and, indeed, one of the main reasons why new HTSF entrepreneurs 'spin off' from existing large firms (discussed above) is a desire for freedom of action, which is a gratification often more important than salary level to very committed individuals with a flair for both technical ingenuity and enterprise. Moreover, on a more general level, the jobs created in HTSFs tend to provide better job satisfaction than in other workplaces and, whether blue- or white-collar, tend to be comparatively well-paid, particularly when located in a successful cluster. In addition, because, by definition, most of the jobs created in HTSFs are in 'start of cycle' industrial sectors, they are not likely to be the subject of job losses associated with obsolescence of various types resulting from a decline in competitiveness experienced in mature sectors. This is partly because in 'start of cycle' industries that have not matured, competition is less (and in some very specific areas of high technology, non-existent). Thus, the medium-term longevity of jobs is relatively secure in HTSFs, notwithstanding the problems of start up and early growth noted above and later in this book.

Thus, due to the youth of HTSFs and the new sectors they are forming, they are often targeted by national and regional development agencies of developed and developing nations as prime vehicles for industrial growth. Particularly when clustered in areas of increasing geographical size in incubators, science parks or sub-regional or regional clusters, biotechnology, electronics, healthcare and many other high-technology sectors are chosen to act as the basis for new industrial developments (Oakey 2003c). The promise of 'start of cycle' technologies that would produce high-quality jobs to replace aging sectors in decline adds balance to any portfolio of industrial development in which the main goal is well-paid jobs with assured longevity. Although the problems of using public expenditure to replicate 'naturally formed' clusters, which had previously emerged over long periods of time, are very real, with perseverance, success can be achieved (Porter 1998).

This key point regarding perseverance is not only relevant to regional planning, but even more relevant at the national level. The promotion and development of HTSFs are of utmost importance to national governments for two major reasons. First, for nations that perform substantial basic R&D and discover new technologies of the future with strong commercial potential, there is a long-term strategic need also to anticipate and plan for the development of the new industrial sectors that will grow and produce the major downstream wealth benefits through the manufacturing that such basic scientific developments currently promise. In this context, HTSFs, and especially academic spin-off HTSFs, are clearly relevant vehicles for such future growth as part of any long-term national industrial development plan. Second, due to problems with the early-stage funding discussed above, and dealt with in greater detail in later chapters, it is unlikely that the desired HTSF development will be achieved without some public sector financial support, in partnership with the private sector. Although adequate investment in HTSFs is a continuing problem, noted below under negative factors, with adequate national government financial support, HTSFs can be a strong positive factor in the future development of both developed *and* developing national economies.

1.4.2 Negative factors

A basic problem, both for the academic study of HTSFs, and for policy makers seeking to promote them, is the lack of a common definition on which all can agree and use with confidence. For academics, a major initial problem concerns arriving at a robust definition of discrete HTSF sectors that all interested parties can agree on, a definitional problem where government statisticians usually take the lead. However, defining these new sectors is inhibited by the reality that, in many cases when new HTSF sectors are emerging, the normal time lag of a few years over which government statistics emerge for industrial sectors is exacerbated by a protracted delay in specifying exactly of what activities a new high-technology sector is composed (e.g. biotechnology; nanotechnology; multimedia). Beyond the problem (discussed above) of the best measure of what constitutes a high-technology sector (e.g. inputs or outputs), many sectors that are used widely in policy debates and in the media do not appear in government statistics because they have not yet been defined, even after several informal years in existence. This problem deprives both academic and government planners of data on the relative prosperity of the high-technology sectors they are attempting to promote, while some 'sectors' could exist in either the service or manufacturing sectors (e.g. contract R&D; computer software). However, this definitional problem is more an irritant than a barrier to progress, since difficulties in defining what 'biotechnology' or 'multimedia' sectors are in statistical terms do not detract from the reality that firms in these sectors have great growth potential, which is the important point to note.

The difficulty of how to replicate artificially HTSF growth (often in clusters) is another more important challenge. While replicating phenomena that occur naturally through artificial means is not an easy task, it is made substantially more difficult if the mechanisms that caused the phenomena in the first place are not properly understood, or are misunderstood. An example of this dilemma is the way in which the role of academics has been over-played in many academic texts, and by government planners. In terms of the manner in which universities act as accretion nodes for HTSF clusters, their ability to offer technical help to HTSFs, and the roles that have been anticipated for academic enterprise (often in the guise of incubators or science parks), there has been a gross misunderstanding of the process at work in HTSF creation, and the potential for universities to aid this objective through academic entrepreneurship (especially in Europe). This is not to argue that universities have no role to play in HTSF formation and growth, but rather that this role has been overstated in the past and too much faith has been put in their power to increase the rate of academic enterprise.

However, the most significant and enduring negative factor to inhibit the formation and growth of new HTSFs since the 1980s in Europe in general, and the United Kingdom in particular, has been the HTSF funding gap. Because Chapter 7 of this book is devoted to a detailed consideration of this problem, it is sufficient here at the outset to note that the long lead times and front-end funding problems that often accompany HTSF start-ups have beset this sector since the early 1980s (Oakey 1984b, 1995, 2003a, 2007a). The retreat of the venture capital industry from the financial support of HTSFs since 1990 has been the subject of many initiatives and enquiries over these years to no good effect.

The underlying problem with HTSF funding is that of 'short termism'. Because new high-technology products often burst suddenly onto the world market, uninitiated observers assume that the R&D work that preceded such an event was also short-lived. In fact, in most cases, new HTSF development takes at least five years, while the successful development of some new products can easily take up to 15 years. Put simply, success in high-technology industry in general, and HTSFs in particular, while often revolutionary in terms of a product's success when launched, is often the result of a long and prosaic process of meticulous industrial R&D. The key point to note here, however, is that early over-optimism regarding the ability of HTSFs to deliver spectacular success has subsequently led to the disappointment of investors and government policy makers alike, who have then retreated from this area of investment because their originally unrealistic expectations of rapid return were not realized.

1.4.3 The future

Taking all the positive and negative points made above together, it is clear that, provided a long-term view of potential progress is taken, HTSF development should remain a key strategic goal for any developed or developing economy. In a similar manner to the way in which national governments fund university research on curiosity-based projects that may or may not have future economic potential, they should also take a long-term view of the potential of the HTSF that is longer than the private sector investors can be expected to contemplate. Thus there may be potential for greater numbers of public–private partnerships in which long-term economic prosperity would be the 'return' to be derived by government, while medium- to long-term financial returns would be enjoyed by private sector investors. This type of collaboration will be a major theme for the remainder of this book.

2 The role of the technical entrepreneur

2.1 The key qualities of technical entrepreneurship

The vast majority of entrepreneurs beginning new small firms in high-technology industries are technical entrepreneurs. Empirical research has found that there are very few instances in which an entrepreneur with no technical skills hires technically qualified staff, who then produce a new high-technology product or service for the founder to exploit (Oakey 1984a, 1995; Roberts 1991). The great strength of technical entrepreneurs, either when working alone or in teams (e.g. Steve Jobs and Steve Wozniak, the founders of Apple Computers), is that they often have a deep technical understanding of what they are basing their business on, and therefore a clear vision of how the new technology they have created can be applied in a commercial context. Clearly, although such enthusiasm may be misplaced, causing the demise of the new HTSF in question, on a more positive note, it can also mean that the technical entrepreneur founder (or founders) of a new HTSF has (have) the 'in-house' ability to produce leading-edge novel technologies with which to create new areas of industrial production in technical niches where competition previously was sparse or non-existent, and through their enthusiasm, often found new industrial sectors to the benefit of all consumers. Such technical entrepreneurs are frequently the harbingers of disruptive technologies that revolutionize or supplant existing industrial sectors (Schumpeter 1939; Christensen 1997; Christensen and Bower 2004).

One of the best examples of this phenomenon is that of Steve Jobs and Steve Wozniak, who founded Apple Computers in the mid-1970s. As technical entrepreneurs, acting as a team, they were able to persuade both investors and marketing experts, whom they involved in the business at an early stage, to believe in their 'dream' of producing a low-cost desktop computer that anyone could afford to own. This unique ability to both invent a new product and entrepreneurially develop a business based on a new idea in a 'seamless' manner, in which invention moves from the laboratory bench, through development and into the marketplace, is a key strength of the technical entrepreneurial process. The combined technical and entrepreneurial skills of the individuals involved produced results that would be difficult to achieve in a more formally managed large or small industrial firm. In the case of Jobs and Wozniak, their new computer company achieved spectacular growth that, together with other new firms of a similar type (e.g. Compaq; Dell), undermined the virtual monopoly of mainframe computers held by IBM, and offered personal computing to the world at a price that, increasingly, customers could afford. However, as noted previously in Chapter 1, it must be acknowledged that this 'rags to riches' independent growth of a new HTSF from birth to large size in a few years is very rare. Nonetheless, while many technical entrepreneurially led new firms are often subsequently acquired by larger competitors, technical entrepreneurs play a key role in radically changing the technological agenda of existing industries, and strongly contribute to the creation of new industrial sectors. Moreover, although technical entrepreneurship in HTSFs is a key driving force behind the development of new high-technology industries, in common with many other features of high-technology industry (e.g. clustering), this phenomenon is not new and was widespread at the time of the Industrial Revolution and the subsequent Victorian era in the United Kingdom. Most of the key entrepreneurs of this long period from 1700 to 1900 were not only major inventors of new technologies, but were also entrepreneurs who often derived ideas for new technologies by observing how existing technologies did not work efficiently when they were employed in (or owned by) traditional industrial enterprises (e.g. Arkwright in the textile industry; Watt in steam power generation; and Brunel in transport engineering). Precisely in common with their later fellow technical entrepreneurs (noted above), their key advantage was their skill in effectively combining their technical abilities with entrepreneurial competence in order to take an embryonic idea through development and production to offer their customers either a new process invention that enabled existing products to be produced at less cost to the consumer (e.g. cotton textile machinery; steam engines) or a desirable new product that large numbers of customers could afford.

Because of this ability to produce, at the very least, a new area of industrial activity within existing sectors and, at most, whole new industries, the governments of developed and developing nations have been keen to identify and support such entrepreneurs. However, the supply of such individuals is not abundant, because not all technically proficient researchers have the business skills sufficient to become successful technical entrepreneurs while, as noted above, very few entrepreneurs with good business skills have the technical ability to produce leading-edge best-selling new technology products. Chapter 1 has observed that the main sources of HTSF entrepreneurs are higher education establishments and 'spin-offs' from existing large high-technology firms. Figure 2.1 exemplifies the problem of suitability in that many potential academic or industrial 'spin-off' entrepreneurs have high levels of technical ability (position B – top right of the matrix), but very poor business acumen (Oakey 1984a). However, as discussed above, other individuals may have high business acumen, but little technical ability (i.e. non-academic entre-preneurs: position C – bottom left of the matrix); the ideal technical entrepreneur might be an individual who has both technical and business skills (position D – bottom right of the matrix). An entrepreneur in position A (top right of the matrix) with no business acumen or technical ability is likely to avoid beginning a new business, or rapidly fail, if tempted into founding a new firm. The problem for the development of increased technical entrepreneurship is that, although 'bottom right' people do exist, when one emerges (as with all successful entrepreneurs) we tend to over-publicize this phenomenon as if it were common, and ignore the reality

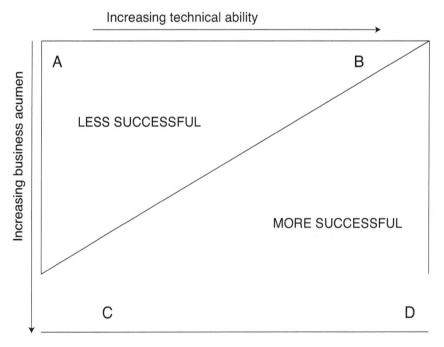

Figure 2.1 An entrepreneurial matrix
Source: Oakey 1984a: 32

that these people are rare exceptions who prove the general rule of poor business acumen among many potential HTSF entrepreneurs (i.e. position B – Figure 2.1).

Many technically qualified individuals, whether in the R&D departments of large firms or academics in universities, choose a technical role because they enjoy a research environment in which non-financial job satisfaction is gained from intellectually rewarding research. Many such individuals are not interested in becoming entrepreneurs, while for others, as Figure 2.1 illustrates, any attempt to do so might result in failure due to their unsuitable temperament and lack of relevant entrepreneurial skills. Perhaps the most famous example of an excellent scientist who tried to become an entrepreneur and failed (as noted in Chapter 1) was that of William Shockley, who left Bell R&D Laboratories to form the Shockley Transistor Company in 1955. This new company was short-lived due to the poor management skills of Shockley, and most of his original recruits, including Gordon Moore and Robert Noyce, subsequently left to form the Fairchild and the Intel corporations (Cardullo 1999).

It is also true that multiple technical entrepreneurship is often more effective than single entrepreneurial effort since such group acts offer a wider skill base and are inherently more democratic. A major reason why entrepreneurs begin new firms is to obtain the non-financial goal of freedom of action (Oakey 2003b). While this can be a positive attribute if the autonomy is aimed at allowing *all* employees of the firm to share in the benefits of a more democratic approach (notwithstanding the ultimate need for managers to manage), it is less attractive (certainly to external potential investors such as venture capitalists) if the freedom motive exposes an *autocratic* preference for control by a single founding entrepreneur. As Figure 2.2 illustrates, founding entrepreneurs who have a strongly autonomous approach are often not very successful since they remain introspective and driven by a strong need for control of all aspects of the firm's operation. Such individuals often prefer to remain small and survive on retained profits, rather than take a more democratic approach in which they share control with other executives, and allow external investment into the business in exchange for equity. These 'controlling' entrepreneurs maintain their HTSF on the basis of 'a good living salary' to be derived from the firm. Many HTSF niche producers of specialist equipment can survive indefinitely (and are often family concerns that continue for several generations) with this type of strategic approach. However, it is clear that such a firm would not be, and could not seek to be, the 'stellar growth' type of HTSF normally associated with HTSF success.

The technical entrepreneur

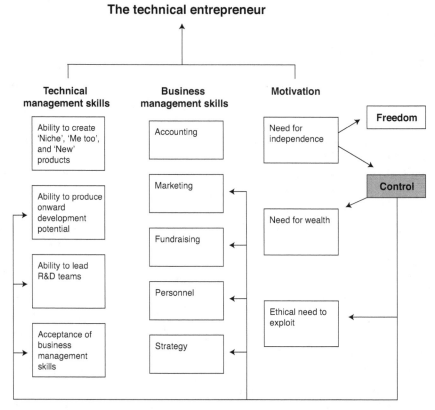

Figure 2.2 The technical entrepreneur at formation
Source: Oakey 2003b: 682

2.2 The role of the technical entrepreneur in technological progress

> The process of creative destruction is the essential fact about capitalism. It is what capitalism consists in and what every capitalist concern has got to live in.
>
> (Joseph Schumpeter 1942: 83)

Acknowledgement of the work of Joseph Schumpeter is an appropriate manner in which to begin this consideration of the role of technical entrepreneurship in facilitating technological progress. His work was revolutionary in many ways and, although not perfect in all respects, Schumpeter's basic assertion that much technological progress was (and remains) attributable to the 'creative destruction' delivered by entrepreneurs through innovative behaviour was a major advance in economic theory (Schumpeter 1942). Before Schumpeter, the traditional view, inherited from Victorian economists (e.g. Marx 1961 [1867]), was that industrial growth was determined by the rate at which the 'key' inputs of capital and labour were invested in any given industry. Schumpeter was of importance to the continued relevance of economics as an evolving academic discipline because he strongly asserted that the introduction of new products and process innovations through technological progress were major determinants of economic growth, in both developed and developing economies. Moreover, he asserted that, during this process, there would be both 'winners' and 'losers' in that, as the above quote implies, outdated industrial and/or commercial practices would be destroyed, since more efficient methods of manufacture would be introduced to replace them by progressive entrepreneurial action.

Schumpeter's key assertion was that existing industries needed to be innovative in order that the capitalist system should survive and prosper, either by spawning completely new industries, or by helping existing industries to become more efficient, and consequently more competitive and better able to survive. However, this key creativity 'variable' that should have been, from the beginning of the Industrial Revolution, included by economists in any credible industrial growth 'equation', and which was clearly at least as important as inputs of capital or labour, was slow to be acknowledged by mainstream economic theorists (e.g. Marris 1964). Given such importance, it is difficult to understand why many economists have often ignored the significance of the 'technology variable' in their teaching of undergraduates, and in equations seeking to model economic performance. This is especially surprising since technology has been argued to be not only a significant variable in explaining the economic performance of economies, but the *most important* determinant of economic growth (Solow 1957; Denison 1962; Freeman 1982). Moreover, this intellectual 'blind spot' is additionally surprising given the increased importance of science and technology in dictating the future direction of industry and commerce since the Second World War, in circumstances where the pace of technological change has substantially increased (Thwaites 1978). However, it should have been obvious to Karl Marx and other nineteenth-century economists that most of the major growth spurts that occurred during this period were due to the innovative behaviour of key technical entrepreneurs, of which there are many examples from England during the early stages of the Industrial Revolution (e.g. Newcomen's atmospheric engine [1712]; Arkwright's water frame [1769]; Boulton and Watt's steam engine [1786]). Indeed, it was a common feature of the introduction of many of these new inventions that the labour input variable, so important to the economists of the time in explaining economic growth, was often severely reduced in importance by the *labour-saving* process technologies introduced by these entrepreneurs. Moreover, with the exception of Arkwright's invention of the water frame, it is significant to note that the other inventions mentioned above not only created new industries to manufacture these products, but also delivered efficiency gains in a wide range of technologically unrelated industrial sectors. For example, Boulton and Watt's steam engine was used to deliver efficiency gains as a source of power in a wide range of industrial and commercial activities, while the steam engine principle was later adapted to produce locomotive power, which was also a major provider of efficiency gains in multiple industrial *and* commercial sectors. These key characteristics of rapid efficiency gains and the broad applicability of such advances were to play a major role in Schumpeter's later explanation of Kondratiev's world-trade-cycle fluctuations (Kondratiev 1925) in terms of the introduction of key innovations, of which static steam power was a major example (Schumpeter 1939). These individuals were clear early examples of technical entrepreneurship, well before the advent of contemporary high-technology industry, demonstrating a seamless link between the scientist/inventor and the entrepreneur, because they clearly possessed both qualities in equal measure.

There can be no doubt that Schumpeter has played a major role in raising the profile of technological change as a major determinant of economic growth. However, his work has attracted some valid criticism, on at least two major grounds relevant to this book. First, his later work, often termed 'Schumpeter Mark II', might be seen to contradict his earlier arguments on the importance of new small-firm entrepreneurs in promoting creative destruction. Put simply, while the early writings of Schumpeter were concerned with the way in which small-firm entrepreneurs, through innovation, could disrupt the status quo, his later work, after his move to the United States, put more emphasis on large firms as the drivers of innovation. In the absence of strong government regulation, there is a tendency for large firms, on becoming large, to operate as monopolies or oligopolies in circumstances where prices and technologies can be fixed by one provider or a small group of providers. Indeed, since Microsoft recently has been accused of such behaviour in a contemporary high-technology context, it is difficult to see how large-firm dominance of a sector would allow the competition necessary for Schumpeter's creative waves of destruction that HTSFs often produce. One of the major advantages of Schumpeter's 'Mark I' approach was that he implied that the capitalist system was kept honest by new entrepreneurial small firms destroying the cosy oligopolistic or monopolistic tendencies that large firms seek to establish. This was a key theoretical advance that he subsequently appeared to abandon in his 'Mark

II' work when he argued that dominance by large firms would be the natural endgame of any process of creative destruction (Schumpeter 1942).

Second, and of central importance to this book, Schumpeter failed to acknowledge a strong link between *invention* and entrepreneurship. He appeared to believe that scientists or layperson inventors invent, while entrepreneurs innovate. In other words, it is the role of the entrepreneur to exploit new ideas or present existing intellectual capital in a different way, not that a single entrepreneur might *both* create completely new entities *and* then exploit them. Christopher Freeman, when discussing Schumpeter's approach to innovation, detected this neglect of a link between invention and innovation by observing Schumpeter's approach to be as follows:

> The ability and initiative of entrepreneurs (who might or might not themselves be inventors, but more usually would *not* be) [emphasis added] created new opportunities for profits, which in turn attracted a 'swarm' of imitators and improvers to exploit the new opening with a wave of new investment, generating boom conditions.
>
> (Freeman 1982: 208)

Schumpeter's attitude is doubly surprising: first because the evidence of history shows that some of the most important inventions of the Industrial Revolution were introduced by individual technical entrepreneurs, who both invented and entrepreneurially introduced the radical new inventions that changed the way existing industries operated, or created completely new industrial activities. Second, such an 'artificial' separation of invention from entrepreneurship is surprising because it is often the lone entrepreneur, entering a sector from outside an industry, who delivers the most resounding destructive impacts that disrupt the large-firm dominance of existing technological paradigms as argued by Schumpeter in his 'Mark I' writings. Steve Jobs and Steve Wozniak might again be cited as an example of how two 'outsider' technical entrepreneurs could, with other small-firm entrepreneurs, revolutionize the world computer industry that had become dominated by large-firm producers (e.g. IBM), virtually overnight (Rothwell and Zegveld 1982).

2.3 The technical entrepreneur and the process of technological disruption

Recently, instead of the term 'creative destruction' advanced by Schumpeter, there has emerged a tendency for researchers engaged in work on technological change to use the term 'disruptive technologies' when discussing the manner in which radical new technologies upset the given technological status quo. This term, generally attributed to Christensen (1997), is intriguing since, in most contexts, it would imply that a previously virtuous regime had been interrupted by an unwarranted aberration, similar to the manner in which a flight schedule of an airport might be 'disrupted' by bad weather. However, the logic of such an interpretation must be questioned since, in most cases involving technological progress, such 'disruptive' technologies, at worst, invigorate the technological status quo through a better rate and trajectory of advancement for existing core technologies; and at best, completely *replace* the status quo with a better technological solution, often invented by technical entrepreneurs operating from a completely different (possibly new) area of science (e.g. the replacement of conventional mail with e-mail communication). In this sense, such 'disruption' might be construed as constructive. However, these technical advances, often championed by technical entrepreneurs, although desirable in theory, are frequently blocked by various forms of industrial inertia, sometimes involving an unwillingness to abandon known ways of doing things, but most importantly, also through the monopolistic (or oligopolistic) behaviour of large firms in circumstances where one producer (or a small number of producers) within a sector deliberately inhibit technological progress in order to continue to enjoy 'super profits' from existing technologies based on extensive previous (inertia-causing) investment (Geer 2003).

The tendency to describe technological progress as 'disruptive' may partly stem from a natural individual (or group) human dislike of the uncertainty engendered by surprise events (in this case, technological revolutions). However, in most cases where technology is concerned, we have an illogical desire *both* for stability *and* for the fruits of rapid technological progress – where we, for example, value the benefits that mobile telephones bring, but complain when others use them on public transport. From a psychological viewpoint, there appears to be a 'glass half full/half empty' problem in that we often view technological change rather schizophrenically as *both* desirable *and* damaging, depending on whether we are using the phone or being irritated by its use. The central argument here is that technological change is unavoidable, and is increasing in pace. Indeed, it is stasis that might be seen as a more often disruptive force since, if progress proves to be generally desirable to the consumer, its inhibition in the manner described above, can prevent beneficial human progress.

2.3.1 Reasons for 'disruption'

Most of the evidence that exists on technological change suggests that, even in a perfectly responsive market where no monopolistic distortions exist, often it is not easy for new technologies to replace (or disrupt) the status quo (Schumpeter 1942; Kamien and Swartz 1983; Oakey 1993; Christensen 1997*)*. Consumers are often reluctant to change, and are not easily persuaded by the forceful advertising of products, as witnessed by the initial massive success of mobile phone technology when this offering was of high utility and reasonable cost, and the subsequent relatively slow uptake of its 3G 'next generation' replacement, which was expensive and performed poorly in its initial form. The consumer has a very well-developed sense of what has high and widespread personal utility (e.g. the basic mobile phone) and of technological 'improvements' that are, by comparison, 'cosmetic' (e.g. 3G phones incorporating cameras, etc.). Since 'disruptive' technologies will only be strongly disruptive if what they offer is *substantially* better than what already exists, we should not worry that substantive disruption resulting from spurious technological 'advances' will occur, causing the inconvenience of change without benefit.

Freeman (1986) has illustrated this problem succinctly when examining Schumpeter's work on the data produced by Kondratiev (1925) on 'Long Wave' theory, which attributed 'upswings' in the world's economic cycle to crucial technological inventions (Schumpeter 1942). Looking to the future, Freeman argued that, for any new technology to have broad impact (and be commercially 'disruptive'), it must possess three major attributes: first, an ability to achieve rapid reductions in the cost of its production (say in less than ten years); second, a *concomitant* achievement of a rapid improvement in performance of the new technology (or specification) (see Figure 2.3); and third, partly as a consequence of points

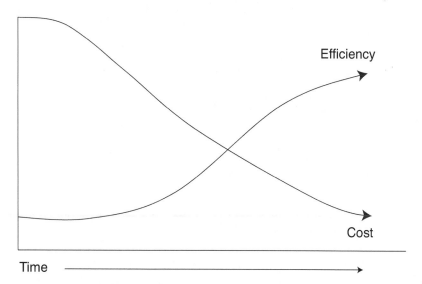

Figure 2.3 The growing impact of commercially disruptive technology over time

one and two above, the new technology should have a wide impact, not only by creating a completely new type of industrial activity, but by reducing operation costs across a wide range of other existing industrial and commercial sectors. Freeman argued, with both strong theoretical logic, and widespread evidence from the industry, that semiconductor technology had adequately fulfilled the three above requirements, and has produced massive impacts in the factory (e.g. robots) and the office (e.g. word processing, etc.). While these achievements, often by technical entrepreneurs, have 'disrupted' (and destroyed) some industrial activities (e.g. thermionic valve and typewriter production), the overall net gain to the world economy in efficiency has been substantial and widespread (Freeman 1986).

2.3 Philosophical perspectives on how new knowledge is created and absorbed

There are many parallels between the manner in which scientific knowledge is generated and absorbed into academia and the manner in which industry utilizes new technology. In this context, the use of the term 'paradigm', defined as a regime of knowledge, has often been used in both academic and industrial contexts (Dosi 1993). Perhaps one of the greatest arguments in the philosophy of science, which has relevance to the current concern for industrial technological change, occurred between Karl Popper (1965) and Thomas Kuhn (1962), in which both authors made telling contributions regarding the manner in which scientific knowledge evolves over time. These views are of concern here, both because, as noted above, the principle of a 'dominant paradigm' is useful in describing knowledge accumulation in academia and industry, but also because the results of academic discoveries often form the basis for new industrial products (or whole industries). Thus the contrasting arguments of Popper and Kuhn, on how science progresses, can be directly applied to an understanding of how industrial technological progress occurs. Popper's argument on 'progress' (implying improvement) provides a more useful and accurate description of what science and industry achieve than Kuhn's more limited proposition on 'change', since in areas such as medicine and manufacturing we can point to examples of real progress (e.g. the invention of anaesthetics; the semiconductor) (Magee 1973; Harvey 1973). Nonetheless, intriguingly, Kuhn's conceptions of 'normal science' and 'paradigm shift' are equally useful, and offer a compelling alternative model of scientific change.

Figure 2.4 provides a simplified comparison of Popper's view of progress with that of Kuhn, to show how 'progress' might be achieved, either steadily

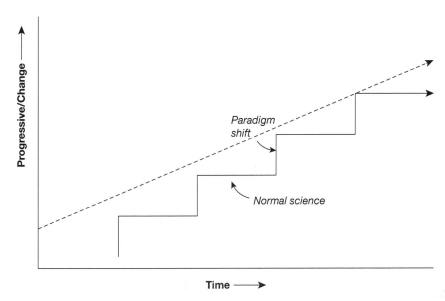

Figure 2.4 Step change versus smooth technological progress

over time (dashed straight line), according to Popper, or through changes by means of a series of 'steps' (solid lines), according to Kuhn, in which periods of 'normal science' are punctuated by sudden 'paradigm shifts', when revolutionary progress is achieved almost 'overnight', and old regimes are replaced by 'young Turks'. Kuhn adds that such change in science within academic institutions is often of a generational nature (Kuhn 1962).

However, as noted above, although these concepts were developed to explain how changes occur in basic science, they have equal utility in explaining how change can occur in industrial contexts. In both the academic and industrial instances, progress is often inhibited in order to serve the narrow imperatives of 'power elites', against the general interests of the public. However, it is significant to note that, in an industrial context, it is generally the brief periods of paradigm shift that produce progress, while 'normal' periods, although stable, do not deliver benefits. Thus, it is through periods of 'disruption' that progress is achieved: 'disruption' is the healthy *norm* for industrial behaviour (as noted in the quote by Schumpeter at the beginning of this chapter), and, by implication, stasis is an aberration. This observation fits well with the views of both Schumpeter (1939) and Christensen (1997), discussed above, in which respectively 'waves of creative destruction' or 'disruption' were seen as key deliverers of radical technological progress.

Another means of depicting progress in an industrial context is to view the principles expressed in the preceeding discussion of Figure 2.4 in terms of sequential product life cycles (or sigmoid growth curves) in which a mature 'existing technology' is supplanted (or disrupted) by a radical new and more efficient replacement technology (see Figure 2.5).

Significantly, the 'destruction or disruption' of one product by another could be seen as a traumatic event (often causing a collapse in the original product's sales, a subsequent loss of jobs, and the possible demise of the whole industry). However, Figure 2.5 implies that, in many cases, there is a strong evolutionary dimension to the process of technological progress, which is likely to bring major medium- to long-term benefits to the consumer in circumstances where an individual might be both damaged by the technological progress (i.e. made redundant), while benefitting from such an advance as a consumer. The diagram depicts the relationship between two product life cycles in terms of efficiency/sales over time (as only part of a possibly longer evolutionary trend). For Product 1 (P1), basic research creates the new technology on which the product is based, while

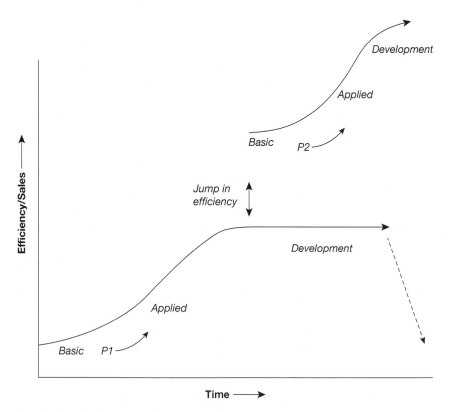

Figure 2.5 The disruptive impact of evolving technologies

applied research delivers the most rapid period of efficiency gains as the new technology is honed, and performance and production problems are eliminated. Subsequently, development R&D is mainly concerned with 'fine tuning' of the product design and performance, and is largely 'cosmetic', since few efficiency gains are achievable at this mature point, due to the 'law of diminishing returns' setting in during the latter stages of any product life cycle, which might ultimately lead to obsolescence (dashed lined arrow in Figure 2.5).

At the point where P1 has reached the stage of only marginal gains in efficiency at the top of the curve, a number of possibilities exist. First, in some cases, due to arriving at a technological 'brick wall', progress is not possible for technical reasons (at least for some time), and Product 2 (P2) does not come 'on stream' to replace P1 (e.g. the lack of a replacement for Concorde). Second, due to monopoly (or virtual monopoly power when large firms act in consort) – where a substantial proportion of an industry-level output is dominated by one firm (or a small number of firms operating oligopolistically) – there is no impetus for manufacturers to produce a replacement for P1, due to the inertia caused by past investment in P1 (i.e. production equipment, sales facilities and servicing – e.g. motor vehicle production based on the internal combustion engine), the high profitability of the status quo and lack of competition. Significantly, in such circumstances, the interests of the customer can be neglected. Looked at from the theoretical perspective of the conflict between 'demand pull' and 'innovation push' as a motive for technological change, any 'innovation push' on the manufacturer tends to be negated by a highly seductive status quo position in which high profits and low uncertainty are enjoyed at minimal R&D cost, while 'demand pull' is also curtailed by the inability of the public to obtain better-performing products under conditions of monopolistic (or oligopolistic) power in which market and technology 'fixing' is achieved by a single producer or a small group of producers acting in concert (Oakey 1993; Geer 2003).

There are two major ways in which this hiatus position of a 'log jam' in technological progress might be broken to restore a more normal and healthy position of general technological competition. First, the market can 'free itself' through actors with no stake in the monopoly status quo breaking into the market with an alternative technological solution to restore competition; often these are new small-firm technical entrepreneurs (this option will be considered in detail below). Second, governments may restore the competitive equilibrium, either through anti-monopoly legislation (common in Western developed economies) or through entering into the market as a customer/manufacturer, to promote the development and production of a particular technology determined to be of economic, military or a combined strategic importance to the nation or a group of nations acting as a consortium (e.g. Airbus Industries in Europe).

If we return to Figure 2.5, this diagram can be used to illustrate a 'real life' example of how government 'demand pull' spending has provoked a much-needed new technical solution in which P1 was superseded by a much better technical solution in the form of P2. A major impediment to the development of early computers was the use of thermionic valves to provide the electronic switches necessary for the construction of computer functions. Because, in order to improve the memory and operating functions of computers, thousands of electronic switches were required, the early computers were huge, with banks of valves that filled large rooms. There was intense demand from the military establishment, especially in the United States, to find a new type of electronic switch to replace the thermionic valve that would be cheaper to produce, more robust and, crucially, much smaller, in order that computer memory power in particular could be rapidly improved (Morse 1976; Freeman 1982; Cardullo 1999). If this example is imposed on Figure 2.5, P1 equates to the thermionic valve in circumstances where the 'flat' (small residual progress) development stage of the product development curve was reached by about 1950. An inability further to develop the thermionic valve led to intense *demand pull* from the United States military establishment to produce an alternative, a motive that, for 20 years between 1950 and 1970 was successively driven by the Korean War, the Cold War and the Space Race (Rothwell and Zegveld 1982; Cardullo 1999). The United States government funding of research aimed at improvement of the thermionic valve (P1 in Figure 2.5) throughout this period – as a means of increasing the power of computers used to control aircraft, missiles and eventually the space shuttle – initially prompted development of the transistor in the late 1940s (P2 in Figure 2.5), and through progressive miniaturization, development of integrated circuits, and the microprocessor family of products in the late 1960s.

The replacement of the old technology by the new, as Figure 2.5 depicts, afforded an immediate 'jump' in efficiency; this was subsequently augmented by the fact that this new solution was only at the *beginning* of a new product development curve where gains for a given input of R&D investment throughout the 'applied' phase of product development (see Figure 2.5) would be rapid during the steep part of the development curve. Moreover, the miniaturization of silicon-based electronics, unlike many defence-induced technologies, found widespread use in terms of *civil applications* and, as noted above, has led to efficiency gains in many existing forms of production (e.g. robots in the motor vehicle industry). This has been the enabling core technology that has allowed new products to emerge, often led by new technical entrepreneurs (e.g. word processors; mobile phones; the internet) (Freeman 1986). This was a case where government defence spending's 'demand pull' triggered a radical 'breakthrough' invention that heralded a generally 'smooth', efficient development of the 'electronic switch' function through semiconductors and integrated circuits to microprocessors between 1945 and 1970.

However, from a broader perspective, the above example indicates that, although the arrival of P2 is highly 'disruptive' to sales of P1, the far less desirable option of the non-disruption of P1 (i.e. in this case a continuance of the inefficient thermionic valve option) would be, in itself, a disruption to technological progress; thus suggesting, as argued above, that periods of stasis in terms of the process of technological change are the disruption, and not the process of change. Moreover, it is also probable that, without the 'demand pull' intervention of the United States government over 25 years, competition between large existing electronics firms, steeped in thermionic valve technology, would not have produced such substantial progress.

Thus, to draw together the arguments of the previous paragraphs, Figures 2.4 and 2.5 may be amalgamated in that the step changes of Figure 2.4 can be broadly superimposed on the product cycles of Figure 2.5 (see Figure 2.6). Here, the periods of rapid progress (i.e. the applied stage of the product life cycle in Figure 2.5) can be broadly equated with the 'paradigm shift' step change of Figure 2.4. Clearly, the curved line of product efficiency growth in Figure 2.5 is less abrupt than the vertical line of efficiency growth in Figure 2.4. However, it should be noted that while the step-change concept is a *simplification* of reality in order to aid explanation, it is also true that, in many fast-moving high-technology sectors, complete product life cycles last less than five years (Oakey 1984a, 1995), implying a 'blip' shape to the product life-cycle curve in that both rapid growth *and* decline occur, with almost no development phase, over a very short product life cycle.

Similarly, the 'normal science' flat section of Figure 2.4, where little or no efficiency gains occur, is directly synonymous with the mature 'development stage' of the product life cycle in Figure 2.5. As noted above, in both instances, institutional inertia can be proposed as a possible cause of stasis. While Kuhn (1962) viewed 'normal science' within academia as a stage in scientific development when institutional inertia was often caused by an 'old guard' of scientists protecting the received wisdom status quo (which was often generational in nature), it has been suggested in this chapter that, in an industrial context, monopoly power (or virtual monopoly power involving oligopolistic behaviour) can achieve the same static result. In both instances, the key common point to note is that, although

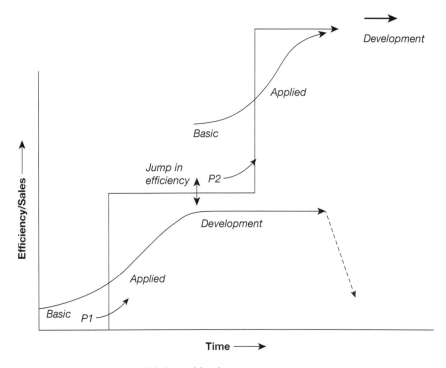

Figure 2.6 Figures 2.4 and 2.5 combined

steady progress is clearly generally beneficial, and desirable from the consumer viewpoint, there is often a critical divergence between what is desired by society (i.e. steady progress), and what might be advantageous for large firms in sectors that they dominate, which is often preservation of the status quo, from which only colluding large firms exclusively benefit.

2.4. The catalytic role of the technical entrepreneur

Although paradoxical, it is often the case that the longer a period of arrested industrial progress continues, the greater the shift that will be caused when a 'revolutionary change' eventually occurs. It is analogous to, for example, an earthquake, where a long period of stasis is often not evidence of stability but, more dramatically, represents as yet unreleased 'under the surface' pressure for change. Thus, a long period without an earthquake is often an indicator of an eventual radical event. It is perverse in an industrial context that, as pressure for progress builds – caused, for example, by poor product performance, or poor safety or pollution concerns

– manufacturers who produce the products that are causing such concern often resist this need for change, because they find the status quo profitable in an industrial sector that they dominate, and they are afraid of being swept away by a sudden technological change that they fear will be both dramatic and irreversible. Moreover, a sudden change in the direction of technological progress might mean that such a manufacturer did not possess the necessary R&D competence, and would not be able to compete in this radically new technological environment (e.g. the destructive impact on high-street music shops delivered by music downloads through the internet). The much-reported difficulties experienced by Frank Whittle in the late 1920s when attempting to promote his new jet-engine design to United Kingdom aircraft manufacturing firms, steeped in piston-engine technology, bear witness to the potency of the above-noted phenomenon of resistance, in this case, to an *inevitable* shift away from a piston-engine technology paradigm that had, by the late 1930s, reached its efficiency ceiling. Although Whittle's patents were eventually successfully exploited, the delay in developing jet-engine technology bears witness to the power of such inertia, sufficient to seriously damage the United Kingdom's Second World War effort. More recently, the initial reluctance of IBM to develop desktop and laptop computers and of Kodak to exploit their early invention of digital camera technology is further good evidence of this phenomenon.

However, resistance to technological progress by large well-established firms is not a universal phenomenon. For example, in the pharmaceutical industry, large firms commonly invest massive sums of capital into R&D aimed at producing new 'world-beating' drugs, in circumstances where their share price can rise or fall rapidly, depending on the optimism of reports from field trials or analysts on the progress of the new drug under development. Nonetheless, there remain other sectors of industry where large firms dominate in circumstances where necessary technological change (often demanded by social and political pressures) is slow to make progress. In sectors as diverse as banking, energy, and motor vehicle production, large firms often offer goods and/or services that are worryingly similar in both type and price, under conditions where called-for necessary changes deemed beneficial to the public are slow to appear (e.g. banking – interest rates, loans to small firms; energy – wind and solar power; motor vehicles – electric power, fuel cells). Indeed, desirable changes, which large firms may be reluctant to undertake, can often be achieved 'overnight' by governments that unilaterally declare, for heath or other reasons, that a technological change is mandatory (e.g. the change to lead-free petrol engines in the United States during the 1970s) (Rothwell and Zegveld 1981).

Notwithstanding these variable large-firm behaviour patterns, a major mechanism for change provided by the free market system is that of entrepreneurial action. In circumstances where technological progress on the part of large firms has been arrested by a tactical unwillingness on their part to adopt and develop existing basic scientific discoveries (or invent totally new technical solutions), technical entrepreneurs, who have no interest in the status quo, often destroy existing technological paradigms and clear the way for a new period of rapid technological change-led growth (Schumpeter 1939; Dosi 1993). These individuals are often disenchanted 'spin-off' entrepreneurs from existing large firms (Oakey *et al.* 1988), or academic entrepreneurs from universities (Roberts 1991).

The technical and/or managerial fragility of the status quo maintained by large firms can often be detected in the simplicity of the technical change that is used by entrepreneurs to destroy current dominant paradigms, and create market shares for themselves when entering long-established areas of product- or service-based industry. For example, James Dyson, after many years of sectoral stability, revolutionized the vacuum cleaner industry by inventing the 'bag-less' vacuum cleaner. Similarly, Peter Wood launched Direct Line Insurance in 1985, which grew to be a major player in the United Kingdom insurance market by using well-established telesales techniques to sell insurance by telephone – a unique juxtaposition of two well-known concepts that produced a new business model which delivered convenience to the consumer, while increasing operating efficiencies in the insurance industry. In many ways, the simple nature of these inventions and/or innovations, that significantly could easily have been introduced by large industry-leader firms, indicates how complacent many large-firm dominators of a sector of industry or commerce can become, rendering them an easy target for aggressive new entrepreneurs, who initially operate from a relatively poor competitive capital base.

In other instances, the invention of new technologies can have very radical impacts on existing product- or service-based industries. In some cases, the new radical technology arises from within an existing sector, and is known, but not properly exploited, by major players in this industry. An example of this phenomenon is the inability of IBM to respond adequately to the potential of the microprocessor, of which they already had detailed knowledge, as a basis for desktop computers in the early 1970s (partly because they were distracted by historically high profits gained from the sale of the mainframe computers that the desktop computer was destined largely to replace). In other instances, entrepreneurs seek to exploit a new technology by *invading* sectors where a new and damaging technology did not previously exist. Recent high-technology examples of this tendency are the destruction of traditional photography (camera and print-developing technologies) by digital camera and printing technology; while the internet has impacted on many areas of business in what appeared to be, before such impact occurred, distant technological and operational contexts, such as postal deliveries, high-street shopping and music retail outlets (Christensen 1997; Christensen and Bower 2004). While the progress of many of these new internet-based technologies depends, to a large extent, on the adoption levels and rates of related enabling technologies (e.g. more powerful desktop computers; broadband rather than 'dial-up' internet connections), their eventual dominance cannot be doubted. Significantly, many of the firms leading this broadly based new technology revolution are new enterprises founded by technical entrepreneurs, beginning from modest resource bases, which have grown large at a rapid rate on the basis of specialist skills that impact upon unrelated sectors where they are not well understood (e.g. Google; eBay; Cisco Systems).

Clearly, existing large firms, which have suffered in this conflict with new technical entrepreneurs, do not willingly surrender lucrative areas of business to new entrants. It has previously been mentioned that complacency and a desire to preserve monopolistic or oligopolistic profits derived from a well-established and heavily invested-in technology all contribute to a failure to keep pace efficiently with technological progress in their own and relevant related areas. However, particularly in modern technologically complex and rapidly changing circumstances, the process of choosing the correct path for investment in R&D in large firms is inherently difficult and consequently risky. Moreover, it is a characteristic of many of the most radical technological revolutions that they often emerge on the boundary between technological disciplines, or where technologies intermingle and overlap. Here, many technically entre-preneurial small firms exist, while the core large firms of the overlapping two (or more) sectors involved tend to occupy their respective distant 'centre grounds'. Indeed, as noted above, many of the most severe technological revolutions emerge from totally different technological areas to that of the large firm that feels the impact of such change. This implies that the affected large firm could not have avoided the damage involved by such penetration through engaging in traditional *intra-sectoral* R&D, since this research would have not been directed at the correct area of related science. For example, it is possible that future development of computing 'brain' power will take place in biological science through research on how human brains process information biologically, and not through the further development of electronic-based solutions, especially since the potential for further efficiency gains in performance through the progressive miniaturization of electronic circuits is reaching its physical limit.

While corporate venturing allows large existing firms scope for investing in new firms working in adjacent areas of technology that are of potential future relevance to their main area of operation (e.g. the interest of large pharmaceuticals firms in their small biotechnology counterparts) (Oakey *et al.* 1990b), the relevance of technical entrepreneurs to the development of new areas of technology in young industries, and radical technological departures from well-established areas of production, remains strong. It is the key role of technical entrepreneurs to expose gaps and weaknesses in the status quo, invent new and better ways of meeting existing needs, and create new needs that currently do not exist; especially in circumstances when large existing firms cannot, or will not, perform this function. In terms of economic theory, it is the role of the technical entrepreneur to *repair* the economic system when the competition-driven process of technological progress may be blocked (for the reasons discussed above). Put simply, in this way, entrepreneurs help to keep the economic system 'honest'.

2.5 More subtle attributes of the technical entrepreneur

Because so many technical entrepreneurs emerge from a research environment that is typically either an R&D department of a large firm or a university, the type of entrepreneurship they bring to HTSF formation and growth consists of a quite unique set of skills and attitudes not found in other areas of industrial entrepreneurship. Many technical entrepreneurs are as much (if not more) interested in the technical solutions they are able to deliver as the financial rewards they subsequently receive, to the extent that they often regard the financial rewards involved as an *additional* reward for inventing the product that made them millionaires, and that finding technical solutions to problems was enough reward in itself. This broadly 'academic' approach has a number of ramifications that explain many of the characteristics that have been found to typify HTSF entrepreneurship in general, and the clustered areas in which these HTSF founders are often located. Examples of this difficult-to-'pin-down' phenomenon are presented below.

As noted earlier in Chapter 1, technical entrepreneurs often emerge from universities or 'spin off' from existing larger high-technology firms, usually when they are in their mid-thirties, after they have acquired enough technical knowledge to create a new product or process technology that would be the basis for a new firm. A ramification of this process is that such individuals will typically have spent several years working with other researchers in structured or semi-structured teams. Moreover, technical entrepreneurs who begin new HTSFs after working in the university sector come from a tradition where the fruits of academic research are often made freely available through publication in academic journals, in circumstances where kudos, and not direct financial benefit, is the 'currency' that will bring reward through promotion within the academic system. Although this regime of disclosure has been somewhat eroded by recent government pressure on universities to generate internal funds by protecting the intellectual property they create (and this is particularly contentious in the medical research field), academic research is typically conducted in an environment in which collaboration between individuals and universities continues to be encouraged through informal networking, seminars, conferences and subsequent related journal publications. Thus, in all the above contexts, regardless of whether the new HTSF entrepreneur is a university or a large-firm 'spin-off', there is a predisposition to collaborative, collegiate behaviour, in which it is often the case that 'democratic' teams of technical entrepreneurs, rather than autocratic individuals, 'spin off' to form new firms; these collaborative characteristics render such new firms more attractive to potential venture capital funders, as noted above in this chapter, and in Chapter 3 below.

However, there are also a number of more subtle ways in which technical entrepreneurship can create a conducive environment for HTSF growth, often within clusters. First, a major reason why the local venture capital industry was so critical to the formation of Silicon Valley in the 1970s and 1980s through its financial support for new HTSFs was the simple fact that, not only were the new-firm founders technical entrepreneurs, but also many of the venture capital firms (run either by an individual or a small group) had also previously been technical entrepreneurs. In many cases, these investors had gained experience by growing an HTSF within Silicon Valley, and then 'selling out' to a large multinational firm, thus providing the capital for their subsequent venture capital business. Apart from these new venture capitalists being able to 'speak the same language' as their entrepreneurial clients, they were also able, through their relevant past technical expertise derived from this 'silicon-based' technical cluster, to evaluate more accurately the potential of the new product they were being asked to invest in, and give good 'hands on' strategic advice based on their own experience of running an HTSF in a relevant high-technology manufacturing sub-sector. Indeed, it has previously been noted that a major shortcoming of the United Kingdom venture capital industry when it was established in the early 1980s was that managers of these venture capital funds tended to be ex-bank managers or accountants with no technical expertise relevant to the HTSFs in which they were investing (Oakey 1984b, 1995). In these circumstances, such individuals tended to revert to what they knew best (which was the need to secure their investment through physical assets, rarely possessed by HTSFs), while ignoring the potential of the technology being developed, on which they were not qualified to comment, and which was often the HTSF's only asset. In Silicon Valley, where it was frequently the case that both the investor and investee had technical entrepreneurial experience, the evaluation of HTSF potential was much better informed (Bullock 1983).

Second, the collegiate atmosphere of the pre-formation work locations of the HTSF entrepreneurs often continues after 'spin-off' in circumstances where these new entrepreneurs continue to network with each other, both informally on a bilateral basis, and more formally through technical conferences and sub-sectoral industry events for specialisms within the HTSF technical area (e.g. biotechnology; electronics; software). These networking relationships can not only operate in a dispersed 'virtual' sense, but can also manifest themselves in physical clustering. Indeed, if the biotechnology sub-sector of high-technology industry is considered, although there is no strong functional reason for the firms to be physically concentrated, due to the international origins and destinations respectively of their inputs and outputs, they, nonetheless, are often physically concentrated in clusters. A major reason for this clustering behaviour is not logistical, but behavioural (or tacit) in that 'being in the swim', where key staff and their ideas can move within the cluster, is more important than economic manufacturing efficiency considerations. This is partly because much of the biotechnology sector remains quasi-academic and is often located near to major universities (e.g. Cambridge in the United Kingdom) (Oakey *et al.* 1990b; Oakey 1995).

Third, a perhaps more subtle adjunct to the need to network on technical matters, HTSFs and their larger high-technology counterparts, for all the reasons given above, often collaborate on an informal basis in certain restricted circumstances. The clusters of the Silicon Valley type that HTSFs have been known to form are unusual in that they involve *both* collaboration *and* competition in the same environment (Oakey 2007b). Some writers on high-technology industries have virtually suggested, through the use of such terms as 'technology transfer' and 'spill over', that new technology is almost a 'free good', often obtained through the extensive local networking of cluster entrepreneurs. However, in clusters such as Silicon Valley, the environment is clearly very competitive in circumstances where, for example, small and medium-sized local sub-contract manufacturers compete with each other on price and quality, to the benefit of their local large-firm customers.

At first sight, maintaining the arguments that collaboration and competition both create cluster advantage would appear to be extremely contradictory. Nonetheless, this apparent contradiction can be resolved by a consideration of Figure 2.7, in which it is clear that any cluster is

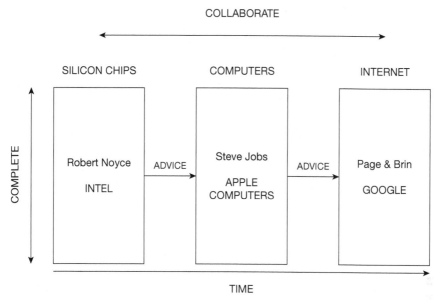

Figure 2.7 Collaboration and competition in HTSF clusters

comprised of many HTSFs, all working in high-technology industry, but divisible into many discrete technology-based sub-sectors (or sub-sectoral silos). Generally speaking, in a cluster, firms tend to vertically compete *within* the sub-sector in which they are operating, but may collaborate horizontally *across* unrelated sectors. This phenomenon can be illustrated by an example from recent history from Silicon Valley, indicated in Figure 2.7, where Robert Noyce, the chief executive of Intel, was happy to advise Steve Jobs when he was in the process of co-founding Apple Computers. Jobs was, in turn, happy to give advice to Larry Page and Serge Brin, the founders of Google (Berlin 2005). However, it would be unlikely that Robert Noyce would have helped a rival silicon chip manufacturer, or that Steve Jobs would have assisted a computer manu-facturing competitor. Indeed, one reason why this chain of advice occurred was clearly that Jobs was subsequently a customer of Intel, and Apple Computer, Inc. benefitted in sales terms from the spread of the internet, assisted by Google. In reality, this well-documented chain of advice probably had both social and hard-headed business stimuli, but it must also have been derived from the fact that all those concerned were technical entrepreneurs with similar views on how technical entrepreneurship should be conducted, involving a degree of the fraternal and professional collegiality noted above, when strategically appropriate.

2.6 Chapter summary

Certainly in terms of the emerging high-technology industries that will form the basis for industrial production in the future, this chapter has made it clear that the technical entrepreneur will play a major part in this process. It was also noted that this phenomenon is not new, and should have been taken into account by Victorian economists when they were attempting to explain the reasons for economic growth at the height of the Industrial Revolution. The importance of technical entrepreneurship is partly caused by the ability of HTSFs founded by technical entrepreneurs to conduct R&D aimed at the development of new products in a highly efficient manner; and partly because they begin businesses based on radical new technologies which have the potential to challenge existing technological paradigms that are frequently maintained by large multinational firms.

Consequently, due to the strategic importance of new high-technology industries to future national industrial development, it has been readily apparent that governments in developed and developing countries throughout the world have sought to encourage the birth and growth of technical entrepreneurially based new firms, often by seeking to tease out more technical entrepreneurs from universities through academic enterprise. However, it was strongly argued that attempts to force increased entrepreneurship would be a dangerous practice since not all technically qualified scientists and engineers are interested in beginning a new firm due to their maximization of non-financial rewards for the technical work they perform. Nonetheless, when technical entrepreneurs do emerge, either from a university or as a 'spin-off' from a large high-technology firm, they often have the intellectual capacity to handle both the technical skills required and the entrepreneurial drive that will make the firm a success. Moreover, in instances where academics and industrial scientists begin new HTSFs, their previous experience, if working in teams, often means that groups of entrepreneurs combine to form new HTSFs, a democratic approach that is often very attractive to venture capital investors.

The central passages of Chapter 2 explore in some detail the role of technical entrepreneurship as a key catalyst in fostering technological change. Inevitably, this discussion involved a consideration of the work of Joseph Schumpeter, since he was one of the first economists, and certainly the most famous, to place the entrepreneur at the centre of the process of technological change, and, by implication, economic growth, by introducing the concept of 'waves of creative destruction'. A consideration of Schumpeter's theoretical approach involved some criticism of his arguments, and in particular his separation of invention from innovation, in that he believed that the entrepreneur was more important in innovation than invention. From a technical entrepreneurship viewpoint, the ability of an individual (or group of individuals) to *both* invent *and* then innovate is a key characteristic, although this approach was, surprisingly, not supported by Schumpeter. However, examples from the Industrial Revolution were cited to argue that technical entrepreneurship is a long-standing phenomenon in which invention and innovation are frequently performed by a single individual to great and very efficient effect.

The relevant work of Schumpeter on 'creative destruction' was then combined with that of Christensen on 'disruptive technologies' to delve deeper into the role of technical entrepreneurs in delivering new technologies to the customer and keeping the capitalist system competitive. In this context, ideas from the philosophy of scientific method were marshalled to argue that, if we agree that technological progress is the natural way in which capitalist systems should behave, 'disruptive' technologies are not actually disruptive, but it is periods of stasis that disrupt the otherwise steady trend of progress. Reasons are suggested as to why the arresting of progress occurs, mainly based on the activities of large dominant firms either acting monopolistically or oligopolistically to preserve the 'status quo'. It was strongly argued that it is often technical entrepreneurs entering an existing market from outside the sector who revolutionize the number and quality of products available to the customer (e.g. music downloads taking the place of high-street shops), thus playing an essential role of keeping the economic system honest by disrupting outdated ways of doing things and protecting the interest of the consumer, who is most keen to receive improved product choice at the cheapest price possible.

The chapter concluded by discussing a number of more subtle aspects of technical entrepreneurship that produce advantage, especially when HTSFs are founded in clustered locations. It was noted that the availability of venture capitalists in clusters (e.g. Silicon Valley) was greatly enhanced by the tendency for many of the investors to be ex-technical entrepreneurs. This means that such individuals had substantial experience of evaluating the technological potential of a new HTSF, based on technical entrepreneurship, which also enabled them to provide relevant strategic advice. In this way, the success of a cluster is reinvested in the cluster and does not leak away to other locations. In a similar vein, there is a somewhat collegiate dimension to the technical entrepreneurship expertise – evidence exists that informal mentoring takes place within a cluster, whereby new technical entrepreneurs receive advice from their well-established successful counter-parts. Such mentoring was used to explain the apparent contradiction in which a cluster can both benefit from collaboration and competition. It is argued that, in general, collaboration can take place among different technological sub-sectors of the cluster horizontally, while competition takes place vertically between firms in the same sub-sector of the cluster.

3 Clusters, incubators and science parks

3.1 A theoretical context

3.1.1 The importance of proximity

As discussed in Chapter 2, it has long been evident to location theorists, especially when observing the earliest beginnings of the Industrial Revolution in the eighteenth century, that many nascent forms of industrial production have tended to coalesce into, and benefited from, clustered locations (e.g. iron making at Coalbrookdale in Shropshire; cotton textile production in North Cheshire and Lancashire in England) (Marshall 1920; Riley 1973). Later key growth industries of the Victorian era (e.g. clock making in London [Martin 1966]; gun and jewellery making in Birmingham [Wise 1949]; and furniture manufacturing in East London [Hall 1963]) were similarly co-located, in vertically disintegrated agglomerations, where individual parts of the production process were performed by several independent firms, working towards final assembly in 'hub' enterprises.

Perhaps not surprisingly, early explanations for such clustering focussed upon the critical role played by skilled labour. The main conclusion of Weber (1929) was that a concentrated supply of skilled labour would distort a least-cost optimum factory location, as determined by minimum transport costs for input raw materials. Such arguments were later modified by other theoreticians, who emphasized that the market for industrial products was the main location determinant (Hotelling 1929; Losch 1954). Yet more recent writing has emphasized the importance of *both* input *and* output local linkages in agglomerated urban-area locations (Wood 1969; Taylor 1971). This more balanced approach to suppliers and customers did not, however, contradict Weber's earlier assertions on the importance of labour, since the coincidence of markets and skilled labour living largely within urban areas was a strong reason for the metropolitan location of much

Victorian industry. Indeed, people (i.e. by virtue of their buying power, entrepreneurship and technical knowledge) were the basic 'feedstock' of such clusters, as both the creators of goods and customers for them, living increasingly in or near urban centres. These early conceptualizations of clusters are very relevant to the subject matter of this book on high-technology entrepreneurship since local material linkages and skilled labour are major reasons why modern high-technology clusters have emerged (e.g. Silicon Valley) (Oakey 1985a).

Nonetheless, as the twentieth century progressed beyond the Victorian era, the relevance of industrial clustering appeared to decline. A period of post-Second World War enthusiasm for industrial redistribution in the United Kingdom through 'mobile industry policies', triggered by a system of grants (i.e. 'carrots') and licences (i.e. 'sticks'), fostered the view that modern industry was 'footloose' and indifferent to the locational cost advantages of agglomeration (Luttrell 1962; Townroe 1971; Keeble 1976). However, by the early 1980s, it began to become clear in evidence from the United States that the modern emerging high-technology industries were showing strong signs of agglomerative behaviour by developing in clustered locations (e.g. Route 128; Silicon Valley – see Oakey 1984a, 1985b; Saxenian 1985). Moreover, more recently, eminent mainstream economists have, perhaps because of this tendency for modern industry to cluster, discovered clustering and, although largely ignoring the long-standing wealth of previous work by fellow locational economists in this area, have begun to acknowledge the existence of geographical clustering as a key determinant of production efficiency (Krugman 1991; Arthur 1994). Apart from the point, obvious to industrial geographers, that such awakening to spatial influence is rather overdue, more serious criticism has been levelled, mainly on the grounds that, although economists have begun to acknowledge clustering as a factor influencing production efficiency, their treatment of it lacks the necessary complexity that would give it full value within any 'equation' designed to measure the locational advantage of clustering (Martin 1999).

Nonetheless, Michael Porter, who approaches clustering from a strategic perspective, has recently successfully promoted the cause of clusters, particularly to government policy makers, for which he deserves much credit. Porter has also produced valuable research evidence on various types and stages of clusters in the United States and other nations (Porter 1998). However, his work, while strong in identifying links between clustering advantage and the competitive behaviour of larger (often multinational) firms, as they seek to drive down production costs, pays less attention to the role of entrepreneurial small firms in originally creating and delivering the efficiency advantages of clusters. In a high-technology context, this is achieved through HTSF inventions and innovations that change existing technological paradigms, and in so doing, provide new products based on new technologies that take industrial standards onto a higher and different level, not achievable by the incremental improvement of the conventional technologies offered by well-established larger firms (Oakey 1993).

3.1.2 Cluster-causing factors

Studies of many industrial clusters across different time periods, in different sectors, and in different countries, have isolated only a few common key determinants of cluster advantage. Prevalent among these are:

  local risk capital (private and public);
  local entrepreneurs;
  local skilled labour (blue- and white-collar);
  local industrial services.

Critically, all the four factors noted above, either directly or indirectly, involve different forms of human capital (Cooper 1970; Oakey 1984a; Saxenian 1985; Oakey *et al.* 1988).

If these factors are considered in turn, public or private risk capital is provided as a result of decisions made by local private and/or public sector investors to accept risk, an advantage (together with critical technological knowledge of the technology to be supported) that may vary in geographical extent and can become specialized in particular locations (e.g. the funding of HTSFs in Silicon Valley) (Mason *et al.* 2002). In the context of the United Kingdom, it is clear that venture capital availability is itself clustered (implying scarcity in non-clustered locations). Indeed, it is widely acknowledged that the presence of aggressive and technically well-informed private venture capitalists was critical in the development of Silicon Valley in the vicinity of San Francisco, an advantage that was not available in other locations within the United States (Cooper 1970; Bullock 1983).

Similarly, the existence of successful local entrepreneurs is both an obvious cause and an effect of a good localized labour supply, partly through the tendency for successful entrepreneurs to become venture capitalists, as, for example, in Silicon Valley. However, the occurrence of initial entrepreneurs in areas where labour specialization has not yet occurred (e.g. William Shockley in the case of transistors in Silicon Valley) can create an upwardly spiralling 'virtuous circle' of entrepreneurship, in which subsequent entrepreneurs learn technical and/or business skills from their entrepreneurial employers, and then 'spin off' to create new pools of skilled labour and enterprise in the local area. This process is exemplified by the group of employees that spun off from Shockley Transistor in 1957 to form Fairchild, which, in turn, spawned a plethora of spin-off 'Fairchildren' that complemented 'spin-off' from firms of a previous era (e.g. Hewlett-Packard) (Mason 1979; Cardullo 1999). Indeed, in a number of cases since the beginning of the Industrial Revolution, many industrial clusters have owed their existence to the efforts of single dynamic entrepreneurs (e.g. motor vehicles – Henry Ford in Detroit, William Morris in Oxford). Conversely, it has also been observed that 'blue-collar'-dominated regions with a limited history of, or potential for, entrepreneurship are unlikely sources of new entrepreneurial self-employment (e.g. parts of North East England and Scotland) (Keeble 1976; Cameron 1979).

Although less entrepreneurially dramatic, skilled labour in the form of white- and blue-collar employees is similarly a key advantage of a cluster in that such workers provide the local manufacturing and professional skills that support business founders. The local availability of sales staff, engineers, technicians and machinists, when specialized in a particular industrial sector, assists entrepreneurs to grow their businesses. For example, specialist staff in high-technology marketing have given Silicon Valley firms many subtle advantages over those in other regions that lack such local skills (e.g. the early marketing assistance given to Apple Computer, Inc. by Regis McKenna), and indeed, local skilled labour may even attract manufacturing competitors to a burgeoning cluster from other regions or nations (leading to an inflationary impact on labour costs – see sub-section 3.2.3 below). Such accumulated workers are further augmented by other new workers who individually migrate into the agglomeration from other national and/or international locations in a cumulative manner (Oakey *et al.* 1988). However, notwithstanding unavoidable wage inflation, the 'body of knowledge' inherent in a multi-talented workforce provides a creative and technical skills 'edge' for the initial clustered firms, the later 'spin-offs' noted above, and immigrant firms, over competitors in non-clustered locations.

Finally, industrial services, noted to be a key benefit of the Silicon Valley cluster (Oakey 1984a; Oakey *et al.* 1988), are advantages enjoyed by one cluster firm through trading with an adjacent counterpart within a cluster. Whether production takes place 'in house' or is sub-contracted to a specialist local supplier is a strategic decision, which is sometimes marginal. However, in many cases, when a firm is located within a cluster, the ability to find a local supplier who can perform sub-contracted tasks of high quality at competitive prices is a major advantage that often renders 'in-house' production unnecessary, and creates competitive and disintegrated networking advantages for a cluster firm over non-clustered competitors in other regions.

3.2 The sustainability of clusters – some key contradictions

Much of the above discussion has understandably concentrated on the benefits that sectoral specialization in a local geographical concentration of production can deliver. However, while there are many historical examples of successful clusters, it is also true that, in many cases, the dramatically prosperous clusters of the Victorian era no longer exist. There are a number of behavioural, technological and economic reasons why clusters ultimately may fail. These are dealt with in turn below.

3.2.1 Behavioural factors

As discussed above, clusters often owe their existence to the individual efforts of one or more key entrepreneurs. Indeed, in many cases, the most vital period of growth within a new industrial cluster may largely coincide with the most productive part of an individual entrepreneur's career. In this context, Henry Ford in the United States and William Morris in England might again be cited as good examples of how motor vehicle clusters were established in specific geographic areas during the active careers of these key individuals in Detroit and Oxford respectively; without them, the geography of motor vehicle production in these two countries might have been very different. A more modern example might be that of Gordon Moore and Robert Noyce at Fairchild, and then Intel, who have provided technical and business leadership to this core Silicon Valley firm for over 40 years (Cardullo 1999), and were the source of many other subsequent 'spin-off' firms (Mason 1979).

The key to evolutionary success for any cluster is that such core firms act as early incubators from which 'spin-off' firms can be founded locally (e.g. Hewlett-Packard and Fairchild in Silicon Valley), and that such firms should move from an entrepreneurial, often family-run structure, to a more formally managed enterprise with a full range of profession-ally managed functions (e.g. finance; marketing; strategy, etc.) before the original entrepreneur retires (Oakey 2003b). Step changes to the growth of regional industries are often brought about by the actions of one or more particularly dynamic entrepreneurs (e.g. in Silicon Valley). Unfortunately, however, without the consolidation of their achievements into professionally managed businesses, such radical achievements are often generational in nature, and can decline after the retirement of the founder.

3.2.2 Technological problems

Some aspects of the technological arguments for the formation of clusters are counter-intuitive. While an initial cluster might gain advantage from a close-knit locally concentrated group of entrepreneurs, both collaborating and competing with each other (and creating a technology 'hot spot' offering local advantages over less advanced locations), there is a danger that such a concentration eventually may become too 'technologically myopic' and introspective. There are a number of reasons for such an outcome. First, early success may create unjustified arrogance in which other approaches in other locations (often overseas) are ignored on a 'not invented here' basis. Second, a focus upon local networking might have the unwanted impact of tending to produce common, but wrong (e.g. outdated) methods of solving the problems of future technological development that confront manufacturing firms in general and high-technology firms in particular, thus leading to a ponderous or incorrect technological development trajectory within the cluster. Third, strong early technological success and subsequent high (often virtual monopoly) profits may have a dampening impact on the desire for reinvestment in radically new technological progress. The reluctance of IBM to diversify away from mainframe computer production in the early 1970s and embrace the new microprocessor-based technology that would have enabled them to produce early desktop computers is a good example of this phenomenon. Particularly given the 'short termism' of current financial markets, there can be a reluctance to plan research over long time horizons (of, say, up to 20 years). It is often not until a previously successful firm is in financial crisis, due to a lack of price and product-specification competitiveness, that the need to reinvest in future technological development is realized, by which time technological advantage has been lost to other regions or nations, and new capital investment becomes difficult to raise.

3.2.3 Economic problems

Only rarely can an unequivocal case for location within a cluster be made. In all successful clusters (e.g. Silicon Valley), for the cluster to continue to survive and prosper, the strong technical and networking advantages that clearly have occurred must outweigh the equally clear economic disadvantages of success. Major among such drawbacks are three types of rising cost. First, since it has been noted above (sub-section 3.1.2) that all types of skilled labour are critical to the success of a cluster, such success implies that, with the growth of the cluster, there will be a sharply increased local demand for labour. Since it is often through the 'poaching' of local white- and blue-collar labour that firms acquire highly-skilled specialist R&D production workers from other local competitor firms (i.e. by advertising jobs at a premium level above average local pay rates), labour costs within the cluster often rise steeply above national rates for a given job (Oakey 1984a; Swann *et al.* 1998). Second, as the cluster intensifies, local property costs will also increase, both for industrial use and domestic housing. While, as in the case of Silicon Valley, such high costs do not necessarily deter higher-order key functions of the firms from being located in the cluster (e.g. headquarters and R&D functions), less sophisticated tasks are often relocated to cheaper and lower-labour-cost locations in other regions or abroad (e.g. standardized mass-production assembly tasks) (Oakey *et al.* 1988).

Similarly, a third related cost of the cluster is increasing congestion and pollution. Congestion causes negative impacts, both at the workplace and in adjacent local areas; while increased 'journey-to-work' times due to local traffic congestion, and delays with the receipt of inputs and dispatch of outputs respectively to and from production facilities, cause increased costs. Again, for the cluster to survive, the benefits of a location predominantly within the cluster must outweigh such disadvantages. However, on balance, if all the above issues are viewed in general terms, it might be considered that most planners would prefer to have the difficulties that arise from rapid cluster growth than grapple with the more intractable effects of long-term decline within a local economy (discussed below in sub-sections 3.3.1 and 3.4.2 on 'inherited clusters'). In most of the cases of increased costs discussed above, the challenge for any development agency involves the anticipation of these various problems, which can be predicted to a greater or lesser extent, and the enactment of policies to ensure that a given cluster expands steadily and is sustained at an optimum level over a protracted time period by avoiding the worst impacts of such growth pains.

3.3 Clusters in practice

3.3.1 Cluster types

It is clear from close observation of any regional economy that not all clusters are alike in terms of activity, origins and age, nor how development authorities might best promote them. Thus, the cluster policy of any development agency must pursue dual but conflicting goals: the allocation of resources, of preserving and promoting the best of what exists in 'inherited' clusters in terms of existing industrial and commercial stock, while being prepared to think 'outside the box' and promote completely new (often high-technology) cluster developments. This can be achieved by selecting as vehicles for cluster development new leading-edge technologies that currently do not exist within the region in terms of production but where there is a basis for dynamic manufacturing clusters of the future, due to local nascent R&D skills with potential competitive advantage (often in local universities). From these general observations, it is possible to propose three specific cluster types found in most mature industrial regions, as follows.

Spontaneous clusters

There are two main causes of spontaneous clusters. First, as noted above (in sub-section 3.2.1) regarding behavioural factors, one or more catalyst entrepreneurs living in his or her home location may initiate a new cluster, using new or established technologies. In the case of newly invented cluster technologies, or those brought in by immigrants from other regions or abroad, such technologies are often new to the host region concerned (e.g. Huguenot weavers and clock makers in London). However, it is also possible that such clusters might be triggered into existence by an imaginative local 'boy or girl made good', who exploits new methods of producing or selling a well-established product (e.g. Lord Leverhulme, founder of Sunlight Soap, in Lancashire). Spontaneous clusters also may be formed by individuals who, in their capacity as inventors, change the technological status quo through unprompted invention and innovation 'push' behaviour and make technological 'breakthroughs' that provide the basis for totally new industrial and/or commercial activities. Silicon Valley provides many examples of entrepreneurs who, through their personal drive and inventive behaviour, have added to the industrial growth of this cluster, often aided by subsequent serial 'spin-off' activity noted above (e.g. Hewlett and Packard; William Shockley; Robert Noyce and Gordon Moore; Steve Jobs and Steve Wozniak).

Second, clusters may be originally created, mainly in the service sector, by changes in a combination of both technological progress and fashion (Drucker 2007). Changes in methods of transport brought about by new technologies can both create and destroy clusters as part of a constant evolutionary process. For example, it was common for new commercial and industrial developments to be prompted by the locating of the new major railway lines and stations in the Victorian era, while the growth of air transport in the mid-twentieth century has changed the locations of long-distance mass-transport termini from coastal dock locations to inland airports. Improvements in road networks and the widespread ownership of motor vehicles have led to the growth of clustered 'out of town' retail centres in the post-Second World War period as shops have progressively gravitated from the traditional high-street sites to new spacious retail parks where mass car parking is possible. As in the Victorian era, the locating of service-sector transport nodes (e.g. airports; railway stations) that may subsequently act as accretion nodes for further businesses has led to the growth of multifunctional clusters around them, in which subsequent commercial and industrial activities have taken advantage of good communication links, and in turn, enhanced the overall strength of the clusters concerned. This phenomenon is also obviously true for modern airports, where not only directly linked commercial activities (e.g. airlines; catering) but also manufacturing industries (especially high-technology ones) locate near such a facility in order to have easy access to international suppliers and customers (Oakey *et al*. 2001). Although these clusters are usually not initially entrepreneurially driven, they mirror entrepreneurially derived clusters in that success tends to breed success as the cluster strength grows in a cumulative manner.

Inherited clusters

An inherited cluster is often an aging example of the spontaneous cluster type discussed above, in which the 'beginning of cycle' industrial phase ended long ago, and gradual decline is occurring over many decades, often through technological obsolescence, and/or exacerbated by strong competition, based on low-cost labour. However, it is important to note that, in common with the spontaneous case discussed above, evolved clusters are *not chosen* by development agencies for their growth potential since, as their history suggests, such clusters have naturally evolved from long-standing geographical and sectoral areas of specialization. An example of this phenomenon might be the historical development of heavy mechanical engineering in the North West of England out of the textile machinery and steam engine industries that were developed, respectively, to manufacture and power cotton textiles production in the nineteenth century. For regional development agencies dealing with such an evolved cluster, policy simply should be concerned with planned gradual decline to a smaller, but hopefully sustainable, level, often through specializing in 'niche' high-value-added forms of production. The North West England cotton textiles cluster might be cited as an example of a rationalizing cluster in which the objective of the regional development agency is not to regain the peak production size of this sector, but to concentrate future production on a reduced, but more specialist, competitive cluster of (often higher-technology-based) niche activities.

Planned clusters

In both of the foregoing examples of clustering, 'development' policy has been concerned with coping with unplanned existing clusters. However, there are a number of examples of new clusters being created on 'green-field' sites within regions. From the construction of 'Science Cities' in the former Soviet Union, through the Research Triangle of North Carolina in the United States and the Twente region of the eastern Netherlands, to the high-technology development of Sophia Antipolis in southern France, specialist high-technology clusters have been planned in areas where such activities were not previously present, often in an attempt to diversify away from an inherited cluster dependency on declining industries as noted above. Thus, a cluster may be initiated in 'virgin territory' on the basis of public and/or private sector investment, often to promote regional regeneration in areas of industrial decline, in locations where it is assumed that a favourable, attractive personal local environment for high-technology executives and their employees will help the cluster to become established (Oakey and Cooper 1989). A high-technology-oriented example of this type is Sophia Antipolis, located in France near Cannes on the Mediterranean coast, where both climate and communications are excellent. While subsequent 'spin-offs', foreign direct investment and future formation of new firms might be expected further to enhance cluster strength in a cumulative and causative manner, this approach to cluster formation in areas without any previous significant high-technology industry is essentially costly and very risky.

3.4 Cluster evolutions – cases from North West England

3.4.1 The genesis of early clusters

As discussed above, one of the most intriguing features of the clustering phenomenon is that the basic causal mechanisms of any cluster have not changed substantially since the Industrial Revolution. The fundamental drivers of the major Lancashire cotton textile cluster differed little from the reasons for the development of Silicon Valley; namely, local entre-preneurship, local investors, the development of local labour expertise and regional geographical factors (e.g. climate, culture, etc.). In the case of North West England, the close juxtaposition of skilled local technical entrepreneurs with favourable geographical features provided suitable conditions for the development of the region's two major early industries of the Industrial Revolution, namely chemicals and cotton textiles. Salt provided an early mineral catalyst to the development of both the chemicals and cotton textile industries, since it was a raw material for synthetic alkali manufacture, a key ingredient for soap and dyes for textile production.

Although cotton was not a locally derived raw material, there were enough early regional attributes (damp atmosphere, water power, local technical entrepreneurs) to fix nascent textile production to water-powered sites in North West England when factories replaced dispersed 'cottage' industrial production in the late eighteenth century (Riley 1973). The increased use of coal within industry as a result of steam power from 1800 onwards did nothing to thwart the development of the Lancashire cotton textile and chemicals sectors. Indeed, the relocation of textile production to coalfield locations merely altered sites within the North West, while coal by-products further aided the development of the chemicals industry, which in turn produced outputs of use to cotton textiles production (e.g. dyes for cotton finishing). Thus, by 1900, two North West cotton textiles and chemicals clusters were at their peak; acting at once both as strongly independent entities and, to some extent, as close collaborators where mutually technological advantage could be found.

For much of the twentieth century, there was a general trend towards a movement of 'newer' industrial production out of urban areas into industrial estates on green-field sites in the suburbs and beyond. However, one of the major recent growth areas of the North West economy has occurred in the inner urban parts of Manchester, based on strong growth within service, and quasi-service, activities. The early development of financial services in Manchester has been gradually strengthened to the point where it rivals Leeds and Edinburgh in northern Britain. These services have been augmented by additional higher-order functions, including legal services, insurance and other professional activities. As a regional capital, Manchester has also developed higher-order media functions where Granada Television and BBC Manchester (latterly augmented by the movement of a substantial number of staff from London to Salford, in Greater Manchester) have acted as 'accretion nodes' for a wide range of media-related activities, including advertising, information technology, video, film and television production facilities.

The other great urban clustering success of recent years has been that of higher education in both Manchester and Liverpool. Again occupying central urban locations, the six universities in these two cities form a major national and international education cluster, this North West group of universities forming the most concentrated cluster of higher education in

Europe. With relevant science parks, incubators, and commercially oriented departments, these centres of high-technology expertise have strong potential to create the 'spontaneous' high-technology clusters of the future noted above. One clear example of this potential is the development of biosciences in the region, in both Manchester and Liverpool, out of strong initial strengths in university-based expertise. Although much of the output of this new area of commercial activity at this stage involves 'findings' rather than saleable products, and is based upon development programmes with long lead times, many of these new developments, particularly in the biomedical area, have strong long-term potential. They may form the basis of a strong 'niche' of future specialist biotechnology production. The long-term interrelated development of all the above activities is illustrated in Figure 3.1.

3.4.2 North West England sectors that exemplify the three cluster types discussed above

For the broad range of manufacturing and service activities that exist within the North West region of the United Kingdom, three sectors at different stages in their life cycles illustrate the three cluster types discussed above. They will be discussed in the same order in which they have previously appeared.

A spontaneous cluster example: Manchester Airport

Manchester Airport, located on the southern edge of the city, has been a major success story for the region. It has grown steadily from its beginnings as a military airport during the Second World War to become the largest United Kingdom civil airport outside the South East of England. In a recent report to Manchester City Council, it was claimed that the airport currently employed 18,500 workers, of which 16,520 were full-time employees, and that the airport indirectly supports 41,290 jobs in the local area through 'affiliate companies such as airlines and catering suppliers' (Manchester City Council 2010). As in many other United Kingdom and international instances, this airport has acted as an accretion node for a plethora of directly related (e.g. airlines; hotels) and indirectly related (e.g. warehouses; export-oriented manufacturing and service-sector businesses) firms that have been founded near, or relocated to, this growing transport-inspired cluster.

Significantly, from a conceptual viewpoint, the growth of this cluster can be termed 'spontaneous' in that the growth achieved was largely not artificially stimulated by government planning agencies, but mainly resulted from spontaneous demand – both the desire by the public to travel by air to

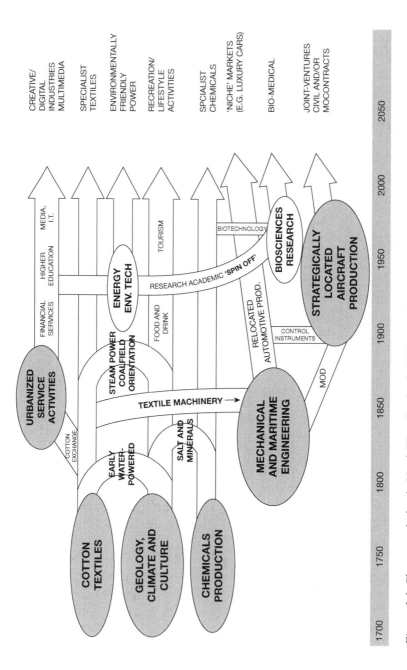

Figure 3.1 Cluster evolution in North West England: 1700 onwards

Source: Oakey 2003c

national and international destinations and the need for industry and commerce (especially high-technology forms of production) to be nearer an airport, to benefit both from airfreight facilities and the access for executive and marketing staff who need regularly to travel abroad on sales trips (Oakey *et al.* 2001). Indeed, most of the expenditure by the airport authorities has been in response to this ever growing demand for air travel in circumstances where regular increases in capacity have been required to accommodate growth, best exemplified by the construction and opening of a second runway in 2002. Seen from a regional development agency perspective, this type of success is very similar to the development of Silicon Valley in that the new business cluster virtually 'kick starts' itself (thus involving meagre government promotion costs), while any costs that do occur are the result of success (e.g. congestion, involving the need to build new roads and infrastructure), and can easily be offset by the additional local taxes that the increased cluster business activities generate.

An inherited cluster example: cotton textiles

A major dilemma confronting any modern regional development agency in countries with a long industrial history is often how to deal with 'residual clusters' which were the 'Silicon Valleys' of the Victorian era. As noted above, since such activities are inherited and often have been in long-term decline for many years, the role of a development agency is to manage this contraction in the best manner possible. Indeed, although decline may have been long term and substantial, residual employment may remain significant. For example, in the case of North West England, manufactured textiles production declined over the decade between 1991 and 2001 from 43,780 to 29,359 workers (Office for National Statistics 2004), a 33 per cent decline. Nonetheless, although in decline, it should be remembered that the residual workforce of such a cluster remains substantial. Since the decline observed is largely due to cheaper foreign competition, often involving lower labour costs, the popular response is to retreat to niche markets (as discussed above), such as high-value-added specialist textiles (e.g. for medical or military use), in order to preserve a shrinking, but still substantial, workforce.

In essence, any overall cluster development policy is a spatially focussed sector development policy, similar to that advocated by Perroux (1955) in his early and influential 'growth pole' approach, in which industries for which a nation had a comparative advantage would be targeted for special encouragement. This principle was later adapted by others to apply at a regional level, when spatial clusters were planned around new steel plants or oil refineries where these new activities would act as accretion nodes for later 'downstream' related production activities (Nicholls 1969; Chapman 1973). However, a major problem with this approach was that the targeting of selected industries in local areas for special encouragement, as part of the overall sectoral specialization policy, would mean that other forms of manufacturing in other local areas within a region would be abandoned. Moreover, the abandonment of particular mature industries in decline would have severe political ramifications in the local areas in which this policy was enacted, both because there might be an electoral 'backlash' through the ballot box, but also because the industries targeted for abandonment, although in decline, often could continue to provide a substantial, although reducing, level of employment (as in the above instance of textiles).

Thus, because employment losses in the industry from which public financial support might be withdrawn would be severe in specific local areas, industrial development agencies have often rejected the radical abandonment approach that would be required by a more focussed sectoral policy. Consequently, new high-technology clusters are encouraged while development agencies continue to maintain older declining clusters at a reduced level of employment. While this inclusive approach is more democratic and practical in the short term, it conflicts with a basic tenet of 'growth pole theory' which argues that resources should be focussed on a limited number of sectors for which a region or nation has comparative advantage (or can have in the future). Spreading the limited resources of a regional development agency over too many inherited and newly planned clusters carries the risk that they will be spread too thinly, thus jeopardizing *all* the clusters involved, a problem that was anticipated by Perroux, and the reason why he insisted on targeting a *limited number* of sectors with the best chance of success. Put simply, cluster policy is merely Perroux's aspatial growth pole policy with a spatial dimension.

A planned cluster example: biotechnology

It is not surprising that most new planned cluster developments tend to be based on 'state of the art' high technologies since they (certainly more than the declining sectors noted above) have the potential for strong future industrial growth in the new millennium. For example, biotechnology is one of the most popular vehicles for new cluster development. Certainly in terms of Europe and the United States, most regions have at least one biotechnology cluster, and the North West of England is no exception in that the various biotechnology activities of this region exist in a 33-mile-long corridor that links Liverpool with Manchester. These activities organizationally have been grouped together to constitute an overarching cluster called Bionow. Based around the University of Liverpool and the University of Manchester, the cluster comprises a number of private R&D facilities and government-funded research centres, together with incubators and science parks, mainly located at or near one of these two universities. The physical shape and size of the cluster is not very compact, being mainly located along the M56 motorway axis.

Although the Bionew cluster's management claimed to have a turnover of £4.9 billion in 2008/2009, most of the activities carried out in this cluster could be defined as research rather than manufacturing. Indeed, more than 30 years after biotechnology was first heralded as the successor to semiconductor production as the next big high-technology manufacturing sector to employ the industrial workforces of developed nations, this sector continues not to have a European Union *manufacturing* Standard Industrial Classification (SIC). The research focus of this cluster reflects the inability of the sector to move from near-market research into actual manufacturing production, a promise foreshadowed by many eminent commentators in the 1980s (Office of Technology Assessment 1984), but slow to materialize (Oakey *et al.* 1990b). Such an observation, however, is not a criticism of the slow pace at which technological change occurs, since Silicon Valley took at least 50 years to develop, but, significantly, provides more evidence of how patient government planners and politicians may need to be in order to reap the benefits we all seek from encouraging high-technology sectoral development. It will be a recurrent theme of this book that, while high-technology industry may be a solution to the manufacturing needs of developed nations in the future, it will not be an 'overnight' success.

3.5 Practical measures to promote new cluster formation and growth – a critique

As observed previously in Chapter 1, both developed and developing countries suddenly realized in the late 1970s that the recent rise of Silicon Valley and Route 128 in the United States was a glimpse of what the future might hold for the high-growth industries of the twenty-first century. In order to share in this new wealth- and job-creating phenomenon, the governments of these countries realized that replication of what had occurred in the United States was essential. However, as noted earlier in this chapter (sub-section 3.3.1 on 'spontaneous clusters'), it is far easier for governments (in this case, the United States) if high-technology industrial clusters form in a natural manner without direct government financial stimulation. Moreover, although some high-technology industry was well established, often in the most prosperous parts of national economies, with zones of high-technology production in a number of national sub-regions (e.g. the M4 and M11 corridors in the United Kingdom running respectively west and north of London; Grenoble and Sophia Antipolis in France), much of the impetus in terms of regional development policy was directed at using the development of new high-technology sectors to ameliorate unemployment and the decline of manufacturing industry in less favoured regions of national economies, often in peripheral geographical locations (Oakey and Cooper 1989; Porter 1998).

However, a major problem in development regions with declining older industrial structures was that – although it was clear that high-technology clusters, once formed, tended to expand through self-sustaining (often exponential growth) – getting started, especially in development regions where relevant skills and infrastructure were absent, was a major problem. At least part of the reason for the causal link that was forged in Europe between high-technology clusters and universities as nodes for further high-technology accretion was that, in many development areas, universities were the only focus of high-technology knowledge and skills. Moreover, many observers of the famous clusters in Silicon Valley and on Route 128 in the United States had noted that Stanford University and MIT were, respectively, in the centre of these developments, which led them to conclude that there must be a degree of causality between the presence of universities and the emergence of high-technology clusters in their vicinity. Thus, it was concluded by many planners and politicians that universities could act as nodes around which new high-technology industry could develop in depressed regions, led by academic 'spin-off' onto adjacent incubators and science parks, while attracting high-technology production to such sites through the promise of R&D consultancy collaboration with relevant university departments (Trinity College, Cambridge 1983).

However, early evidence on the links between universities and their local high-technology firms in the United Kingdom and in Silicon Valley in the United States showed that the relationship between universities and local high-technology firms was not as simple as supposed above. Conversely, it was noted that, in terms of spin-off, the majority of new high-technology firms had spun off from previously established industrial firms in the cluster (e.g. Hewlett-Packard; Fairchild) and not Stanford University. Moreover, for the firms that largely had spun off from these pre-existing large firms, their subsequent R&D technical contacts with Stanford University were minimal (Oakey 1984a; Oakey *et al.* 1988). Research indicated that the reasons for the lack of high-quality technical interaction between the university and local HTSFs were twofold. First, the idea that there was a need among HTSFs for important external R&D contacts clashed with research findings that close internal teamwork was a major asset, and the cause of higher efficiency when compared to large firms (Rothwell and Zegveld 1982). Such firms were very specialized, sophisticated and introspective, working on close-knit in-house teams, thus rendering the potential for collaboration with a local university unlikely. Second, in the areas in which these firms performed R&D, they were often the world-leading experts. Thus, any idea that they could pick up the phone and have problems solved in their narrow, but highly sophisticated, area of technical expertise by a university professor 'virtually overnight' was totally unrealistic (Oakey 1985b; Oakey *et al.* 1988).

Nonetheless, despite the supporting evidence of later works that the additional advantages of a university science-park location were minimal (e.g. Westhead and Cowling 1995), incubators and science parks have remained the mainstays of high-technology industrial development in Europe and South East Asia. By the early 1990s, for example, most United Kingdom universities had a science park and at least one incubator. Moreover, notwithstanding the above reservations concerning incubators and science parks, they remain major policy instruments for local and national governments throughout the developed and developing world, and are widespread in the United States in regions where 'natural' high-technology economic growth is absent. For this reason, a more detailed consideration of these policy instruments is given below.

It is surprising that, although R&D collaboration between HTSFs is at best rare and difficult to organize (Oakey 1984a; Oakey *et al.* 1988; Oakey 1995), and at worst avoided, so much international policy towards promoting this scale and technological type of firm over the past 20 years has been collaboration-based, most recently within various types and sizes of proposed clusters. Beginning with the trend for the establishment of United Kingdom science parks in the early 1980s, and culminating with the recent enthusiasm for incubators and clusters throughout the 2000s (particularly fostered by the work of Michael Porter, 1998), a set of nested geographical policies, based partly on the advantages to R&D management of localized R&D networking, have been established. While the principle of a proximity-based development policy has merit, since the reality that HTSFs readily cluster is well established (Oakey 1985a; Saxenian 1985; Porter 1998), the notion that such clusters promote research collaboration between firms through networking is, however, a proposition that is difficult to accept, since it is often found by empirical studies to be absent (Oakey 1985a; Massey *et al.* 1992; Westhead *et al.* 2000).

It is common for practitioners charged with the task of promoting HTSF regional development through a clustering approach to view HTSF promotion in terms of stages of development, in which there is a relationship between the age of firm and the size of cluster in which it exists, ranging

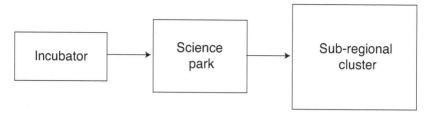

Figure 3.2 Nested entrepreneurial clusters at increasing spatial scales
Source: Oakey 2007b

from the incubator when nascent, through the science park when entering production, and on to a local sub-regional cluster when established. However, from an R&D management perspective, the value of such policies strongly depends on the validity of 'local interaction' arguments, which assert that the internal R&D of HTSFs will be substantially improved by meaningful collaboration with other large and small local firms, often in the same industrial sector, and local providers of capital and infrastructure support. Figure 3.2 depicts this transition in which a set of 'cluster' policies at differing nested spatial scales can be seen progressively to nurture HTSF success within a region to the point where, after passing through an incubator and a science park, they emerge into a sub-regional cluster within the regional economy, possibly in an urban or suburban area. Since there has been a tendency to emphasize local R&D collaboration as a key feature of the advantages of all these developments within sequentially linked concentrations, this assumption will be examined below in terms of the extent to which incubators and science parks effectively generate HTSFs' formation and growth, sufficient to cause high-technology cluster formation at the sub-regional level.

3.5.1 Incubators

The intended role of the incubator is, quite simply, to provide very small premises for nascent firms (usually HTSFs), together with other various forms of logistical support, and to provide an opportunity to collaborate (or network, especially with regard to R&D) with other people inside and outside the incubator in the local area. While the 'services' part of the incubator package may provide material advantages (e.g. shared office support, access to finance, etc.) with little difficulty, the R&D networking component of the concept has proven to be more problematic. For while it is common for incubators to provide communal areas in which incumbent entrepreneurs can network, it is often the case that new-firm founders are reluctant to discuss their new product ideas with other entrepreneurs in case their intellectual property is stolen, while wider links with other local interested parties often tend to be underdeveloped (Albert *et al.* 2002; Pittaway and Robertson 2004).

Although the argument that the proximity offered by an incubator will breed friendship and collaboration is often advanced, not only does concern for the need to protect intellectual property detract from the free flow of ideas on R&D, but also many other subtle forms of friction between individuals may mean that 'familiarity breeds contempt' (Stockport and Kakabadse 1994). While the incubator concept is not totally flawed, it is argued here that many of the assumptions that underpin their avocation – in particular, the idea that technological collaboration to improve R&D management at informal or formal levels can be triggered by the close proximity of similar HTSFs – is over-simplistic and not based on strong empirical evidence. Moreover, given the tendency for HTSF founders to be introspective, and reluctant to share the business idea on which they sought to base their new firm, a converse case for success based on minimal collaboration and networking could be made, since external involvement is likely to distract attention from the 'all important' internal collaborative R&D effort among work colleagues (Rothwell and Zegveld 1982).

3.5.2 Science parks

Although most science parks are open to any new or established HTSFs, they also may include 'academic spin-offs' from an adjacent associated university. A science-park location is also an obvious 'next step' for a successful local incubator firm that has become too large for its small incubator premises (often when production is embarked upon). Such a move is often not physically far, frequently involving only a transfer across a university campus. There is much common thinking behind the ethos which drives incubators and that which drives science parks in that the provision of support services, begun in the incubator, is continued on the science park (e.g. shared office accommodation; links with local support agencies, etc.). Again, much emphasis continues to be placed on internal science-park and local external collaborations of various kinds, especially with the host university, when R&D is concerned.

However, in common with the experience of incubators, actual R&D collaboration between science-park firms, and university science departments, is often lacking. When science parks were reaching their peak in terms of formation adjacent to major universities in the United Kingdom during the 1980s, the value of technical links with university science departments was frequently proposed as a 'unique selling point' in favour of a science-park location (e.g. Trinity College, Cambridge 1983). However, as noted earlier in this chapter, such an avocation of external involvement, either with other science-park firms or university consultants, contradicts the acknowledged strong tendency for introspection, and for working confidentially in tight-knit teams within HTSFs. Previous work has observed that the notion of unlocking the undeniable knowledge of university staff and easily applying it to good effect in science-park HTSF R&D is simplistic in the extreme and rarely occurs in practice (Oakey 1985b; Lindholm-Dahlstrand and Klofsten 2002). Furthermore, a plethora of other logistical reasons why academics do not engage with HTSFs on adjacent science parks, such as their limited availability, lack of commitment, or unwillingness to become involved in personal financial risk, have ensured that academic technical support for science-park firms has proven to be rare (Oakey 1984a; Massey *et al.* 1992; Lindholm Dahlstrand and Klofsten 2002). Moreover, studies concerned with the overall benefits of a science-park location, when compared with off-park sites, have shown that a science-park location does not offer any major measurable advantages (Westhead and Cowling 1995; Westhead *et al.* 2000), thus rendering their utility marginal when compared with off-park sites that frequently offer lower rents.

As in the case of incubators, science-park advocates have made the major mistake of misunderstanding the main ethos of R&D management in HTSFs. This process is not strongly influenced by external resources, but is heavily dependent on internal expertise and motivation. Science parks have been frequently promoted on the premise of technology transfer from adjacent universities to science-park firms. This 'benefit' was strongly promoted in the United Kingdom during the 1980s, partly triggered by falling university funding (which might be ameliorated by science-park rents and perceived R&D collaborations), and pressure from the government to make universities more relevant to industry in the area of applied research. Empirical work, nonetheless, has shown that the main academic reason for HTSF clusters near to universities in the United States was the contribution made by early academic 'spin-off' of a small number of key individuals from universities (e.g. Hewlett and Packard from Stanford University) who acted as subsequent incubators for 'spin-off' firms over several decades, and not technical interaction through R&D collaboration once academics had 'spun off', which was found to be low, in common with the United Kingdom (Oakey 1984a; Oakey *et al.* 1988).

However, the importance of this observation here is that, while the experience of HTSF growth in clustered locations in the United States formed the basis for United Kingdom science-park formation, this attempted replication was based on the misconception that clusters were caused by R&D collaboration between firms and universities in the local area, thus intensifying locational advantage. This approach, which predicts strong informational R&D linkages between universities and incubator and/or science-park firms, has been seriously questioned by both academic research (Oakey 1985b; Massey *et al.* 1992; Westhead and Cowling 1995) and by the daily experience of firms located on incubators or science parks across Europe where university–science-park-firm links were found to be universally rare (Albert *et al.* 2002; Pittaway and Robertson 2004).

3.6 Chapter summary

A context was provided to the parts of this chapter that dealt with high-technology clusters by making it clear that clustering was not new, and that many of the major industries of the Industrial Revolution were strongly clustered. Moreover, these past clusters had many common features with modern high-technology clusters in that key local entrepreneurs often played a major role in the genesis and subsequent growth of specialist clusters where new inventions provided by technical entrepreneurs brought technological advantages to the cluster, both in terms of new product and process inventions. These arguments led to a conclusion that there are a number of enduring features that render all clusters advantageous, regardless of their age, including skilled labour, input and output local linkage advantages, and locally available venture capital, which often takes the form of wealth accumulated by successful local entrepreneurs who further sustain the cluster by their reinvestment of past profits in future new ventures.

Following a chronological path, discussion moved on to a period after the Second World War when much of the modern industry of the time was considered 'footloose', meaning that it was not constrained to any location and could be equally profitable at any site within a national economy. This approach to industrial location was probably never true for all types of industry and, for example, some big mistakes were made in the 1960s in relation to relocation of production to development areas in the United Kingdom's motor vehicle industry. However, by the beginning of the 1980s, researchers in the new high-technology industries began to realize that, far from being 'footloose', the new high-technology industries based on semiconductor technologies were highly clustered, due to local locational advantage. Moreover, as noted above (sub-section 3.1.2), many of the locational advantages that were key features of Victorian clusters were found to be present in these new high-technology clusters (e.g. skilled labour; venture capital; local linkage economies). But perhaps of most importance was the discovery that technical entrepreneurs played a major role in the birth and subsequent growth of these high-technology clusters, especially through various forms of 'spin-off' activities, since large more-established firms acted as (voluntary or involuntary) incubators for new entrepreneurs who had gained experience at these incubating firms.

In order to balance the strongly positive attributes of a high-technology cluster, this chapter moved on to discuss problems of general cluster sustainability. Cases were cited in which a cluster was formed by a particularly dynamic entrepreneur, only to decline following the retirement of the founding father. This instance led to a broader problem with any cluster in that it is clear, as witnessed by many of the thriving clusters of the Victorian era in developed countries, that the strengths of a cluster can become its weakness if care is not taken to remain technologically vigilant. There is a danger that entrepreneurs within a cluster can become both rather introspective and complacent in circumstances where, if a new technology is 'not invented here', in their view, it cannot be a success. The decline in the cotton textile cluster in the North West of England was partly caused by an unwillingness to take seriously competition from abroad, initially from the United States, and latterly from Asia. These observations are important because we have noted that many of the advantages of high-technology clusters are similar to those of the Victorian era that have subsequently declined; so too might the subsequent demise of some of these Victorian clusters be the fate of currently clustered modern high-technology industries. A final problem of modern high-technology clusters was noted to be (ironically) the fruits of success; namely, local inflation of production costs caused by competition for labour and land (both for domestic and business use) and local congestion. Silicon Valley in the United States is a good example of how these costs have escalated as a result of prosperity. Nonetheless, in most cases, any inflation in costs of a strong cluster is usually outweighed by the many advantages, mentioned above, of a clustered location which is viewed as 'the right place to be'.

A more detailed consideration of cluster mechanisms proposed three major cluster types that government development agencies are likely to encounter: 'spontaneous clusters', 'inherited clusters' and 'planned clusters'. Following a description of each of these types, their relevance to a regional economy is considered through a detailed case-study of the North West of England. The case-studies were prefaced by a discussion of the evolution of the North West region's economy from the birth of the Industrial Revolution to the present time. From the contemporary industrial scene in this region, three examples of current economic activities – namely, Manchester Airport, cotton textiles and biotechnology – were chosen respectively to represent spontaneous, inherited and planned cluster types. This chapter makes the point strongly that different types of policy are required for each of these clusters with different origins, ages and potential for future growth. It is argued that policy towards the airport is merely a case of providing resources that are needed to continue the growth of a transport-based cluster which has been a major success since its beginnings as a military airport after the Second World War. This spontaneous cluster is the type of development that planning authorities are very keen to encounter in that it required very little planning and grew in response to very strong commercial and private demand for air travel in recent decades. In this sense, this cluster is very similar in planning terms to the Silicon Valley success story.

An example of an inherited cluster is provided by cotton textile manufacturing, which once dominated the industrial structure of the North West of England. This now steadily declining sector nonetheless remains a significant employer in the region, and a process of managed decline is in place in which higher-value-added niche production is sought for the remaining pockets of textile manufacturing activity in the region.

Finally, an example of a planned cluster was provided by the biotechnology sector in the North West, existing in an east–west corridor between Manchester and Liverpool. This cluster is in embryonic form and mainly consists of various types of R&D activities in a cluster of university laboratories, incubators and science/industrial parks. This is possibly the most difficult type of cluster to assist since its very high-technology nature requires substantial long-term financial and political support in circumstances where the leading-edge nature of many of the potential products ensures that success cannot be assured, and successful exploitation always proves to be a much longer process than originally envisaged.

Following from this example of a planned cluster, the chapter concluded with a consideration of how planned clusters are fostered. In particular, this inevitably involves consideration of incubators and science parks in their role as major 'building blocks' of high-technology activity that, it is hoped, will lead to a sub-regional cluster of highly profitable high-technology industrial production, an optimism that is questioned by this chapter.

4   Research and development

4.1 The power and the pitfalls of HTSF research and development

Although, in any given HTSF sector (e.g. electronics; biotechnology; software), there will be firms that are engaged in relatively unsophisticated tasks based on disintegrated forms of sub-contract assembly work, or contract research and development (R&D) for another, usually larger, company (especially in biotechnology), the typical new HTSF will devote substantial resources to the creation, through in-house R&D, of a new product on which the early survival of the firm will be based. This new product is often not only new to the firm concerned, but new to the industry in which this firm operates and, significantly, new to the public. Such novelty has strong implications that are both positive and negative. Clearly, it may be a major potential strength of such a firm that this product is leading-edge in terms of technology. This may well mean that the new invention has potentially strong competitive power, delivered through a specification that renders it highly desirable on technical grounds, in circumstances where financial cost to the customer is not a significant consideration. This performance advantage will allow a new product to command a high unit price, based on its ability to be more effective than the products of existing competitors (Oakey 1984a). Moreover, as noted in Chapter 2 (see especially sub-section 2.3), new products of this type may have disruptive potential to the extent that they can occasionally revolutionize the industrial sector or sub-sector into which they are introduced (e.g. the disruption to the mainframe computer market caused by the development of small desktop machines in the 1970s). In these infrequent but important instances, HTSFs, by introducing such disruptive new ideas, have the power to achieve rapid market domination, and the 'super profits' that such domination brings. This success may occasionally lead to actual or virtual monopolies. For example, Microsoft emerged as a disruptive new HTSF in 1975, and has progressed to a dominant position in the world computer software market.

In practice, there is clearly a relationship between the level of investment made by HTSFs in R&D and the rewards obtained in terms of intellectual property generated. As observed above, HTSFs perform many functions within a given high-technology sector, ranging from sub-contract assembly work at the low end of the R&D scale, where R&D is virtually absent, to leading-edge, very high-technology full-time R&D involving a team of permanent researchers at the high end of this R&D investment continuum. There is also an obvious relationship between the extent of R&D investment and risk, both in terms of the amount of capital invested and the long time periods over which the investment can be required to take place, which greatly increase the risk involved. To some extent, however, the level of R&D that any HTSF needs to perform largely depends on the niche they hold in any given high-technology sector. For example, a sub-contractor in the electronics industry performing component assembly would not need to perform extensive R&D, since much of the technical information necessary for this firm to operate would be provided by the (often larger) firm for which the work was performed, notwithstanding the fact that many sub-contractor firms have aspirations to become product-based, a strategic move that would enable them to command higher 'value added' for a given amount of productive effort (Oakey 1984a, 1995). However, the 'bitter' dimension to the 'bitter-sweet' nature of all new high-technology product-based firms is contained in the fact that the spectacular success stories, often attributed to HTSFs, are most frequently the exceptions that prove the rule of expensive failure. Many new product-based HTSFs are founded on the premise that, in their early years at least, these firms essentially will be research organizations. Business plans, often produced by HTSFs to obtain venture capital, frequently anticipate protracted periods of R&D at the beginning of the firm's life, *in advance* of any sales. For this reason, new HTSFs are often termed 'front-end loaded' since a substantial period of patient investment is required of investors in advance of any financial returns. For this reason alone, as discussed previously in this book, venture capital is the most appropriate form of funding for new R&D-intensive product-based HTSFs, since a bank loan of, say, three years, would not be a long enough period over which to fund R&D between the initiation of the research project and revenue from any sales of the ensuing product that would be needed to repay the loan. Indeed, in the case of a humanly ingested biomedical product, the period between the beginning of R&D and the achievement of initial sales could easily be more than ten years (including a substantial period of controlled field trials on human volunteers).

Figure 4.1 illustrates the range of types of R&D provision that exists among HTSFs. Generally, with progression from the bottom left to the top right of Figure 4.1, there are increases in *both* financial cost *and* risk. As noted above, relying on technical information from customer firms in a sub-contracting relationship is both low cost and low risk, but with low relative reward. Performing contract R&D involves a high level of financial cost in terms of the employment of skilled workers and/or equipment, but the risk is low because, in this case, the HTSF is contracted to perform the work, and the major risk involved in commissioning the work is usually met by the client. Various other solutions to the technical needs of the firm include part-time R&D (often performed in nascent HTSFs by the firm's owner in his or her spare time), licensing, and hiring external consultants to perform R&D, where both the risk and the quality of the reward in terms of outputs tend to be reduced. However, the most risky form of R&D commitment is full-time internal R&D, which is the type of research most frequently performed by leading-edge HTSFs when seeking to develop new highly competitive product ideas. Nonetheless, this type of R&D can also be the most rewarding in that any genuinely important technological breakthrough that such firms may achieve may be highly valuable (e.g. a new life-saving medical treatment in the biomedical area), although, as noted below, these types of product development may be extremely 'front-end loaded', implying long periods of patient R&D investment *before* any returns from sales are achieved.

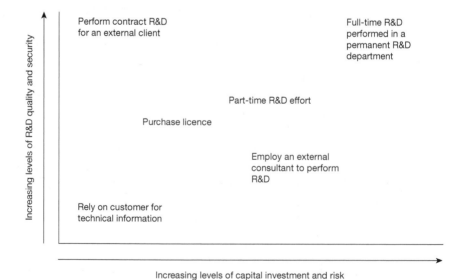

Figure 4.1 The relationship between R&D risk and reward in HTSFs

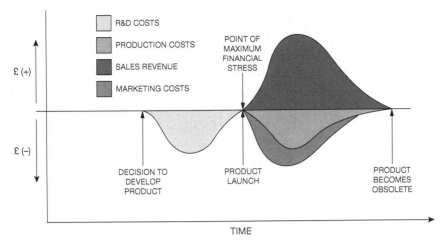

Figure 4.2 Factors influencing survival and growth in small firms based on a complete product life cycle

Source: Oakey 1991

This problem is graphically illustrated in Figure 4.2, where a typical HTSF product development process is depicted. In the current context, the 'decision to develop a product' might be taken as concurrent with the founding of a new HTSF. As can be seen, a period of substantial R&D prior to the product launch causes substantial cost, which, in the absence of any sales, will cause problematic 'red numbers' on the firm's balance sheet (i.e. in the pounds minus area below the 'zero' line in Figure 4.2). Moreover, even at the point of product launch, (i.e. the 'point of maximum financial stress'), the costs of production 'gear up' and marketing must be added to extensive R&D expenditure. In such circumstances, it is not difficult to envisage instances where the costs (below the line) can exceed any subsequent profits above the line, thus causing a long and protracted R&D and product launch process to become a financial disaster. Significantly, it is not only the duration of the R&D period that will determine how the benefits will relate to costs, but also the specification of the final product produced by such R&D. This point is exemplified by the fact that a product offering a very high level of improvement over what is currently available in the marketplace will influence the extent to which marketing costs will need to be incurred. Clearly, a new product that beats the competition on performance and is also cheaper in price (the desktop computer is again probably the best recent example of this phenomenon) might virtually 'sell itself', subject to a degree of customer education, discussed in sub-section 4.4 below. The potential potency of a new HTSF product under development in terms of international competitiveness is also likely to influence the attitude of investors in terms of second- or third-round additional financial support.

However, in many instances, the combination, noted above, of a lower price coupled with improved specification is necessary to ensure a healthy sales performance. High-technology small firms are often the antithesis of 'me too' businesses in which the product specification and production technology employed are generally known, and barriers to entry are low, resulting in extreme price competition (e.g. restaurants; furniture making; food processing). In many specialist areas of high-technology production, where barriers to entry are extremely high due to the leading-edge technology embodied in HTSF products, meeting the exacting technical requirements of customers may be far more important than a low price. For example, being able to manufacture pressure transducers for the aircraft industry at a very high level of sensitivity might enable an HTSF manufacturer to charge a premium price for a small number of these devices. In an aircraft costing several million dollars, the unit price for a small component of this type is not significant in financial cost terms, the key issue being whether the technical specification required can be met, which otherwise might be a major technical barrier to the success of the product to which it is added. Indeed, in many instances, HTSFs manufacture products or systems in a bespoke manner, where the product is made to order on a 'one-off' basis to a customer's specifications (Oakey 1995).

The extremely high 'value added' incorporated in many high-technology products, in which a product that is costly to produce commands an equally high sales price, ensures the economic viability of many forms of HTSF R&D and subsequent production. This is a very important mitigating feature, given the high cost of R&D in high-technology sectors. The ability to produce a product that is completely, or relatively, unique means that its price can be set at a level that renders high-cost R&D economically viable. Moreover, venture capital investors are often aware of this real potential advantage and are prepared to be patient over the 'front-end loaded' funding periods indicated in Figure 4.2, because they know that when the researched product becomes a success, the returns will be as high as the risk they take in funding such a venture. For example, in the biomedical area, the invention of a new cure for a major disease would be extremely lucrative, regardless of whether the developing firm moves into full production 'in-house', or sells on the embryonic new-product technology to a major international pharmaceuticals company (see sub-section 6.3.2 in Chapter 6 for further discussion of the role of strategy regarding the protection of intellectual property).

A final point worth noting regarding HTSF R&D and risk is that an additional uncertainty is the high rate at which technological change occurs in many high-technology industrial sectors. Indeed, large firms in these technically sophisticated industries (e.g. semiconductors) often do not patent their new products, since they know that the technology in their sector is changing so rapidly that, by the time any competitor would be able to 'reverse engineer' and copy a device they had manufactured, the product would be obsolete and not worth copying. The short lives of the MiniDisc Player and the Zip Drive bear witness to the high attrition rate of products in high-technology consumer markets. Indeed, in many high-technology sectors, product life cycles may be as short as three to five years (Oakey 1984a). This frenetic rate of change, and the stress it causes, is endured because of the high profits that can be made over these very short time periods. What this means for large and small firms alike in high-technology sectors is that the simplified product development example, depicted in Figure 4.2 above, is only one of many product life cycles that may need to be, at the very least, conducted in slightly overlapping cycles in order to ensure that, as older products become obsolete, they are replaced by new alternatives. However, the high pace of change is particularly risky since the need to produce new and improved products in extremely short cycles not only increases the risk of failure (compared to a product that has steady sales over a number of years), but such rapidity throughout a given sector also means that the chances of being beaten to the marketplace by a competitor's product, superior to the technology under development, is increased.

Moreover, the life cycles of products that have been launched and achieved success in the marketplace may be suddenly curtailed by the subsequent introduction to the marketplace of a better, more attractive, product from a competitor in terms of specification and/or price. Thus, both new products under development and those already in production may be rendered obsolete before the cost of substantial R&D can be recouped. Although financial returns in these frenetic conditions may be high in some cases, such volatility is generally not conducive to ensuring support for HTSFs from the venture capital industry. This is especially the case for early-stage HTSF funding, given the reality that unspectacular average returns of between 25 per cent and 30 per cent are achieved by venture capitalists from a portfolio of investments in lower-technology established firms, returns which presumably would be yet lower if more risky early-stage HTSFs were supported (see Chapter 7 for further discussion of this phenomenon). Investment in early-stage HTSFs, it is reasoned by venture capital investors, would reduce the overall returns further.

Although the investment of venture capital in HTSFs might remain attractive in theory, due to the high value that any purchased equity in a very successful HTSF might deliver from the major success of a new high-technology product, the high risk and the often long periods of patient investment that a venture capitalist is often asked to endure frequently render new HTSFs unattractive in practice. In this very real sense, R&D costs lie at the heart of why HTSFs are difficult to plan for, either as an HTSF owner or an investor since, while it is a *necessary* condition that R&D expenditure needs to take place before any success can be achieved in terms of product invention or innovation, *sufficiency* is only achieved by success: the key point being that there is great scope for long and expensive R&D pro-grammes to end in the total failure of the proposed product development. In this context, business-plan projections regarding the time periods and subsequent costs for programmes of R&D and the final sales forecasts for the new products that result from this research (especially in new highly technological areas where there are no existing equivalent products against which to 'benchmark' the new product idea) are often wildly inaccurate. This frequent inability to predict or control R&D costs has profound impacts on other areas of HTSF management covered in later chapters of this book: including marketing (Chapter 5), due to the uncertain saleability and marketing costs of the finished product resulting from R&D; strategy (Chapter 6), because the extent to which any new product under develop-ment is successful will determine the degree to which HTSF managements will be able to control their own destiny (e.g. in terms of staying independent, growing the business to sell, and when to sell if this option is chosen); and finance (Chapter 7), since the length of any R&D programme is directly linked to its financial cost.

4.2 R&D in an HTSF environment

Consideration of the unpredictable nature of R&D in new HTSFs in terms of cost–benefit, noted above, is continued here since, in counterbalance to the many pitfalls involved in conducting and funding HTSF R&D, it is generally accepted that R&D in the HTSF environment is often more effective than when conducted in large enterprises (Rothwell and Zegveld 1982; Rothwell 1994; Roberts 1991). The documented success of well-known high-technology technical entrepreneurs who grew their businesses from small beginnings bears witness to the fact that the early basic R&D that these individuals performed in their new HTSFs was more efficient, and their strategic approach more perceptive, than in the larger firms that dominated the markets they subsequently invaded to great effect with their disruptive R&D outputs (e.g. Steve Jobs and Steve Wozniak at Apple Computers and their impact on IBM). Indeed, the R&D effectiveness of the HTSF environment has been readily acknowledged by large firms through their frequent strategy of rejecting their over-bureaucratized in-house R&D facilities in favour of establishing small subsidiary companies in which to develop specific new technologies that might be a future threat to their current 'core' business activities. These subsidiaries are intended to mimic the close-knit R&D environment of HTSFs (Oakey 1984a). In addition, large multinational high-technology firms are equally keen to tap into the R&D expertise of innovative HTSFs by taking equity stakes, either in HTSFs in their own high-technology sector, or in those in adjacent sectors (e.g. pharmaceuticals firms taking stakes in new HTSFs in the emerging biotechnology industry, where biotechnologies are often replacing chemically-based products) (Oakey *et al.* 1990b). A minority stake can be expanded into a full acquisition if the firm in which they have invested becomes successful and strategically important to the growth of a new industrial sector, or alternatively, there is a decline of the sector in which the large firm currently operates (Faems 2012).

A major characteristic that renders HTSFs particularly efficient at performing high-technology R&D is the simple fact that the founding entrepreneur has often 'spun off' from a high-technology research post where he or she has gained expertise, either in a university or a large existing high-technology firm, where valuable experience gained is given 'full rein' in a new unfettered HTSF owned by this individual. Indeed, a new HTSF may be formed by a small group of entrepreneurs, for example, when three founders with complementary skills (e.g. R&D, production, and sales) act as co-founders. It appears that both individual technical entrepreneurship and group technical entrepreneurship are often highly productive, since there is little physical or organizational distance between general management and the development of a product idea created, either prior to a firm's launch, or developed in the firm's R&D department after formation. Experience has shown that there are very few HTSF founders who are not also technically knowledgeable (Oakey 1984a, 2003b) and in these cases, the technology for founding the new firm is typically developed by one or more of these technical entrepreneurs.

Indeed, such individuals are often driven to begin an independent new firm because they found the R&D environment of a previous employer, either in a large firm or a university laboratory, stifling and bureaucratic. This HTSF R&D environment tends to allow strategic freedom and a sense of common purpose for both general management and R&D, and a strong teamwork ethic that increases effectiveness, inside the firm when developing new products, outside the firm when convincing, for example, venture capitalists to invest in a new HTSF, and, critically, when persuading customers to buy the new product. It is a well-established fact that every new product, whether in a small or large industrial firm, needs a product champion. This observation is given added impetus when the product champion is an individual, or a group of technical entrepreneurs, who invent the new technology, understand and believe in its potential, and develop it within a new HTSF to which they are highly committed, often by virtue of personal ownership of equity in the firm.

Another key characteristic that distinguishes R&D in HTSFs founded by technical entrepreneurs is the belief that these individuals may have in their ability to identify emerging gaps in high-technology markets. It is often the case, where high-technology entrepreneurship is involved, that before such an entrepreneur is successful with his or her new-technology business idea, potential investors and large firms alike, confronted with the new business idea, argue that it is doomed to fail; but after it is successful, claim that it was an obvious development to make. However, clearly, it was not obvious; otherwise other entrepreneurs or large firms in the relevant technological sector would have taken this step themselves. HTSF technical entrepreneurs often have an almost religious zeal that leads them to believe that what they are inventing will be successful; this enables them to achieve technical breakthroughs that others (especially in large bureaucratic firms) cannot achieve. As noted above, many HTSF entrepreneurs will recall that they took their new idea to the R&D department of a large firm for which they previously worked, and argued that it should be developed; they then began a new HTSF to exploit this technology because their previous employer refused to develop this new idea. Apart from instances where the new idea was rejected outright, large firms that did explore the new idea with their customers often found that, not surprisingly, there was no demand for such a new technical solution, notwithstanding the fact that this new idea was potentially far more efficient that the technical status quo (Oakey 1995). Indeed, it has been noted, in the context of disruptive technologies, that a major reason why well-established large firms are happy to sell traditional products to their customers, and not introduce new technology options, is that customers tend to be very conservative, and are happy to continue using traditional solutions with which they are comfortable (Christensen 1997). For example, many large industrial and commercial enterprises, when offered word-processing technology in the mid-1980s, were not keen to abandon their electronic typewriters. However, by the mid-1990s, the world typewriter industry had been destroyed by HTSF entrepreneurs who saw the potential of linking computers, relevant software and electronic printers to invent the word processor. It is often HTSF entrepreneurs who drive these changes through and, in doing so, benefit all consumers.

4.3 External R&D contacts

Previous sections of this chapter have made it clear that the main focus of R&D in new and established HTSFs is on a strong internal R&D effort, often originated by an individual technical entrepreneur, or a group of founders, in a small, but productive, internal R&D department. Therefore, it should not be surprising to note that when functioning HTSFs are investigated, external R&D contacts with similar research organizations in terms of research specialization (e.g. a biotechnology firm with a biosciences department of a university) are secondary and supportive in nature, rather than of primary importance (Oakey1984a, 1995; Roberts 1991). While strong R&D links may occur in a number of specific high-technology industrial sectors between HTSFs and large firms through contract R&D (as noted above and in Figure 4.1), most of the research information in this case tends to flow from the HTSF to the large firm in a relationship in which the HTSF is technically dominant, but financially dependent. In other instances, while advice in a general sense might be sought by an HTSF R&D department from a university professor, or technical information might be gleaned from a government research establishment in support of internal R&D, strong formal collaborative R&D into complex basic and/or applied research with external bodies is uncommon. Apart from the benefits HTSFs derive from working internally in close-knit teams, which might be disrupted by external R&D collaboration, there is other evidence to indicate why external R&D contacts are not strong.

Indeed, a similar pattern of very weak, or non-existent contacts, has been found regarding R&D joint ventures (Oakey 1984a, 1995; Klein-Woolhuis 1999). The high costs and high-risk nature of HTSF R&D, noted above, might initially suggest that a collaborative sharing of the onerous burden of R&D costs between two or more HTSFs, or an HTSF and a large well-established firm would be popular. Certainly, in terms of combined resources that might be deployed towards an agreed programme of R&D aimed at new product development, joint ventures initially might appear attractive. However, if the previously noted characteristic in HTSFs of a strong preference for working in-house in close-knit teams is taken into account, the involvement of external actors might prove less appealing. While shared costs and risk might seem attractive in theory, making sure that the inputs of resources to the R&D effort between two or more collaborators are fair, and just as importantly, that the ensuing intellectual property outputs from a joint venture are also divided in proportion to the resources invested, is a task that, in practice, is extremely difficult to achieve equitably. Even when academics work collaboratively on research, for which the only output is kudos, there are often acrimonious arguments over attribution. Thus, it is not surprising in the case of HTSF R&D that, when capital is introduced into the R&D input–output 'equation' in the place of kudos, that collaborations which begin on a highly positive collegiate basis, can end in disagreement and the involvement of lawyers when the fruits of joint R&D are to be shared between collaborators (Klein-Woolhuis 1999). But perhaps the main reason why joint ventures are not very popular with HTSFs is that a major benefit which HTSF executives gain from working together is an 'us against the world' ethos, in which the very difficulty of their condition in terms of the high risk of failure galvanizes them into making efforts that a more loosely organized team, such as a joint venture, could never achieve.

Previously, in Chapter 3, when discussing the role of science parks and incubators adjacent to, or on, university campuses, the point was generally made that the widespread premise, particularly held in Europe during the 1980s, that universities play a major role in the development of clusters such as Silicon Valley, was flawed. Since much of the reasoning for the conduciveness of strong local university links with cluster HTSFs was based on assumed R&D collaboration, the detailed reasons why this collaboration rarely occurs in practice are discussed below.

Although HTSF owners and university professors operate in sharply different 'worlds' with different aspirations that are likely to inhibit interactions, other more subtle organizational and cultural problems inhibit university–HTSF collaborations on R&D. Perhaps the most pervasive difference between a university and an HTSF is practical. While the management of an HTSF may have invested substantial personal capital in their firm, and face bankruptcy if their firm fails, a university professor employed as a consultant to advise an HTSF R&D team would not solely rely on any income from this work, and the failure of any HTSF research in which he or she was collaborating would not be financially disastrous for such an individual. Moreover, other commitments within the university that a university-based HTSF consultant might have (e.g. teaching; academic research, etc.) would usually mean that meeting deadlines relating to HTSF research in general, and showing the same intensity of effort displayed by full-time internal HTSF R&D staff in particular, would be unlikely. Moreover, there is also an ethical issue in terms of different goals here, in that the main aim of university research is curiosity *per se* (which may not have any implications for financial gain), while HTSF R&D is aimed specifically at achieving financial returns.

A final point to make on the potential for collaboration between HTSFs and relevant staff of local universities is that any close contact with the R&D staff of HTSFs would reveal that, in the narrow area in which small firms specialize, such firms are often 'world leaders'. The idea that, when an R&D problem arose regarding their next product, such an HTSF could, almost overnight, enlist the support of a local university professor, and he or she could solve their problem, is a grossly simplistic interpretation of how industrial R&D functions (Oakey 1995). Nonetheless, such an unrealistic relationship was widely predicted when universities were attempting to attract HTSFs to their newly acquired associated science parks in the mid-1980s (e.g. Trinity College, Cambridge 1983). However, detailed research at the time, and subsequently, has shown that the technical interaction benefits between an adjacent university and HTSFs, argued in science-park promotion material, have often been shown to be extremely rare in practice (Oakey 1985b; Westhead and Cowling 1995).

Research and development in new and established HTSFs remains a largely intense internal exercise, which has major benefits, both in terms of the quality and focus of R&D work performed. Moreover, it should always be remembered that the function of any HTSF is to produce innovative leading-edge products for sale as a result of effective R&D, and that a crucial part of this R&D process is *confidentiality*. The high cost of R&D (discussed above) can only be justified if the intellectual property produced, and contained in the products sold to customers, can be protected. Therefore, another key advantage of internal R&D in HTSFs is that R&D outputs can be more easily protected to ensure that the advances made in the research laboratory have maximum impact where it matters, in the marketplace. This is why much of the promotion material for science parks and incubators is flawed, because it fails to acknowledge that R&D in HTSFs, at any stage in their development, is a process not conducive to external relationships, either with university professors or with other small or large HTSFs around a table in an incubator's communal coffee area (Oakey 2007b).

Given the potentially high value of the products produced by HTSF R&D, and the long period of R&D that precedes their emergence, the protection of intellectual property is clearly a key issue for any leading-edge HTSF. While patents can be taken out on new technology development in some cases, in others, notably in terms of computer software and specialized areas of biotechnology (e.g. genetics), protection of new high-technology developments may be difficult for HTSFs to achieve in technical terms. This is partly because it is often difficult accurately to describe what has been invented, or to define its specifically novel features (when compared with what has been invented by others) in order to gain either copyright or patent protection (e.g. in the genetics sub-area of the biotechnology industry). To the technical problems of definition and novelty must be added the fact that most new HTSFs, although often technologically strong, are usually financially weak, and their ability to finance legal actions that might result from, say, an infringement of a patent that had been taken out to protect a new invention, is often severely limited (Macdonald and Lefang 1998; Oakey 2003b).

While there is much folklore concerning the new HTSF that disrupts the technological dominance of a large firm to become a major player in an established industry, or in a new industry that replaces what went before, in reality, although such instances do occur, most new HTSFs, sooner or later, are acquired by larger competitor firms. This may even be a strategic option deliberately taken by a fast-growing HTSF in order to gain the protection that a large multinational firm might bring. This important issue for HTSF strategy will be a major concern for the section on strategy in Chapter 6. It is sufficient here to note that if a new HTSF is able to invent a new technology that has very strong technical potential, and consequent high financial value, it is very difficult for such a firm to protect its new invention, due to the almost inevitable attempts of other (often large) competitor firms legally (or illegally) to acquire this highly attractive technology. This is why many new HTSFs are formed on a 'grow to sell' basis in which a trade sale to a large firm is planned for some specific point in the future, thus avoiding the problem of an HTSF needing to protect valuable technology with its very limited financial resources.

4.4 HTSF R&D and the conflict between 'invention push' and 'demand pull'

4.4.1 Context

There has always been much debate in the theoretical literature on technological progress as to whether new technical advances are delivered by the 'demand pull' of the consumer (Schmookler 1966) or the spontaneous 'invention push' of, for example, inventive entrepreneurs (Schumpeter 1942). In reality, however, the evidence from the study of many past technological developments is that there is no clear pattern of behaviour that would exclusively support either view. For example, it has been observed that the development of the family of increasingly sophisticated products, beginning with a single transistor, progressing through the integrated circuit, to the microprocessor, was driven by the financial 'demand pull' of the United States government over a long period of time, particularly from the early 1950s until the late 1960s as a key part of an attempt to gain a 'Cold War' advantage in the small computers that controlled missiles, space craft and much other military equipment. This non-commercial defence spending was key in stimulating growth in Silicon Valley, and was a crucial factor in the formation, and subsequent success, of The Fairchild Corporation, founded by 'spin-off' staff from Shockley Transistor in the late 1950s (Cardullo 1999).

However, even in this example of the development of microprocessor technology, the overall picture is not clear-cut in that this initially 'demand-pull'-derived technology was subsequently seized upon in the early 1970s by HTSF entrepreneurs working in Silicon Valley and used to produce a succession of new products (e.g. video games; desktop computers; word processors) that were subsequently 'invention push' in nature, based on serving civilian markets, that had not been triggered by the defence needs of the United States. Clearly there is an interactive link between 'demand pull' and 'invention push' in which the key unifying feature is a growing discontinuity between the performance of a technology in a given technical area and the efficiency of the tasks to which it is asked to be put. Put simply, an aging technical solution may increasingly become unable to perform the tasks that existing customers for the product require. In reality, it can be *either* the consumer (i.e. 'demand pull') or the supplier firm ('invention push'), or a mixture of both, that can identify this discontinuity.

4.4.2 The implications for HTSF R&D

The term 'high technology' implies that any firm given this title will be at the forefront of invention and/or innovation in its chosen field whether it be, for example, electronics, software or biotechnology. High-technology small firms may occur at the exploratory forefront of existing sectors (such as electronics), emerge to create totally new sectors for which there has been no industrial classification code to define them (e.g. software; biotechnology), or develop in the margins between two or more existing sectors to create a new industrial sub-sector that might grow to become a sector in its own right. For example, in California, a new high-technology sub-sector has grown in which expertise in computer hardware, software, publishing and the moving image is coming together to create a high-technology multimedia sector based on an amalgam of these disparate skills (Scott 1993; see also Figure 4.3). The 'blue sky' nature of R&D in these overlapping industrial, commercial and artistic activities implies that multimedia firms will mainly be involved in novel types of R&D that seek to extend and exchange knowledge in order to offer new products to the public that could not have been independently developed by any one of the three industrial sectors involved.

In terms of Figure 4.4 and the invention push–demand pull dichotomy, HTSFs are mainly clustered at the basic or applied science end of any new industrial life-cycle curve. Since most of the R&D they perform is concerned with inventing or applying new inventions, they are rarely concerned with 'development' R&D, which is the honing of

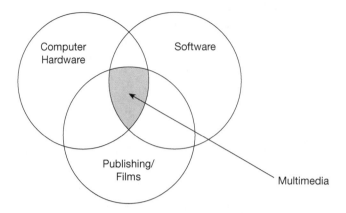

Figure 4.3 Multimedia, the birth of a new industrial sector

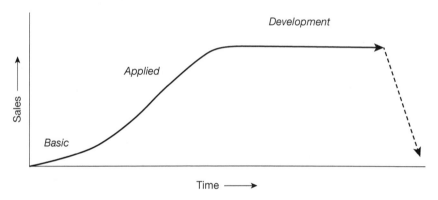

Figure 4.4 Changing types of research during a typical industrial product life cycle

well-established products, such as occur in, say, the motor vehicle industry, where 'add-ons' such as satellite navigation and anti-lock-breaking features can refresh well-established products to give them revived interest. Because many HTSFs are concerned with 'invention push', their interaction with potential customers usually concentrates on finding ways in which their new invention can be improved to render it more 'user friendly'. However, customers may also have input to 'development' R&D in the more stabilized phases of a product's life, when it has existed for some time. Relatively small problems with performance can be fed back from customers in order to 'pull' the supplier towards a better, more refined product, which benefits the supplier in terms of competitiveness, and to the benefit of the customer from a 'value for money' standpoint. However, this type of information is *particularly* advantageous to the supplier, since it is often free and collected by sales staff during sales visits.

As noted above, customers are rarely involved in demanding completely new inventions from their suppliers, since it has been acknowledged that they are often very conservative in their purchasing behaviour. Indeed, it has been previously observed to be one of the reasons why large firms are slow to take advantage of subsequent disruptive technologies (Christensen 1997; Christensen and Bower 2004). Although most HTSFs are engaged in the development of leading-edge new technology-based products, it is ironic to note that the very newness of these ways of doing things can be a problem for potential customers in that, as noted above (Christensen 1997), they often initially reject new products in favour of the status quo, only to embrace them fully (and in the process enjoy substantial efficiency gains and cost reductions) when the new product finally becomes more widely adopted. In this sense, although such a new HTSF product is an example of 'invention push', there is also the need for some degree of 'demand pull' in order to trigger more extensive acceptance. This is because, in order for the product to gain wide acceptance among potential customers, it is necessary for the HTSF to learn how the basic product idea can be modified to suit specific customer needs, especially in circumstances where the new product has sales potential in a market where the new technology has not been known or used before (see Chapter 5 on HTSF marketing). Therefore it is often advisable for the creators of totally new products to obtain the opinions of potential customers during the R&D stage. This strategy has two main benefits for an HTSF. First, very valuable feedback information is gained on what potential customers find irritating about the prototype they have been asked to trial, thus providing free market research, which can be used to improve the new product. Second, and more subtly, involving potential customer firms in these field trials helps to *educate* the customer to the positive attributes that the new product has, thus reducing the natural aversion customers might have to the unknown. Thus, a synopsis of this overall process might be that invention in HTSFs is mainly a process of 'invention push', with some degree of 'demand pull' in the early stages of the new product's introduction into the marketplace, where potential customers can help refine the product offering.

4.5 Chapter summary

There are a number of R&D options available to new HTSFs, involving widely differing levels of both risk and return (see Figure 4.1). For example, sub-contract HTSFs, and HTSFs performing contract R&D for other, often larger, customer firms (e.g. biotechnology), encounter low levels of risk due to the minimal levels of in-house R&D investment required. However, HTSFs that seek to develop new products of their own, through substantial amounts of in-house R&D, are well represented in all high-technology sectors. Consequently, due to the protracted 'front-end-loaded' nature of much HTSF R&D, capital invested in research is frequently a high-risk exercise. However, the growth and survival of HTSFs has a 'bitter-sweet' dimension in that, while a strong product development orientation may offer the prospect of 'bitter' failure (if the product under development does not perform to the expectation of either the firm's management or the customer), the new product conversely might be highly successful, causing a large new market to be 'sweetly' created (or captured in the case of disruptive new technologies from, often large-firm, competitors). In this sense, while there is a weak overall correlation between risk and reward, in individual cases, rewards can be high.

It was noted that HTSF R&D is of critical importance to the long-term development of national and international economic performance, since the outputs of this R&D have the potential to create the new product offerings that have spawned new industries or revolutionized existing industrial sectors, while disrupting the dominance of large-firm-controlled industries that were becoming oligopolistic or monopolistic through their resistance to technological change. This disruption has been achieved in a number of famous cases by the introduction of new products that have brought the customer radically improved efficiency and choice, while at the same time reducing the price of this better performing new product (e.g. desktop computers). However, specialist R&D performed in HTSFs also has the potential to produce products that achieve profitable sales in conditions where prices do not need to fall in order to achieve acceptable success. Profitability can be produced by HTSFs in conditions where the specification of new products (i.e. their performance quality) is very high, and customer firms are prepared to pay premium prices for products that perform key functions as components of larger products that are highly expensive (e.g. control mechanisms in aircraft).

However, an added important risk factor concerning R&D in HTSFs that constantly threatens the length of product life cycles, and consequently the solvency of firms, is the constant technological change that occurs in some high-technology sectors. This means that the life cycles of the products that HTSFs produce are often very short (e.g. as little as three to five years). Thus, strong and rapid returns from R&D effort must be obtained in order to assure financial success, since it is possible for a product to be rendered obsolete by a more advanced alternative offered by a competitor, even before that new product can be introduced. Such rapidity of obsolescence has a number of impacts on the environment for HTSF survival and growth. It ensures that the decisions HTSF managements make regarding R&D investment take place in circumstances where a lack of stability renders correct decision making difficult. Moreover, this difficulty has a number of ramifications for other areas of management within the HTSF (i.e. marketing; finance; strategy), and there is an additional problem, in that external potential investors similarly find making decisions on financial support of R&D-intensive HTSFs extremely difficult, particularly when estimating risk.

Regarding the day-to-day functioning of R&D within the HTSF, it was observed that there is an overall agreement in the literature that R&D in HTSFs is generally very efficient. This assertion was supported by the manner in which large firms in high-technology sectors often seek to copy HTSF R&D working practices by either establishing small-scale subsidiaries, taking equity stakes in existing new HTSFs, or securing full HTSF assets through complete acquisition. The close-knit environment in which HTSFs perform R&D is one in which there is little organizational distance between management and R&D, often because at least one HTSF founder is a 'technical entrepreneur' who holds a strong financial stake in the HTSF that they have created, implying very strong commitment.

Given the importance of internal close collaborative R&D to many HTSFs, it is not surprising to note that external R&D contacts have generally not been found to be very important. External R&D contacts, when they do occur, tend to be secondary and of a supportive nature. The roles of external research organizations in general, and local universities in particular, are of only marginal importance to HTSF formation and growth and the (often argued for) link between HTSFs and university research facilities were found to be based on a misconception of how HTSFs are formed and how they perform R&D as they grow. This was especially the case regarding widespread support, throughout Europe in the mid-1980s, for the development of science parks and incubators on or near university campus locations. The reasons for the lack of strong research links between universities and HTSFs were attributed to a number of practical and more subtle organizational factors associated with motivation, meeting deadlines, and the differing financial- or kudos-based goals that HTSFs and university staff respectively have in pursuing their research objectives.

Similar reasons were given to explain why joint ventures were not popular among HTSFs. Given the obvious, in principle, attractions of joint ventures to HTSFs in circumstances where risk of failure is high and R&D costs may escalate beyond expectations, it might be difficult initially to understand why joint ventures are not widespread as a means of spreading risk. However, if the strong argument made above, that internal R&D is the main strength of HTSFs, is accepted, it follows that the sharing of research with external firms would create unwanted distance, both physically and organizationally. It is also a major difficulty of joint ventures that, although risk and cost may be shared in theory, it is often hard to determine an equitable balance regarding how much capital each partner invests in R&D, and how the resultant intellectual property is divided between the parties concerned. Moreover, to these logistical problems must be added the issue of confidentiality, which is a consideration in all cases when two independent firms perform joint R&D work.

Indeed, this is why large firms, when seeking to invest in and perform joint R&D work with a new HTSF, often seek a full acquisition of the HTSF in question, rather than an equity stake, in order to avoid problems of intellectual property ownership that might otherwise subsequently arise. Confidentiality, however, is also a wider problem for any new independent HTSF since, together with the need to develop valuable intellectual property through R&D, there is obviously a strong need to protect the valuable R&D outputs, once created. It was observed that many new HTSFs, struggling with limited financial resources from which to produce and market a valuable new product, and confronted with the high legal costs that may be involved in protecting this asset, may decide to 'sell out' to a large multinational competitor, rather than run the risk of valuable R&D assets being 'stolen' by a much larger firm with greater financial resources. It was observed that new HTSFs rarely have the financial resources to take costly legal action if their technology is stolen or a patent is infringed. Indeed, many firms adopt a 'grow to sell' strategy in a business plan devised to attract external capital from venture capitalists, in which an 'out' is planned through a trade sale a set number of years following formation.

In a final section to the chapter, the issue of the 'invention push' versus 'demand pull' concepts of technological progress was discussed. It was concluded that for HTSFs, both concepts have played a part in their development. To exemplify this view, the case of United States defence spending in the 1950s and 1960s was cited as a major 'demand pull' impetus to the formation of many new HTSFs, particularly in Silicon Valley. However, the later exploitation of the semiconductor technology created by this 'demand pull' defence spending was counterbalanced by the commercial exploitation of advanced semiconductors by 'invention push' entrepreneurs in Silicon valley as they revolutionized the technology of the world computer industry. It was also noted that well-established firms in mature industrial sectors cannot be relied upon to 'demand' new technologies from HTSFs, and often prefer to reject change in favour of the less efficient status quo, due to their oligopolistic or monopolistic power to control markets and/or the inertia caused by past investment in aging process technologies.

5   Selling high-technology small-firm products

5.1 General context

Much of the accumulated literature on the geographical development of markets by small firms has only marginal relevance to the selling behaviour of HTSFs, mainly because there has been a long-standing tendency within these studies to adopt a 'stages approach' to selling, in which exporting, it is argued, is finally achieved following a geographical progression through local, regional and national market areas over a number of years (Khan 1975; Olsen 1975; Bilkey and Tesar 1977; Johanson and Vahlne 1977). However, this process is largely irrelevant to most HTSFs, since it is a well-established fact that, for many HTSFs, exporting is an essential *first step* towards developing a viable level of performance. Many high-technology firms are 'born global' in terms of selling, since most or all of their actual and potential customers are internationally based (McAuley 1999; Bell *et al.* 2001; Saarenketo 2004). Previous research by this author has confirmed a very early dependence on exports by HTSFs (Oakey 1984a, 1995), and this has been supported by more recent HTSF research (Ganotakis 2007).

Moreover, another special feature of R&D and production that influences the speed of selling behaviour in HTSFs (discussed in a different context in sub-section 4.1 of Chapter 4), is that, notwithstanding the fact that some HTSF products can take up to ten years to produce, many HTSF product life cycles, *once they reach the marketplace*, are extremely short (and much shorter than the time they took to develop) in competitive and rapidly changing high-technology markets. Certainly, compared with many lower-technology businesses where a product or service, with only minor modifications over time, can be sold for many decades, most 'grow to sell' HTSF business plans anticipate that, following the successful launch of a new product on which a new HTSF was founded, there would be a trade sale, usually in less than ten years. This means that the gradual process of market expansion through local, regional, national and then international sales (discussed above) over several years is a path of development too leisurely for many new HTSFs. Although the duration of product life cycles may vary in total length at the extremes – from, say, three years in the fast-moving semiconductor industry, to decades in terms of scientific instruments production – in most cases, HTSF product life cycles are sufficiently short to preclude any sales strategy that would take place over more than ten years. Thus, both the lives of HTSFs as independent entities and the products they produce tend to be short-lived and volatile, rendering a long-term selling strategy inappropriate.

In this chapter, the term 'marketing' has been deliberately avoided since, for many HTSFs, the process of selling new products is rarely a simple marketing exercise, but more often involves collaboration with potential customers in circumstances where a new product emerges from a series of negotiations on what form and function a new technology should take. Indeed, as mentioned previously in this book (e.g. sub-section 2.3.1 in Chapter 2; sub-sections 4.2 and 4.4.2 in Chapter 4), the adoption of new HTSF products is often preceded by a period of rejection by customers who, initially, are reluctant to adopt change. In this sense, the new HTSF product is often driven forward by interactive contact with customers and not marketing effort *per se*. Moreover, while it is clear from the arguments of Chapter 4 (sub-section 4.4) that R&D in HTSFs is often initially triggered by an 'invention push' approach of technical entrepreneurs, frequently there is a need to adapt their product ideas to meet customer needs in circumstances where the potential customer is initially totally unaware of the new product's existence prior to an approach by the HTSF in question. In these cases, the entrepreneurial drive of the inventive HTSF entrepreneur is tempered by the needs of the customer, as the product invention or innovation is matched to the range of uses to which a potential customer might put the new technology.

Implicit in the 'invention push' process in many HTSFs is the key role a new idea or technical breakthrough plays as the event that triggers the desire of an inventor to become an entrepreneur in order to be rewarded for his or her technical entrepreneurial abilities. In this connection, as noted in Chapter 2 (sub-section 2.2), such a combined approach involving both invention and exploitation is a departure from the stance taken by Schumpeter (1939), who tended to argue that it was scientists and technocrats who invent, and entrepreneurs who exploit their discoveries. However, more recent academic research (Roberts 1991; Oakey 1995; Cardullo 1999) has strongly argued that technical entrepreneurs are often key instigators of technological progress through their contributions to R&D effort in HTSFs, since they embody *both* strong inventiveness *and* entrepreneurial zeal. This phenomenon is indicated by evidence from studies of academic entrepreneurship, which tend to show that it is most often the discovery by an academic of a new technical development that triggers the decision to begin a new academic 'spin-off' HTSF, rather than any long-standing desire to become an entrepreneur (Oakey *et al*. 1988; Roberts 1991). In these instances, initially, new academic entrepreneurs are frequently rather reluctant business people. Moreover, in terms of this current consideration of selling in HTSFs, such subtle motivational drivers regarding HTSF formation have substantial relevance to the technical entrepreneur's approach to selling an HTSF product, when it has been researched and manufactured. Because so many HTSF owners are scientists or engineers, they tend to have an approach to product success that is more oriented towards 'Will it work?', rather than the more useful selling question, which would be 'Does anyone want to buy it?'. This ambivalence towards selling criteria directly stems from the problem-solving back-ground of HTSF technical entrepreneurs, in which satisfying curiosity is often deemed more important than commercial relevance.

Together with those HTSF founders who emerge from an academic background, where research is *curiosity-* rather than profits-driven (Russell Group 2010), another substantial source of new technical entrepreneurs (especially in the United States and the United Kingdom) has been the defence industries. Large high-technology firms in the aircraft, shipbuilding and military hardware sectors are commonly driven by a need to solve technical problems for their (initially military) customers, which are, although critical to military needs (e.g. the ability to avoid radar), often of no relevance to the selling requirements of high-technology firms serving civil markets. Moreover, for defence contractor firms, customer need is dominated by functionality rather than price, in circumstances where contracts won by tender are often subject to massive cost overruns. Such an environment excites in engineers an already strong tendency to believe that cost to the customer, so relevant in civilian contexts, is not important, provided a good technical solution can be achieved. This is a key observation since such attitudes often render defence industry firms unable to compete effectively in civil high-technology markets.

But most relevant to this present discussion of selling by HTSFs is the tendency for HTSF entrepreneurs, whether they 'spin off' from universities or large defence manufacturing firms, often to have a 'blind spot' regarding customer needs in general, and competitive pricing in particular, when they try to enter new HTSF civil-market environments.

This tendency to neglect the importance of customer needs is further exacerbated by three related and mutually reinforcing factors. First, there is a general 'the customer is lucky to get it' approach in which HTSF technical entrepreneurs believe that the excellence of their genius will be rewarded at whatever price they seek to charge (Gupta *et al.* 1985; Moenaert and Souder 1990). Second, there is a stubborn belief among many technical entrepreneurs that any initial resistance by potential customers is only a result of the customer's inability to understand the merits of what they have produced, and that such resistance will disappear in due course when the full potential of the new technology on offer is recognized. Of course, customer ignorance may prove to be a real barrier to successful selling (Christensen 1997), as argued in other contexts previously in this book (e.g. sub-sections 4.2 and 4.4.2 in Chapter 4). However, if the HTSF owner concerned is unable or unwilling actively to persuade potential customers of the merits of a given new technology, or adapt their new product as a result of customer feedback advice, the prospects for such a firm are bleak.The third and final point is that physical-science-trained technical entrepreneurs from an engineering culture often find it difficult to acknowledge that the success of their new product development might depend on sales staff who, due to their social science background, are often considered intellectually inferior. This is an area of friction previously noted to exist between physical and social scientists, involving a long-standing barrier to better collaboration, which can lead to inefficiencies in areas where physical and social scientists need to collaborate effectively (e.g. in manufacturing where technology and management meet) (Snow 1959; Oakey 2003b).

Although curiosity-driven research has many strengths, it can produce discoveries that have no immediate commercial application, while sales staff, and the customers they serve, conversely look for solutions to very obvious *immediate* problems. In new HTSFs, it is the role of sales staff both to convince customers that brand-new inventions can have a major impact on their performance, while simultaneously feeding back customer needs to enable their colleagues in R&D to modify new technologies to meet the specific needs of customers and invent totally new solutions to problems encountered by them. The intermediary function of sales staff is, however, often difficult to achieve, since it may seem to engineers that sales staff are dictating how they should go about their work, and/or in what areas research should take place.

5.2 Organizational factors that inhibit investment in selling effort

There are also a number of practical resource reasons why selling in HTSFs may not be a possible priority in the early years following formation. First, an initial reason why selling is either not financially provided for, or is inadequately funded, say, in a business plan, is because a product, invented through internal HTSF R&D, can only be sold when it is perfected and safe to offer to the public, which cannot accurately be predicted. As has been previously argued diagrammatically (see Figure 4.2 in Chapter 4), a new product is often only ready for sale to customers after an unpredictably long period of R&D (which may exceed ten years in some cases).

Second, it is often not until the later stages of product development that the management of an HTSF are clear as to what the specification of the new product they are producing will be. Frequently, HTSF entrepreneurs have several, sharply different, potential applications for the new technology they have invented, all of which initially seem to have equal viability. It is only as the product is developed in detail, and shown to potential customers for evaluation, that the function it will best perform becomes fixed, and, importantly, the relevant market for this product becomes clear. This further uncertainty renders the detailed early planning of sales strategies for a new product under development very difficult, since the lack of a clear specification as to what function the product can fulfil renders the production of sales literature impossible.

A third, more tenuous, related reason for not conducting an effective selling campaign for a new HTSF product derives from a range of management inefficiencies often displayed by HTSF technical entre-preneurs. For example, partly for the reasons noted above associated with the lateness of selling in the product life cycle (and the financial ramifications of this), steps to begin provision for selling a new product (especially in export markets) are often not adequately taken because HTSF entrepreneurs maintain an either mental or physical 'things to do' list which they revise on perhaps a weekly basis in order to perform the actions that are most pressing. Although selling provision may be on this list, it frequently does not rise high enough to prompt any substantial action because it is pre-empted by more urgent tasks (e.g. raising additional capital; solving technical problems with the nascent product) (Oakey 2007c). This tendency is exacerbated by a common attitude among many HTSF entrepreneurs, who, as noted above, often feel rather arrogantly that their new idea is so powerful a technology that it will 'sell itself', and will not need a proactive selling campaign.

5.3 The cost of selling

Although the vigorous international selling of a new product is often the best way to ensure that export sales are maximized in order to achieve optimal global product profitability, HTSFs traditionally have not been very effective at conducting well-organized selling campaigns for their new products at home or abroad. They have often resorted to inadequate and unimpressive selling techniques (e.g. mail shots and/or brochures) or a total negation of proactive effort due to a reliance on unsolicited demand triggered by 'word of mouth' that, overall, typifies a sub-optimal performance (Oakey 1984a, 1991; McCartan-Quinn and Carson 2004). Apart from this ambivalent attitude towards selling for products that require a vigorous selling campaign, the *timing* of this type of expenditure by the inventing firm is often extremely problematic. Although the complete selling process begins with the initial conception of a new product idea, and ends in final obsolescence (Oakey *et al.* 1988; Oakey 1991, 1995), successful selling of the resultant product is a key *and integral* later part of this sequence of events (see Figure 4.2 in Chapter 4). However, effective selling may not occur because the point at which the formal R&D process ends and the new product is ready to be sold (implying substantial new costs) may coincide at a juncture when the company is often in severe debt due to previous substantial R&D costs which have overrun, both in terms of time and expenditure (i.e. the point of maximum stress; see Figure 4.2 in Chapter 4) (Oakey 1991). These unique coinciding features of product life cycles in new HTSFs tend to mean that selling provision for any new product under development is not adequately planned for or funded.

5.3.1 Selling existing products

In common with the funding of R&D in HTSFs, spending money on promoting the sale of HTSF products is necessary but not sufficient for success. Sufficiency is only achieved through the successful sale of the product, which can never be guaranteed, and expensive sales campaigns (especially when undertaken overseas) can easily cost large sums of money without any success (Oakey 1984a, 1995). Since many HTSFs are 'born global' in terms of the locations of potential customers for their often very specialized high-technology products and/or services, reaching them is exacerbated, not only by a higher cost (when compared with a domestic customer), but also by additional costs associated with *finding* potential international customers for specialist HTSF products.

The use of 'word of mouth' methods of selling (noted above) illustrates this problem of finding the customer, since the identification of foreign customers can be difficult. In certain niche areas of HTSF production, personal contacts may be useful in selling products. For example, in public and private contract research activities and in medicine, the international interchange of staff may mean that a researcher uses a particular HTSF product in, for example, a United Kingdom hospital, and later decides to purchase this product when he or she returns to their own country. This phenomenon is a low-risk option for this type of purchaser since the product will have been 'trialled' previously, and it is a zero-cost selling method for the HTSF involved. However, such an unsolicited means of selling has limited value, while other methods of selling, noted above, such as the production of brochures and advertising in trade journals, are equally likely to achieve only limited success (Oakey 1991). Until recently, what was needed (but not available) to help HTSFs reach fragmented markets in far-off international locations was a cheap and effective means of making their products known to potential customers. In this context, the arrival of the internet could represent a very powerful *potential* tool for use by HTSFs as part of international selling campaigns.

5.3.2 Selling products totally new to the marketplace

A particular problem experienced by HTSFs as they seek to sell into a new or existing market is that many of their new products are not merely a new version of a product that already exists and has a well-established customer base, but often new HTSF products are completely new to the market. In such circumstances, a considerable body of past literature on invention and innovation diffusion is relevant, since it is generally a well-established fact that adoption rates of totally new inventions or innovations do not follow a smooth, linear, increasing adoption path over time, but are sigmoid in nature: the sigmoidal growth curve passes through three major stages in which adoption is initially very slow, followed by rapid take-up, and slows again when acceptance among the population of adopters approaches saturation (Hägerstrand 1952; Griliches 1957; Oakey *et al.*1990a).

Resistance at the beginning of the selling process by uninformed potential adopters, happy with their existing technologies, needs to be overcome before the product can achieve the success it deserves. It is also the case that the rate of adoption of any given new technology may be inhibited by the adoption rates of other high-technology products that enable the technology in question. For example, the recent rate at which the internet has spread in developed nations has been facilitated or inhibited by the pace at which state-of-the-art computers and fast broadband connections have progressed. Indeed, it might be argued that the 'dot.com bubble' that both emerged and 'burst' in the early 2000s might have been more successful if the international spread of powerful home computers and fast broadband connections had been more advanced at that time. In this sense, the drive to develop internet businesses might have been premature and preceded the opening of the 'window of opportunity' that eventually did open a few years later.

This slow take-up phenomenon is relevant to the current consideration of HTSF selling in that many of the most important HTSF inventions, which have ultimately produced great disruption to traditional markets, have been totally new products sold to new or existing customers either to create a brand-new market (e.g. the mobile phone), or replace obsolete products in an existing market (e.g. the replacement of the typewriter with the word processor in the late 1980s). As noted by Christensen (1997), because customers are often very resistant to change, selling can be extremely problematic for firms with a new invention or innovation that has strong disruptive potential, because persuading conservative customers to abandon a current technology with which they are comfortable in favour of a new HTSF product that might not prove an improvement will clearly be much more expensive in time and capital in the short run than selling a known product into a known market.

Perhaps the best example of confronting, and overcoming, this problem of 'fear of the new' is provided by Apple Computer, Inc. when they invented their first desktop computers in the early 1970s. The computer market at that time was dominated by mainframe computers, of which IBM was the largest manufacturer (Rothwell and Zegveld 1982). In the early 1970s, the embryonic desktop computer market was mainly composed of 'hobbyist' engineers who purchased new desktop computers in kit form, mainly to use experimentally in their spare time. The challenge for the new desktop computer manufacturers was to expand the market away from this 'niche' hobbyist area into mass-market usage in sectors such as education, commerce and manufacturing. Significantly, Steve Jobs and Steve Wozniak, the founders of Apple Computer, Inc., were unusual in that their strong technical backgrounds did not inhibit them from hiring local expertise – Regis McKenna and Mike Markkula in Silicon Valley – to assist with selling. However, this help with selling their new computer did not take the form of 'selling' *per se,* but mainly involved talking to potential customers, offering them computer prototypes to examine, and obtaining feedback on how the product could be improved, in a partial 'demand pull' manner in which the customer helped to perfect the 'invention push'-created product that he or she was eventually likely to buy. This early use of potential customer involvement, subsequent price reductions, and per-formance improvements achieved as the market for this new technology grew, is perhaps one of the best examples of how HTSF technical entrepreneurs can achieve success by embracing customer feedback orchestrated by expert sales consultants during a process of developing and selling new high-technology products.

5.4 The role of the internet in promoting HTSF sales

As noted above, an aggravating factor in the process of developing HTSF sales is the high proportion of the production that must be exported. HTSFs, selling specialist technology-based products, often to a small number of large-firm customers in specialist high-technology sectors spread across the world (e.g. medicine; aerospace; scientific instruments), know they must export more than half (and often more than three-quarters) of their output to become, and remain, viable (Oakey 1984a, 1995). While these international markets may be profitable once established, they are frequently difficult initially to find and service. However, the recent emergence of the internet would seem an ideal *low-cost* vehicle for HTSF international selling, both in terms of making the complex HTSF products known to potential customers worldwide and communicating with them once a sales link has been established.

In principle, the internet should have considerable relevance to HTSFs, since other recent studies of HTSFs have confirmed that *both* inputs to the production process *and* subsequent sales tend to be international in origin and destination (e.g. biotechnology production). Thus, HTSFs now should be better able to compete with larger companies in terms of their international export sales, since accessing distant customers for HTSF products through the internet renders this process very low cost (Santarelli and D'Altri 2003; Molla and Licker 2005). A website, and associated search engines, offer both HTSFs and their potential customers a cost-effective means of finding each other in order to facilitate the sale of very specialized products and, from the perspective of the high-technology supplier firm, help inform potential customers worldwide as to what their products are, what they can do, and how much they cost, in some detail. Indeed, many HTSFs operate in specialist 'niche' markets, where the major challenge is to make their product or service known to a very small number of disparate potential customers who would be eligible to buy their product or service.

However, in recent research on new HTSFs (Oakey 2007c), the reticence noted above regarding the willingness of HTSFs to tackle the problems of selling effectively was again apparent. It was perhaps surprising to discover that, although all the firms in this study had some form of website, a majority of these firms did not use their website to sell their products or services. In these cases, the site merely performed a 'contact us' role and was very basic. Of the firms that did use their website in an attempt to achieve international sales, the pattern of results was scarcely more encouraging, with only a small minority of firms using the internet to any substantial extent. This trend is supported by other recent research evidence on the poor use of internet sales techniques (Ganotakis 2007).

Given the general efficiency of search engines and the worldwide scope of the internet, it is hard to escape a conclusion that, through inadequate sales management, many HTSFs continue to miss this opportunity to find the high-quality and *relevant* customers they seek. This tendency is supported by other previous work on internet adoption by SMEs in general (Jones *et al.* 2003) and among very small (often new) firms in particular (Dandridge and Levenburg 2000). The amount of detail that an HTSF might put on a website regarding a complex product would be easily enough to initiate potential customer enquiries that would permit the internet to trigger consequent sales. The clear fact that, in many cases, the internet is not used as a selling tool, especially when it might be used for promoting the export sales that are crucial to the survival of many new and established HTSFs, implies that a valuable mechanism for achieving international sales continues to be underused, resulting in yet another example of HTSF selling inefficiency.

5.5 Export sales assistance

Despite the reality that international sales are the lifeblood of many HTSFs (Katsikeas *et al.* 1996; Lefebvre and Lefebvre 2001; Lachenmaier and Wößmann 2006), it is surprising that many studies of HTSFs have discovered that a substantial number of these otherwise sophisticated enterprises have no sales staff (Oakey *et al.* 1988; Oakey 2007c). As noted above, such neglect often results not from ignorance of the key role to be played by selling, but more from the distractions caused by funding R&D and production, *and* the very real complexities that inhibit the task of selling abroad. Apart from problems, discussed above, with finding customers, selling abroad involves accessing a large amount of official, legal and business information before any HTSF exports can proceed. Such information is extremely important since any one of the issues discussed below, if badly handled, could cause the firm concerned severe financial and/or legal problems.

There is always a strategic dilemma for any new HTSFs regarding the best way to penetrate a foreign market. While selling directly to a foreign location ensures complete control for the firm concerned, hiring an agent may be less complicated, in terms of contacting local customers, arranging attendance at exhibitions, and gaining advice on local legal and commercial practices. However, a major problem with agents is that they may not effectively promote the product (or products) that the client HTSF has on offer to in-country potential customers. This often means that using an agent can be both expensive and ineffective. Another related problem that may confront HTSFs seeking to export is that of product liability. Any firm seeking to sell a product in their own country or abroad must consider product liability issues, since if the product malfunctions after it has been purchased, and human injury is incurred, severe damages against the firm might be awarded (especially in the United States). In particular, the biomedical healthcare sub-sector of HTSFs often encounters extreme problems in this area. Not only do programmes of R&D often overrun (see Chapter 4), but when HTSF products are ingested by humans, there is an additional need to gain permission to sell the new product in any foreign market. Nonetheless, licence permission notwithstanding, any malfunctions causing death after the product has been approved for sale might yet cause the demise of the firm concerned. Indeed, new biomedical products have been found to be flawed after being launched on the market, notwithstanding extensive field trials and approval by the relevant health authority. This concern with product safety often encourages many HTSFs to develop products only up to the 'proof of concept' stage, and then to sell the intellectual property they have developed to larger firms, choosing not to go on to sell their new invention, due to the costs and risks involved in international selling and international product liability.

There is also a further category of issues that surround the funding of exporting, involving export guarantees, fluctuating exchange rates, insurance and shipping costs. Since all of these expenses constantly vary, it is often very difficult efficiently to confront these issues without expert advice. Thus, since it will be argued in the concluding passages of this book that the encouragement of new HTSFs is a key requirement for any developed nation's industrial strategy into the mid-part of the twenty-first century, targeted assistance from government and/or private sector sources in identifying problems encountered by HTSFs and helping them to exploit foreign markets is indicated. Such external exporting assistance would allow the management of the HTSFs the freedom to concentrate on ensuring that their new product has the correct specification and price characteristics, while the regulatory problems surrounding international sales would be ameliorated through public and/or private sector assistance.

Moreover, research into selling in HTSFs has indicated that the best ways to help HTSFs to sell their products more effectively is to provide 'face-to-face' contact with experts on exporting as a means of solving specific problems that they encounter, rather than general taught courses on selling abroad (Oakey 1991, 2007c). Such assistance might be provided free of charge by local or national government agencies or delivered on a consultancy basis for a fee, as required by local circumstances. However, the key point about such advice is that it should be accurate, provided promptly (since the need to resolve exporting problems is typically encountered in a crisis), and personally delivered by experts with specialist knowledge and experience. As noted above, although effective selling of a new HTSF product is the last part of the product life cycle, if it is performed badly, the whole cost of previous R&D and production 'gear up' will be lost. Selling is the activity with which HTSF owners frequently need the most specialist help since, although they are technically proficient in terms of R&D, they often lack the management expertise to enable them to perform this key final task efficiently.

5.6 Chapter summary

This chapter on the selling of HTSF products and services began with an observation that most of the general accumulated literature on how markets are developed by small firms is not appropriate when seeking to explain the selling behaviour of HTSFs. The main reason for such inapplicability is the difference in time scales that exist between lower-technology small firms and HTSFs regarding the pace at which new products are launched in the marketplace. In the case of HTSFs, the 'stages approach' widely adopted when explaining market development in typical small firms, in which sales are expanded over time in geographical distribution and size from a local domestic base, through regional, national and international markets over a number of years, is not relevant for two specific reasons. First, many new HTSFs are 'born global' in terms of the markets they serve – where highly specialized goods are sold to dispersed customers from the outset on an international basis. Second, in several manufacturing subsectors of HTSF production, the scope for building markets for a new product over a number of years is inhibited by the rapid obsolescence of products in circumstances where product life cycles can be less than five years.

Another early contextual argument of this chapter was that the term 'marketing' would not be used to describe how HTSFs reach their customers, but 'selling' would be chosen instead. This distinction was made because, in HTSFs, the process of selling to customers is partly market-driven, whereby new products are often developed with the advice of customers, and sales are achieved through market-driven collaboration, rather than developed by the seller, and then marketed to customers. It was further noted that a major initial trigger for new product development in HTSFs was the 'invention push' effort of many HTSF technical entrepreneurs: both in academic and defence-industry contexts, the major impetus for new product development was curiosity or specific defence needs, rather than demand from potential customers in civil commercial markets. These stimuli for new product ideas have tended to exert a negative impact on the competitive performance of such firms when seeking to exploit civil markets, leading to a view that the customer is 'lucky to get' any newly invented product at whatever price was deemed appropriate, rather than responding to customer needs at an affordable price. Added to this somewhat elitist attitude to the invention process in some HTSFs, there is a tendency for physical scientists and engineers to have a negative attitude towards sales staff, partly because sales staff are often thought to be intellectually inferior, but also because following the dictates of customers relayed to them through sales staff could involve the firm's R&D agenda being surrendered to the dictates of customers. However, this negative attitude must be countered by the example of some technical entrepreneurial scientists and engineers who have embraced the skills of sales staff and customers, and have been particularly successful as a result (e.g. Steve Jobs and Steve Wozniak at Apple Computers).

When considering why HTSF owners find it difficult to organize selling strategies in advance, it was noted that predicting in advance the cost of selling products to the final consumer was very difficult for a number of reasons. Apart from difficulties associated with anticipating the point in time at which the product will be ready for selling to the customer (since this depends on the progress of R&D), it was observed that it is often not until late in a new product's development process that the precise function of the product is known, and therefore, at what market it should be aimed. Finally, the programming of a sales campaign is often not attempted well in advance for a simple administrative reason. Although selling the product is an essential late phase of a successful product life cycle, HTSF managements are often so preoccupied by the R&D and financial-cost problems of developing the product that selling does not reach the top of a 'things to do' list on which selling strategy is always present, but is not properly addressed.

Concerning provision for the costs of selling, again, many HTSFs are not well organized. Indeed, many HTSFs spend very small amounts of capital on making their product known to customers, often preferring to rely on mail shots, brochures and 'word of mouth' as cheap, but often ineffective, means of selling. Moreover, the point at which an HTSF needs to begin selling a new product often occurs when the firm is at a very weak point financially, where R&D cost has overrun and the investment needed to 'gear up' production often means that there is little capital available to begin a selling campaign for the product. In the above consideration of selling HTSF products, a distinction was made between selling existing products and those that are new to the market. Regarding existing products, it was noted that although the costs and risks involved in expensive selling campaigns are both high, investment in selling is only a *necessary* requirement for success; *sufficiency* is provided by successful sales, which do not always follow, thus implying substantial risk.

The problems involved in selling new products were noted to be yet more difficult, since potential customers often would be totally unaware of the new 'ground-breaking' product about to be offered, and might be actively antagonistic to the (often initial) disruption to their stable technological status quo. Indeed, it was noted that evidence from substantial literature on the adoption of new technologies indicates that take-up of new inventions is generally not smooth, but is subject to considerable resistance at the beginning of the diffusion process, a process that is often slowed by the need also to adopt other enabling technologies before the technology in question can be fully utilized (e.g. fast broadband connections are needed to permit satisfactory internet usage). Often, potential new adopters of the new technology may need to be gradually introduced to the new product on offer through the HTSF management asking potential customers to provide feedback on the performance of prototypes. This approach enables the free acquisition of information on how best to fit the new product to customer needs, while growing familiarity with the new technology during this process lowers any barriers that the customer might have put in the path of a smooth adoption process. The example of Apple Computers was given as a perfect demonstration of how their first computer sales were assisted by potential customers as the market was expanded away from the hobbyist customers into industry, commerce and education.

Given the high cost of sending sales staff abroad on selling missions, it was noted that the recent arrival of the internet was an ideal low-cost potential means by which HTSFs could find international customers and make their products known in a detailed manner. However, in common with the generally poor attitude to the selling of products by HTSFs, noted above, recent evidence gained on the use of the internet by HTSFs was not encouraging. While most HTSFs had some form of website, the use of the internet for well-resourced selling campaigns was not found to be widely used in studies on HTSF marketing.

A major reason for the lack of effectiveness in making sales abroad was observed to be the very real cost of assembling all the financial, technical and legal information necessary before export sales can be attempted. It was noted that, since HTSFs are likely to provide many of the new high-growth industrial sectors of the latter part of this century, it would be prudent for national governments, keen on promoting HTSF development, to assist HTSFs in overcoming barriers to exporting through 'hands-on' assistance programmes. It was also argued that the best way to impart such information would be through 'face-to-face' contact between HTSF executives and expert advisers, designed to deliver assistance on specific problems encountered by HTSF managements, rather than through general courses which, although time-consuming, are found by many HTSF executives to be of little subsequent value.

6 Strategy

6.1 Introduction

Chapter 2 has strongly argued that the history of technical entrepreneurship is illuminated by impressive individuals who, through their personal drive and technical knowledge (much of it self-taught), were able to produce technology that has been the basis for many new industries, from the beginning of the Industrial Revolution in the eighteenth century, to the present day. Before the development of management science as an academic discipline, these technical entrepreneurs were allowing full scope to their imaginations and, during the Industrial Revolution in the United Kingdom, individuals such as James Watt, George Stephenson and Isambard Kingdom Brunel produced inventions that ranged across manufacturing and civil engineering to involve *both* the building of machinery *and* creating the commercial infrastructure in which it would operate.

These men were steeped in the tradition of the cosmographers of the eighteenth and nineteenth centuries where, for example, physics, geography, biology and geology were studied with equal enthusiasm by individuals (e.g. Alexander Von Humboldt; Charles Lyle; Charles Darwin) (Harvey 1973) who believed that their inquisitiveness should not be restricted to one scientific discipline, but could range freely from one area of science to another, unfettered by the need to be 'pigeonholed' into a single specialism. This freedom was partly permitted by the smaller size of the scientific knowledge-base in these early days of scientific research when all the members of the Royal Society could gather in one small room. However, the stress that could be caused by such a wide-ranging approach to science and invention was reflected in the life of Brunel: while his achievements ranged impressively from civil engineering through railway engineering and ship building to mass-transportation service enterprises, taking on all these onerous responsibilities ultimately led to his death from overwork in 1859. Indeed, it might be concluded with regard to Brunel that his genius as an engineer was undeniable, but his command of business management principles was poor, particularly regarding the need to delegate effectively within his portfolio of businesses.

The ethos of 'getting the technology right and the management will take care of itself' remained with many technical entrepreneurs into the twentieth century. This attitude was bolstered by a feeling among a number of physical scientists that social science in general, and management science in particular, was a contradiction in terms (Snow 1959); and that, moreover, 'management science' is not a scientific subject, but merely a matter of 'common sense' and that all the necessary industrial management skills could be learnt through work experience. This view was noted above when considering the attitude of engineers towards the selling of industrial products (see Chapter 5). However, throughout the twentieth century, the steady increase in the size of manufacturing and service organizations, and the complexity of all the competencies necessary to invent, construct and sell a new product invention, increased the unavoidable need for management specialisms in particular, and management science in general.

The subsequent tension between the residual inclination of engineers and scientists to pursue new ideas through 'invention push' and the need for sales staff to hone such inventions through customer 'demand pull' resulted in a fragile equilibrium in which it is sometimes necessary for scientists to move the technological paradigm forwards through radical invention (that the market initially does not want), while sales staff give a technically 'winning product' an extra 'edge' over competitors through including customer-led design features. Nonetheless, despite the growth of a complex international industrial system based on professional management-science principles, and the clear proven value of effective sales campaigns, especially in high-technology sectors (e.g. the case of Apple Computers), there remains a degree of snobbery present in the attitude of many scientists and engineers, when founding new HTSFs, that renders them sceptical of the need for formal business strategies based on strong professional management principles (Oakey 2003b).

6.2 The strategic goals of the HTSF

When considering the strategy of any new HTSF, it is first necessary to consider the main goals of the firm that the strategy seeks to achieve. At the outset, it must be noted that many new HTSFs do not have a formal strategy, and that in the early days, ideas of what the firm seeks to achieve are often obscured by the need to survive. For example, in many new HTSFs, there is not a formally written-down strategic document that is available for all the employees of the firm to read and 'buy into' (except in the case of 'grow to sell' firms – discussed below). Much will depend on the ownership structure of the firm at the time of formation. In the case of the lone entrepreneurial founder, there is considerable scope for confusion and variation in terms of what strategy is to be adopted. This is perhaps why many nascent HTSF entrepreneurs do not write down a formal strategy document, since they are not clear in their own minds what the strategy should be, or what they wish the business to become. In cases of multiple entrepreneurship, where two or more entrepreneurs come together to form a new business, the potential for a clear formal strategy is higher, since prior to beginning the new firm, there must be a degree of discussion among the founders in order to arrive at a common view of what the new firm should seek to achieve. This is particularly the case for the 'grow to sell' firm, where, typically, a business plan will be constructed. Thus, although specific 'day-to-day' goals often are difficult to pin down and may change over time, the overall ethos of the firm and its *raison d'être* are specified. However, despite the rather confused picture of the nature of strategy identification and its implementation, there are some key factors that influence the strategic approaches discussed below.

6.2.1 Independence

In Chapter 2, it was observed that most new HTSF entrepreneurs gain experience, before founding their new firm, in an organization where they accumulate enough technical knowledge on which to base their new business. Typically, such a prior organization will be large, probably taking the form of a university, a government research laboratory, or an incubating, large, existing high-technology firm (common in Silicon Valley) (Mason 1979). Thus, a common reason for beginning a new HTSF is to gain independence from the bureaucracy of a large organization. Indeed, the move to begin a new HTSF may have been prompted by an attempt of an individual researcher to persuade the organization for which he or she worked to develop a new technological idea that he or she had invented. In many cases, after consulting customers, the answer from the employer firm is often negative (Christensen 1997), thus prompting the individual to 'spin off' and use the unexploited technology as a basis for the new HTSF. In many cases, the resultant firm either fails or struggles to survive; but in a small number of important instances, the new HTSF's invention may result in a disruptive technology that offers a new product or service to the customer, disrupts or destroys an existing industry, and promotes rejuvenated market competition (as discussed in Chapter 2).

However, the desire for independence might not only stem from a need to gain freedom from a large bureaucratic organization, or from distaste for bureaucratic control. Indeed, the problem for some introspective entrepreneurs is not that control is disliked *per se*, but that it is in the wrong hands! This type of entrepreneur 'spins off' from a larger organization because of the wish to achieve total control is a key motive for founding a new business. However, these individuals, while providing strong focus and drive for the new business, especially in its early stages, can become a bottleneck to growth as the firm reaches a point where a more formal management structure is indicated (e.g. the appointment of finance and R&D directors). Such a founder often develops a 'not invented here' attitude in which he or she is unwilling to delegate control to other senior staff or take specialist advice from colleagues, but conversely keeps control for him- or herself. For example, such an individual, as a technical entrepreneur, may argue with R&D staff over the direction of product development and/or with the finance director regarding how the finance department should function.

As indicated graphically in Figure 2.2 of Chapter 2, such a founder may have a pervasively bad impact on the firm as it grows, in instances where the objectives of the firm become clouded by the desire for control overtaking the need for strategic and financial success. This is a stark example of how the control of a firm can become more important than the simple rational logical drive for economic success proposed by economists (Marris 1964). However, such an attitude would be no surprise to academics concerned with the 'boundedly rational' choice of entrepreneurs (Simon 1955; Cyert and March 1963; Pred 1966). The potential severity of this problem is indicated by the fact that many venture capitalists operating in Silicon Valley during the 1980s often removed the founder of an HTSF immediately after obtaining a controlling interest in such a firm, because he or she was deemed to be an obstacle to the continued growth of the business as it evolved from an entrepreneurial stage to a more formally managed business (Oakey 1984a; Oakey *et al.* 1988). Clearly there may come a point in the evolution of a new HTSF when the interests of the founding entrepreneur and the 'best practice' management of the firm that he or she has founded conflict, to the detriment of the firm. This negative view of independence, however, should not be overstated. There are clear examples from recent history where the initial founders of a high-technology firm (e.g. Bill Gates; Steve Jobs and Steve Wozniak) have negotiated the difficult transition from the 'hands-on' entrepreneurial early phase of an HTSF's growth to the formally managed stage, where specialist delegation occurs to achieve large-firm status; although it must be concluded that these examples tend to be exceptions that prove the rule of the founder's ejection from the business at some point in its development, either on a voluntary or involuntary basis.

6.2.2 The 'grow to sell' approach

While 'independence' might be viewed more as a somewhat irrational imperative than a formal strategy, 'grow to sell' is an unambiguous strategy for a new HTSF and is the antithesis of the independence principle. Since it has been noted in Chapter 4 on R&D that many HTSFs are 'front-end loaded' in terms of R&D costs incurred prior to making any product sales, the 'grow to sell' approach acknowledges this fact by seeking to fill the funding gap caused by front-end-loaded R&D costs by raising venture capital support at the birth of the new firm. Indeed, in many cases, if venture capital cannot be raised, the proposed new venture will not take place. The 'grow to sell' approach will involve a business plan that will clearly indicate, within five to ten years from the point of the firm's formation, a trade sale of the new firm, thus providing any investing venture capitalist with an 'out' when equity can be redeemed for cash – it is hoped, at a profit. Unlike many HTSFs founded with an independence ethos, where the initial funding of the firm is frequently provided by an individual founder, and the firm is subsequently resourced on the basis of retained profits as and when they occur, 'grow to sell' HTSFs are often founded by a group of entrepreneurs who collectively write the business plan to be 'pitched' at venture capitalists. This is a much more democratic process than the independent approach of the individual entrepreneur, in that it offers advantages to the new firm – a wider range of management skills held by the founding team in terms of manpower and management skills (e.g. typically financial, technical and selling expertise) that is also attractive to the venture capitalist, since it implies more openness regarding inputs from other interested parties and a willingness to share control, in this case with external investors.

While venture capitalists are occasionally prepared to invest in a strongly independent firm as a minority stakeholder under favourable circumstances, the 'grow to sell' option is clearly more attractive to a venture capital firm since both the firm's founder (or founders) and the venture capitalist investor are agreed on the need for a trade sale at the successful conclusion of the 'grow to sell' project. In contrast, the potential for venture capital investment is often sharply different in the case of a strongly independent firm. Here, the desire for independence encourages the owner to be very wary of any external financial involvement, either loan capital from banks (which may close a business down to which they have lent money if repayment cannot be made), or from venture capitalists in cases where a minority equity stake held by the venture capitalist might be increased beyond a 50 per cent shareholding that would transfer control of the firm to this external investor. Such considerations only combine to emphasize the strong difference in sentiment and practical effect between the 'independence' and 'grow to sell' approaches to business formation and growth.

6.3 The strategic approaches of HTSFs to market competition

Although the popular media throughout the world understandably concentrate on the spectacular success stories regarding HTSFs (e.g. Microsoft; Google), any area of concentrated high-technology production, which often takes the form of a cluster as typified by Silicon Valley, contains a number of different types of HTSF in terms of the strategic manner in which they serve the needs of the local high-technology agglomeration and the world beyond the local area. For example, while some comparatively lower-technology firms in high-technology sectors perform service or sub-contract functions (e.g. component making and assembly), at the other end of the production process, large firms design and construct the finished products for which high-technology industry is deservedly famous, implying not only a difference in size, but also in technical sophistication and function (e.g. computers; biomedicines; internet hardware and software). The following section on the strategic approaches of HTSF owners explores the way in which they choose their productive activities, how they influence the markets they serve, their profitability, and their potential for strong growth. This potential is often initially derived from the abilities of the founding entrepreneur (or entrepreneurs) and the way in which such abilities can be applied to the needs of the market to offer a saleable product or service. Three major types of new HTSF are proposed below in terms of strategic approach, together with an explanation of the functions they perform and the advantages and disadvantages they experience in the market segment they serve.

6.3.1 Sub-contract HTSFs

Sub-contract firms are the 'workhorses' of any high-technology sector. They are often founded by entrepreneurs who have greater business acumen than technical ability (see Figure 2.1 in Chapter 2). In this specialist, but generally low-technology area of HTSF production, the ability to organize the business efficiently in order to produce output that is competitively priced is often more important to survival in subcontracting than having leading-edge technical skills. In many cases, such firms provide services to large high-technology firms that the large firms could perform themselves in-house, but do not, either because they do not wish to create this particular expertise or because fluctuating demand means that this type of production is best served by putting out this work to a sub-contractor. In certain cases, work may be sub-contracted because the sub-contractor has specialist facilities to deal with hazardous materials (e.g. asbestos, radioactive materials, etc.). This is a symbiotic relationship in which both the sub-contractor and the sub-contractee benefit, although, from a strategic viewpoint, the position of the sub-contractor is much more precarious than that of a usually larger client firm.

There are three major reasons for such fragility. First, client firms working with a sub-contractor may come to realize that the amount of business being put out to the sub-contractor has become substantial and, as a result, decide to reduce costs by performing the work in-house rather than sub-contracting, thus causing the sub-contractor severe problems in finding other customers. This can be a particular strategic problem when, as is often the case, sub-contractors have a major customer that accounts for over 50 per cent of their business. Second, because, as noted above, large high-technology firms may put out additional work to sub-contractors during periods when the national and/or world economies are booming, this tactic can rapidly reverse if these economies enter into a recession. Such a downturn, at best, will often force large-firm customers to ask for cheaper prices from their sub-contractors; or at worst, cause them to withdraw their patronage completely, often overnight, and move this product in-house. Third, in a more general sense, because the barriers to entry are low in HTSF sub-contracting (due to their generic, often process-based, technologies when compared with more sophisticated HTSFs with leading-edge *product* technologies), competition can be intense, particularly, as discussed above, in periods of recession when sub-contract work is scarce.

For all the reasons discussed above, because of the precarious general position that sub-contractor firms hold in high-technology industry, where the customer large firms have a dominant hold over their destiny in terms of the scope they have for growing their market share, the development of a formal strategy has limited potential. Many sub-contract firms would prefer to evolve from a subservient sub-contract role to develop a new product and become product-based, since this evolution would enable them to achieve better 'value added' by selling a finished product. However, the technical entrepreneurship issue again becomes relevant, since, as observed at the beginning of this section, most sub-contractor entrepreneurs tend not to have the sophisticated technical skills that would enable them to develop a new product. While their often mainly process skills, coupled with a good head for business, enable them to run their firm competitively, in high-technology industry this is no substitute for developing novel product technologies with strong growth potential that can be used as a vehicle for achieving larger size, or be sold to a larger competitor at a substantial profit (as discussed below in sub-section 6.3.3). While external consultants may be used to design a new product for a sub-contract firm, the strength of the technical entrepreneurial role is reflected in the fact that technical entrepreneurs gain confidence from intimately knowing the technology *they* have developed and seeing ways of realizing its potential that a non-technically qualified sub-contractor would not possess if reliant on a third-party consultant (Oakey 1984a).

6.3.2 Niche producer HTSFs

Niche production is another type of HTSF activity that is, again, less glamorous than many large-scale HTSF activities. However, it is, unlike sub-contracting, a more financially stable activity. As will be noted below when discussing product-based firms, a major problem for any new HTSF seeking to exploit a novel product technology with mass-market potential is, ironically, that such strong growth potential is also a problem, since the road from invention to exploitation for such a firm is paved with many potential pitfalls, mainly associated with protecting the intellectual property involved. An irony lies in the fact that the very high potential that the new technology possesses will ensure that large international firms will seek to gain access to this new knowledge, either fairly by seeking to purchase or license the new firm and its technological assets (see sub-section 6.3.3 below), or by deliberately infringing patents by allowing the original producer to enter the market and then 'reverse engineering' its new product to produce an (often improved) patent-infringing copy. Consequently, the small size of the HTSF that is a victim of such predatory action may render preferable a trade sale of the technology involved, often to a large competitor, rather than 'going it alone'. This is a popular way of obtaining value from this new technology, because legally defending any patent taken out by such a small firm would be financially crippling.

However, there is a substantial sub-sector of HTSF production in which small firms are protected by specialization. There are a number of high-technology markets where the scope for mass production does not exist, either because the size of the total market is small (e.g. specialist measuring instruments; laboratory equipment; specialist high-performance electronic components) or because the type of products produced are bespoke in that the specification for the product will vary with each individual customer (e.g. control equipment for industrial production systems or small power stations). While small and medium-sized firms in these types of activities can achieve profitability that offers a good return for the management and workers of an HTSF, such returns would not be great enough to interest a much larger firm. Thus, due to the lack of a threat from larger firms in high-technology sectors and the relatively small size of the market, predatory activity by large firms in this sub-sector is rare.

From a strategic viewpoint, this type of firm has limited potential. However, if the previous discussion in this chapter on the motives of HTSF entrepreneurs is rehearsed, it is clear that not all HTSF founders wish to become multimillionaires. Freedom to be independent and run a modestly successful, but stable, business with a strong financial base and secure customers is often quite enough for many HTSF founders. This niche type of production has many advantages, not least of which is an absence of the problems experienced by HTSF executives who seek to exploit a new product that has high mass-market potential. This will be the subject of the next strategic type of HTSF discussed below.

6.3.3 The new product-based HTSF

The third type of firm, based on a new product with high, or very high, growth potential, is the kind of HTSF most commonly recognized by the public as archetypal, when such firms rapidly achieve large size. However, although there are many examples of HTSFs that have grown into very large multinational corporations, and have dominated the new sectors of industry that they have created, often by disrupting previously dominant large firms (as discussed previously in Chapter 2), the *majority* of new HTSFs do not grow from garage-based businesses to multinational enterprises. Even in successful clusters such as Silicon Valley, most HTSFs either fail, or are acquired by larger firms a few years after formation. In this sub-section, some of the reasons why it is extremely difficult to transform a new HTSF into an industry leader will be explored.

Initially it must be acknowledged that, as indicated in sub-section 6.2.2 above, many firms that have produced a new product with strong growth potential opt for a 'grow to sell' approach to their business strategy; and in these cases, the problems of survival and growth are reduced by an acceptance, at the outset, that the firm will be sold at a predicted point in the business plan, written when the firm was founded. Nonetheless, also as noted above, there remains a substantial group of HTSFs where independence and organic growth are strong strategic goals. However, in practice, the reality is that, whatever strategy the firm adopts at birth, it may be modified to suit changing conditions experienced as the firm develops the product that was its *raison d'être*. For example, a firm that was founded on a 'grow to sell' basis might not be sold at the pre-determined time, remaining independent through buying out its investors; while a firm that was founded on strongly independent principles, if it is successful, will receive many offers of purchase by large multinational firms (e.g. in the biotechnology sector; see Oakey *et al.* 1990a), thus prompting a decision to sell out at an opportune moment (to be discussed in sub-section 6.4 below).

The problems for firms that do have promising new products which they seek to exploit independently to the full are twofold and interrelated: namely, obtaining adequate investment capital to grow the business while remaining independent; and adequately providing intellectual property protection for their embryonic new product. These strategic issues are interdependent because they both relate to the financial strength of the new independent HTSF as it grows. Although this type of firm cannot include the technological assets represented by the new high-technology product under development on its balance sheet (notwithstanding that this is its main asset of value – see Chapter 7 for a more detailed discussion of this subject), the potential return from the sale of this asset remains the main means by which the firm can maintain the financial support of external investors or loans from banks. Put simply, the strategic imperative for such a firm is striking a balance between achieving lucrative sales of the new product when it comes to market and losing the support of funders (e.g. banks and holders of minority equity stakes) who become nervous as R&D programmes overrun and/or market sales do not quickly materialize.

A strategic issue that can often help a new HTSF to survive this 'valley of death' type of growth problem is the age of the industry into which the firm in question is seeking to launch its new product. It is a well-established principle that new HTSFs in an industrial sector that is also nascent often enjoy a window of opportunity when a dominant technology has not been established, and large-firm economies of scale have not yet occurred. The emergence of a new technology onto the international market can take advantage of a period when the established large firms in the relevant industry (if one exists) have not become aware of the existence or potential of the new technology, or are deliberately seeking to ignore it in order to protect existing lucrative market sales of a mature technology they previously have developed (discussed in Chapter 5). For these reasons, a window of opportunity may open for, say, five years, in which a new HTSF, if it can solve its own technological problems and produce a winning product, can grow rapidly to exploit this short-lived gap in the market. In these circumstances, the problems of funding and intellectual property protection are both solved by the rapid increase in profits from sales, and the confidence this creates in banks and investors, who will be keen to provide funding.

Probably the best example of the above phenomenon was that of Apple Computers in the early 1970s. Due to the complacency of IBM, partly caused by its reluctance to disturb its lucrative mainframe market, this new firm was able to exploit a window of opportunity that was open for about six years between 1972 and 1978, and launch its new desktop computer into the market before IBM realized that their mainframe computer market was under threat. By the time IBM recognized the threat, it was too late, and Apple Computer, Inc. was well on the way to becoming a major international player in the world computer industry. However, the coincidence of new HTSF technology with a world-beating relevant window of opportunity is rare, and when many other firms seek to enter, or disrupt, well-established markets where large firms dominate, they are usually resisted by these large firms, causing their closure or acquisition. It is also possible for new HTSFs to emerge *before* a window of opportunity has opened, to damaging effect, and this has been argued above in the case of the 'dot.com bubble' in the early 2000s, when the 'explosion' of internet firms unfortunately preceded the widespread availability of adequate technology (e.g. broadband connections).

6.4 The strategic development options that are open to a new product-based firm

Given the problems that a new high-technology-product-based firm faces when seeking to exploit the new intellectual property it has invented, it is not surprising that they often seek some means of reducing the risks involved in achieving such a goal. The options discussed below (in ascending order of risk) are some of the main strategic alternatives open to new HTSFs as they seek to develop and/or exploit a new technology they have developed.

6.4.1 Sell the intellectual property at an early 'proof of concept' stage, and use the capital raised to develop other projects

This is a conservative option for a potential HTSF founder, in that expensive and difficult-to-estimate periods of R&D, production and marketing are, in this case, avoided by selling the intellectual property at an early stage. This scenario is the converse of the other strategies discussed below in that the major advantage of such an approach is the low risk. The main disadvantage is that a much lower price would be obtained for this intellectual property in its relatively 'raw' state than would be obtainable were it to be further developed, sold to customers, and have achieved a proven track record of performance. This strategy is often adopted by academics who discover a new technology with strong commercial potential, but do not have the experience or inclination to abandon their academic careers, to which they are well suited, in favour of business entrepreneurship, for which they might not be. However, some established HTSFs adopt a deliberate 'no production' strategy for their business, in which they see their main role as developing new technology to the 'proof of concept' stage, and then selling the intellectual property involved to a third-party large firm. This approach is particularly popular in areas of high-technology industry involved with healthcare since, in addition to the normal problems associated with R&D and product development risk, there is an additional difficulty of product liability; in the United States, for example, a healthcare product proving to have negative side effects after entering the market can cause huge damages to be awarded against the manufacturer (Oakey 2007c). Such an HTSF strategy of 'no production' avoids this very large and real risk.

6.4.2 Actively seek the early support of a larger firm

Since many large firms in high-technology sectors have a policy of corporate venturing, it is often possible for new HTSF owners to interest one of these firms in investing in their new enterprise (e.g. large well-established pharmaceuticals firms often invest in new biotechnology ventures). Again, this joint venture strategy has both negative and positive implications for the HTSF. From a negative perspective, while a minority stake taken by the large firm in a new HTSF would not involve a loss of control in the first instance, the HTSF management might reasonably fear that, if continuing financial problems associated with R&D occur, another sale of equity in order to ameliorate their financial difficulties could lead to a further dilution of ownership to a point where control is lost. This might be an important consideration for an HTSF founder for whom independence was an important reason for beginning his or her new business. Positive features of large-firm involvement, however, would be that a continuing commitment to the support of the HTSF would probably be forthcoming in the form of further capital and/or technological assistance, in order to safeguard the investor's equity stake. Moreover, such large-firm financial support would make it easier for the HTSF to bear the legal costs of defending any intellectual property involved, and to support the R&D, production and marketing costs that will be incurred when bringing the product to market. Although this type of arrangement can work well, resulting in either a continued equity stake or full acquisition by a large partner firm, this will largely depend on the attitude and compatibility of the individuals involved, both on the part of the investing large firm and the HTSF; this itself can be a source of unknown risk to any HTSF embarking on this strategic option (Klein-Woolhuis 1999; Faems 2012).

6.4.3 Develop the intellectual property to a more advanced stage, and then sell the business

This approach is basically the 'grow to sell' strategy discussed above. The main advantages of this scenario are that venture capital investors know at the outset what the strategy of this business is intended to be, while the founder (or founders) obtain, at an early stage, the capital investment necessary to enable them to achieve the goal they have set themselves. There is no problem over ownership, since continued independence is, by definition, not an issue. However, friction between the founders and their investors may arise if the actual performance of the firm, especially in terms of R&D progress prior to the product launch, falls short of what was predicted in a business plan. Conversely, if the new HTSF is extremely successful, the founders of the firm might come into conflict with their investors should they decide that selling the business at the agreed time would be sub-optimal behaviour, and therefore seek to continue past the agreed point of sale. However, the investors seek to hold to the original agreement – to sell the business at the previously agreed date and obtain an 'out' that would allow an early return on their investment. While the HTSF founders might be able to raise capital to buy their investors out, this might not be financially possible, which would lead to strategic deadlock. As will be discussed below, a major problem that this impasse illustrates is how to decide at what point the returns from a trade sale will be at their maximum. Without a crystal ball with which to foresee the future, this decision is highly problematic!

6.4.4 Seek to patent the new intellectual property, sell the invention involved and defend it against competition

This strategy is associated with the 'independence' approach to new HTSF formation discussed above. This strategy, when it is successful, gains much misleading notoriety, since such success is often the 'exception that proves the rule' of either failure or acquisition. While the folklore of a founder (or founders) beginning their business in a garage and building it up to become a world-leading multinational firm is an attractive story to tell, the idea of 'winning against the odds' is generally not a rational approach to running a business. As will be discussed below, while the desire to remain both independent and successful may be a preference held by new HTSF founders, logically, this should not preclude consideration of other options both in terms of the overall strategy of the firm and with regard to external advice and external capital investment. Indeed, although many firms pursue a strong strategy of independent growth, if they encounter financial difficulties, a belated decision to seek external help may leave them inexperienced in dealing with agencies outside the firm at a time when they are in a weak position and are in most need of help (Oakey 2003b). These concerns lead logically to the next section, which considers strategic decision making under uncertainty.

6.5 Strategic decision making under conditions of uncertainty

At face value, each of the strategic options discussed above might seem sensible in principle. However, it is a paradox that all these diverse approaches to the development of HTSF businesses might be flawed. For example, without the power of foresight, a decision to sell a new technology at an early stage by negating the option to develop and take this new invention to the market might be *either* optimal (if continuing should lead to the collapse of the new business) or sub-optimal (if continuing to develop and sell the new idea might lead to strong profitability). Moreover, any given strategy, once adopted, can only be judged an absolute failure if closure of the firm is a direct result of its adoption; while success can only be fully confirmed if very impressive progress is achieved by the firm in question. There are many scenarios that would allow a technical entrepreneur to make a sub-optimal strategic decision which, although incorrect in terms of optimal behaviour, led to poor results that did not, however, cause the demise of the firm.

The dilemma faced by technical entrepreneurs when deciding which strategic options to adopt for their firm is graphically indicated in Figure 6.1. An obvious initial decision to be made by a potential technical entrepreneur is whether beginning a new HTSF is a sensible option. As noted above, the case of the potential academic entrepreneur provides a useful example of this initial dilemma. It is relatively common for university academics, who have often accumulated R&D expertise and resultant product ideas on which a new high-technology enterprise realistically could be based, to consider a new academic 'spin-off' firm with which to exploit such intellectual property. Academic R&D outputs with commercial exploitation potential range from the type of radical breakthrough inventions that create, destroy or revolutionize industries, to marginal new discoveries, the potential commercial application (or applications) of which are not clear. Indeed, academic 'spin-off' is often encouraged by universities. However, there may be a further problem of the suitability of academics for an entrepreneurial career. Although there have been notable exceptions where academics become successful entrepreneurs, most academics choose an academic career because they enjoy the educational environment in which non-financial job satisfaction

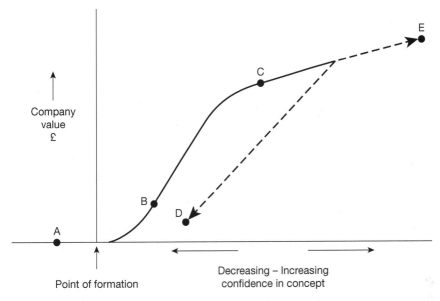

Figure 6.1 The relationship between value and product confidence
Source: Oakey 2003a

is gained from the rewards of teaching and research rather than a high salary. Many such individuals are not interested in becoming entrepreneurs, while for others, any attempt to do so might prove a complete disaster due to their unsuitable temperament and lack of relevant business skills.

Clearly, when entrepreneurs in a free market decide to begin a new firm, the risks that they take are solely attributable to them. However, it is significant that, in cases of academic entrepreneurship where government-funded practitioners are attempting to 'tease out' new entrepreneurial ventures on which *their own* positions and success depend, there is a moral hazard issue present in that such a practitioner, who has no personal risk, may attempt to encourage an academic to take the major step of founding a new enterprise which involves him or her *alone* in personal financial risk (e.g. possible loss of savings, pension or property). This problem is exacerbated by the rhetoric surrounding university entrepreneurship in which, as noted above, the likelihood of success is often exaggerated, although failure is far more likely than success (Storey 1994; Cressy 2006). In general, prospective entrepreneurs are encouraged to have over-optimistic views of how easy beginning a business will be, and consequently, need to be carefully counselled on how risky and likely to fail most businesses are in reality.

Most of the problems associated with the encouragement of risk concern the balance between risk and reward in general, and who is encouraging the risk compared with who is taking the risk. An obvious risk-averse conclusion that could be drawn from the above assertions on the attitude of academics with ownership of intellectual property might be that they should *always* sell such assets without beginning a new business themselves in order to exploit this new knowledge. However, while this would certainly be low risk, more enterprising academics with the potential for developing business skills might decide, with the encouragement of entrepreneurship development practitioners, to attempt to develop the technology they have invented into a new product and form a business to build and sell such a product on the open market. Figure 6.1 implies that, in many instances, it would be optimal for a potential academic entrepreneur not to begin an academic 'spin-off' enterprise, but rather, in keeping with the strategic option outlined in sub-section 6.4.1 above, sell the technology at the 'proof of concept' stage and remain an academic (i.e. point A, Figure 6.1).

For technical entrepreneurs adopting strategies that seek to begin a business and develop the technology further (i.e. strategies 6.4.2 and 6.4.3 in section 6.4 above), a major specific challenge is whether to sell the business at some point in its development (option 6.4.3) or to seek to achieve large independent size by competing 'head on' with existing large firms in the sector concerned (option 6.4.4), notwithstanding that this is a very risky and usually unsuccessful strategy for all the reasons noted above. Moreover, if the 'grow to sell' option is chosen, a key question is at what point in the development of the firm should this sale occur? Figure 6.1 graphically indicates some of the problems associated with making the most efficient decision of when to sell. This essentially involves a 'trade-off' between obtaining maximum value for the business without – in the process of trying to grow the firm (e.g. expand the customer base) – the firm being pitched into a collapse that causes confidence in the business, and its subsequent value, likewise to fail. The possible reasons for such a collapse are discussed below.

Regardless of whether the intention in forming a new business is 'independence' or 'grow to sell', both approaches share a common intention to grow the new enterprise in order that its value will increase, since both independence and saleability can be protected by achieving a strong financial footing for the firm. Thus, Figure 6.1 (above) indicates that by taking the intellectual property beyond point A and forming a new entrepreneurial firm, the value of the intellectual property is increased through B to C. However, by attempting to grow the business to E, the value of the company (and commensurate confidence) may collapse to point

D. Such an outcome can arise for a number of reasons ranging from insurmountable technical problems, through withdrawal of financial support, to the discovery of an alternative technological solution which performs more effectively and takes the envisaged market share of the firm in question (Oakey 2003b).

6.6 The desire for independence – a vice or a virtue?

A summary of the major strategic options open to HTSF founders, noted above, shows that there is a relationship between risk and reward: the ventures most likely to be highly successful are also highly risky, due both to their often radical and disruptive technological potential that might not achieve market success, and the likelihood that large firms will seek to acquire their intellectual property if the HTSF in possession of such technology begins to become successful. However, in contrast to many other forms of business, where much of the success achieved depends on the business skill of the entrepreneur in circumstances where the means to produce the product or service are well known, and barriers to entry are low (e.g. restaurants; food processing; furniture manufacturing), in high-technology industry, the likelihood of success largely depends on the potential of the technology that lies behind the product or service on offer. For example, when Howard Florey developed penicillin in the 1930s, this discovery was so important that it was not a case of whether the technology would be a success, since its value to medicine was readily apparent, but how the highly successful exploitation would occur and who would benefit. Many of the new technologies developed by HTSF entrepreneurs are of this type, whereby the novelty of the technology involved ensures that competition is often absent. This reality is relevant to a major theme of this chapter, which is how best to bring a new entity to the market and ensure the best financial returns with minimal risk.

As noted above, one way in which many inventors think that their new discovery should be developed would be through the establishment of an independent firm, over which they can exert full control. Although this approach to HTSF formation and growth is only one of the four alternative development paths elaborated in section 6.4 above (i.e. option 6.4.4), it is the only strategy that anticipates total continuing independent control of a new enterprise. While the reasons for this attitude may be understandable, given the often mentioned need of new technical entrepreneurs to escape the bureaucratic control of previous large organizations, a degree of unhelpful introspection might also lie behind the drive for such strong independence. A strong logical argument might be made that, in order to maximize the potential for a new HTSF to thrive and grow, *all* options that could help in this regard should be considered. This would include, for example, the raising of external capital through bank loans or equity finance by the surrendering of shares for additional investment funds. An almost irrational compulsion to remain totally independent, rather than being a guarantee of autonomy, may perversely deliver sub-optimal progress, acquisition, or even total failure.

As a business grows, and the economy in which it exists changes over time, an effective strategy must adapt to these, often subtle, variations in the regional, national and international business environments. Having the tools to cope with such changes should include various forms of external assistance, even if this means some loss of autonomy. Moreover, the building of external contacts as sources of, for example, finance, management training, or government assistance (where relevant) is best achieved as the firm grows and becomes prosperous. Particularly with regard to financial support, this is better explored when a new HTSF is not in a weak financial position. Maintaining independence at all costs, only to seek financial help when the firm is in a poor financial state is not advisable. It is far better from the outset to be outward looking rather than introspective regarding external help, since a moderate amount of external help might not lead to loss of control, but help preserve the independence so important to many firms. As observed elsewhere, it is a paradox to call an adopted management approach a strategy, when no other options are available, and only the adopted course of action remains (Oakey 2003b). Keeping a wide view of what is on offer in the industrial environment while in a position of strength is more likely to ensure that future failure will be avoided.

Finally, given the above arguments, even in the case of firms that are founded on a strongly independent basis, managements should regularly consider if selling the business would be better than continuing on as an independent entity (assuming a buyer can be found). An irrational need to preserve the independence of a firm in the face of countervailing economic evidence would not only be illogical, it would be highly dangerous. If a 'golden' opportunity to sell the business arrives, it should not be missed, since Figure 6.1 reminds us that continued onwards and upwards progress can never be assured.

6.7 Chapter summary

At the beginning of this chapter, it was observed that the role of strategy as a sub-discipline of management science has emerged gradually. It was noted that the great entrepreneurs of the nineteenth century tended to follow a 'cosmographer' approach to science in which it was quite acceptable for individuals to possess a number of scientific skills from unrelated disciplines that they deployed in a context where strategy was developed by them, often without the involvement of others. In these circumstances, both the technology under development and the means by which it would be exploited (i.e. strategy) were often accepted to be the prerogative of a single entrepreneur. Isambard Kingdom Brunel, in common with many of his contemporaries, was noted as an individual, originally trained as an engineer, whose skills ranged from engineering across strategic management to commerce. However, this breadth of activity, even by the end of the Victorian era, was not without cost, and the early death of Brunel from overwork foreshadowed the reality that, with the increasing size of all the functions a business needed to perform, there was an unavoidable need to specialize as the twentieth century arrived. Nonetheless, it was also noted that a legacy of this tendency to believe that strategy was 'just common sense' that could be easily handled by entrepreneurs in their 'own heads' continued among some physical scientists into the twentieth century. For example, it was recalled that this friction between the physical and social sciences has endured in the uneasy relationship between engineers and sales staff in many high-technology firms.

Regarding the general strategic goals of the firm, it was noted that many HTSFs founded by individuals with a strong independent approach to the way the business should be organized often do not possess a written formal strategy. While HTSFs founded on a formal 'grow to sell' strategy, by definition, had a better agreed approach to how the firm should be developed, strongly independent firms often lack strategic focus. However, it was strongly argued that 'independence' was a motive force behind the formation and development of many HTSFs. This was largely due to the frustration that individuals felt when working for large public or private sector organizations. Nonetheless, in some circumstances, it was warned that the desire for independence can be a negative factor in that this may also be a symptom of a less attractive need for control of the new firm that is formed. In this context, a new independently oriented entrepreneur can have a 'not invented here' problem whereby a disinclination to delegate is common. This tendency can lead to a more general management problem in which the founding entrepreneur becomes a bottleneck to the future growth of the new HTSF. It was noted that, in extreme cases, many investing venture capitalists may remove the founder of a new HTSF, if they find that he or she is guilty of the 'not invented here' approach to management noted above. Although there are a number of famous examples where transitions have been made by independently minded founding entrepreneurs from HTSF to large high-technology-firm status, an unreasonable desire for independent control of a business can be a genuine problem that often restricts necessary progress towards a more formally managed business.

Conversely, a detailed treatment of the 'grow to sell' strategic approach observed that this was, again by definition, a much more democratic approach to founding and managing a new HTSF. Since an initial act of this type of firm was to write a business plan as a strategic document, and use this information to attract external investors in their new firm, this type of organization was not only more democratic since it was usually founded by a group of entrepreneurs, but, due to multiple founders, it was also able to call on a wider range of skills (typically financial, technical and marketing expertise). This type of firm would also be attractive to venture capitalists since the selling of the business at a predicted point in the future catered for the venture capitalists' need for an 'out' by virtue of a trade sale. This generally more democratic attitude of the HTSF's founding management would also be attractive to a venture capitalist since this approach to founding and running the new HTSF would suggest a more open approach to external involvement in management.

The specific strategic options open to new HTSFs were then considered and three main approaches were identified. First, at the lowest level of technological sophistication, sub-contracting was isolated as a strategic option for a new HTSF. Sub-contracting is essential in any high-technology industrial complex since it provides manufacturing services for usually larger more sophisticated high-technology firms. Mainly based on business-management skills rather than technological expertise, this type of firm produces component parts and/or manufacturing services that supplement identical or more sophisticated production performed in larger customer firms. However, such sub-contracting was observed to be a precarious activity since the amount of work available in a given sector will fluctuate, depending on local, national and world economic cycles. When strong international growth occurs, large amounts of work are available at good prices. However, in times of recession, the volume of work on offer can dramatically decrease, and prices fall. Having a large amount of a sub-contractor's output taken by a single customer (a common phenomenon in these firms) may also be a problem if the customer resorts to taking the work back into their own factories. In many ways, such sub-contracting acts as a 'safety mechanism' that expands and contracts in keeping with the relative prosperity of high-technology industry as a whole. Moreover, an added element of insecurity was noted to exist in the low barriers to entry to which HTSF sub-contracting is subjected. This means that it is easier for new small firms to enter production and compete with existing firms. Generally, such a tendency has the effect of depressing prices. Competitor firms tend to enter the sector during periods of rapid growth, while there are high rates of attrition when a recession occurs. Thus, overall, a steady strategic approach in this sub-sector of high-technology industry is difficult to maintain.

The second type of HTSF strategy to be isolated was that of niche production. HTSFs in this sub-sector occupy market niches where there is steady, but not large, market potential. Such firms are protected from the acquisitive attentions of larger firms because the levels of profitability they might obtain are comparatively small. HTSF entrepreneurs with a strongly independent approach to ownership (discussed above) tend to occupy these types of niche in which a 'good living wage' is the main objective of the owners in circumstances where both profitability and risk are low. These firms tend to manufacture specialist low-volume (often bespoke) types of instrumentation and equipment, including scientific instruments, test equipment and systems for regulatory control.

The final strategic type of HTSF is the product-based firm that seeks to research, manufacture and sell a new HTSF product. Many firms of this type have the 'grow to sell' approach discussed above, and part of their strategy is to avoid the acquisitive attentions (or patent infringements) of large-firm competition by selling out to a large competitor firm at a date agreed in a business plan. However, this strategic type also included the product-based firm that seeks to grow to large size and compete with existing large high-technology firms. It was asserted that, although this type of HTSF is best known by the public (e.g. Apple Computers; Microsoft), such firms are the exception to the rule of failure due either to bankruptcy or ultimate acquisition by a larger competitor. Such firms often become susceptible to acquisition when they run into difficulties in raising capital for development, frequently caused by R&D overruns and/or production difficulties. A technically attractive HTSF with a product that has strong growth potential, but which is experiencing an extreme shortage of capital, is a prime candidate for acquisition by a large existing high-technology firm. Although the likelihood of success can be assisted by a 'window of opportunity' opening when the new HTSF launches its new product on an unsuspecting market, the window usually rapidly closes, meaning that follower HTSFs do not succeed. However, occasionally a new HTSF does become highly successful through seeking to compete with the 'giants' of an industry that is ripe for the introduction of a new disruptive technology. Although this type of success is rare, when it does occur, it can revolutionize a whole industry.

With regard to the strategic options that are open to HTSFs, four potential approaches were identified in increasing order of risk and reward. The first and simplest approach would be for an inventor of a new technology not to begin a business to exploit the new intellectual property, but rather to sell his or her idea to a large existing firm. This strategy has both strengths and weaknesses; its strength is that the level of risk is low; while the weakness is that the value of the knowledge sold probably would be increased by creating a successful firm that could be sold at a later date after a proven product, with customers, was created.

Second, the founding entrepreneur might seek to mitigate risk by founding his or her new company as a joint venture with an existing large high-technology company as a corporate venturing exercise. Clearly, this would not be an attractive option to a highly independent-minded founder, although being acquired by a large corporation would largely solve any intellectual property protection problem.

The third strategic option would be to develop a new firm to the point where the technology involved has been proven and a reasonable level of profitability achieved. This approach would be consistent with the 'grow to sell' imperative discussed above. The main problem with this type of approach is to decide at what point to sell the business (discussed below).

Fourth, a new HTSF founded by an entrepreneur with a strong belief in the potential of his or her new product might decide to develop the firm aggressively, and be prepared to defend the new technology involved against any large firm that might seek (legally or illegally) to acquire the intellectual property involved. In strategic terms, this would equate to the product-based firm noted in the consideration of types of firm above. As noted when discussing product-based firms, although this type of independent new HTSF is the best known among the public, due to the success enjoyed by a small number of high-technology entrepreneurs, in most cases such firms either fail or are ultimately acquired.

The final section of this chapter considered the general problem of strategic decision making under conditions of uncertainly. The problem with uncertainty is that any one of the four strategic options discussed above might be optimal for a new HTSF, depending on the future conditions that occur as that entrepreneur decides either to form a new business or to sell his or her intellectual property rather than founding a new firm. Without the benefit of foresight, any strategy is only the best guess that an HTSF's management can make regarding what they think will happen in the future. Clearly, this view may need to be radically modified in the future as circumstances change. The key point in conclusion to this section was that extreme independence and introspection should be avoided in favour of an approach that seeks to gain as much external information and advice as possible in order to help internal decision making. In particular, it was argued that it is illogical to exclude any option on the basis of prejudice, and that, for example, rejecting the 'sell-out' option without due consideration is not only sub-optimal, it is dangerous. Even if independence is finally judged to be the best future strategic option, it should only be adopted after collaborative alternatives have been considered and rejected on logical grounds. Strategy should be progressive and flexible, and is best determined by a group of managers working together, rather than a single person.

7 Finance

7.1 Introduction

Capital is the lifeblood of any business organization since its investment can produce a wide variety of resources for the firm, ranging from R&D, through production capacity, to marketing effort. However, translating these assets back into capital through profitability in HTSFs is a complex and risky task that renders the raising of investment capital, in the form of either loans or equity funding, a very difficult process. When investors or lenders are contemplating advancing capital to any business, they normally seek maximum returns, over the shortest possible period, at minimum risk. This places small and medium-sized enterprises (SMEs) in general, and HTSFs in particular, at a severe disadvantage, when compared with their large-firm counterparts (especially due to the 'front-end loaded' R&D-intensive nature of many HTSFs – discussed in Chapter 4). Because of the larger amounts of capital that larger firms tend to seek when borrowing or issuing shares, the administrative costs incurred tend to be much lower than for small firms since, for large transactions, the administrative costs to investors or lenders will be lower as a proportion of the sum advanced. Moreover, the risk involved in lending to, or investing in, large organizations is lower due to the greater physical and financial resources that larger firms have available as collateral to secure any capital received.

Thus, it should be no surprise to discover that the financing of small firms has been a continuing problem in the United Kingdom for many years. For example, over the past several decades, a number of government enquiries have sought, with only partial success, to solve the funding problems of SMEs (e.g. Macmillan 1931; Bolton 1971; Wilson 1979: House of Lords 1997). As noted in Chapter 1, in the late 1970s, both in Europe and the United States, concern for the funding problems of small firms was sharpened by the realization that these firms accounted for an increasing proportion of manufacturing and service-sector employment in these developed nations (Birch 1979; Storey 1982; Oakey and Rothwell 1986;

Hughes 1997). This interest in the fortunes of small firms and their employment potential was largely attributable to two major causes. The first was the relative importance of small firms to the manufacturing economies in the United States and the United Kingdom, partly due to a collapse in large-firm employment during the 1970s and 1980s in sectors such as machine tools, motor vehicles, electronics and heavy engineering, as a result of growing competition from emerging economies, led by Japan, and latterly China (Freeman 1986; Oakey and Rothwell 1986). In these circumstances, the contribution of small firms in manufacturing and service-sector employment grew in percentage terms.

A second reason for an increasing emphasis on small manufacturing and service-sector firms in terms of government policy (less evident in France and Germany) was the unwillingness or inability of governments to influence the strategic behaviour of their large multinational firms through public sector subsidies. In the case of successful large domestic firms, there was an increased tendency for them to invest overseas, such that, although the headquarters of a firm might remain in New York or London, much of its investment and employment growth was progressively in countries where operating costs (especially wage levels and environmental standards) were lower, in conditions where existing domestic industrial incentives aimed at locating businesses nationally through the efforts of internal regional policy were often becoming uncompetitive. Clearly this type of outward investment was difficult for national governments to influence since, although domestic employment might be highly desirable, the international competitiveness of national 'flagship' large firms also needed to be respected.

However, it is also true that an unwillingness in both the United States and the United Kingdom for governments to become involved in the strategic development and support of 'problem' industries of the 1980s saw the absolute or relative collapse of many key manufacturing sectors, notably in heavy engineering, consumer electronics and motor vehicles. For example, despite a long history of many successful large firms in both these countries, there are now no domestically owned television manufacturers in either the United States or the United Kingdom. In such conditions, often-heard criticisms in the 1980s of unfair foreign competition, in terms of currency exchange rates or dumping 'exported production' below the cost of production, become irrelevant since, in many cases, no domestic industry remains to meet national demand if imports were blocked. But significantly, although the above criticism might reasonably be made of the United States and the United Kingdom, the governments of France and Germany have taken a more interventionist approach to their large-firm sectors and, as a result, both maintain viable motor vehicle industries dominated by domestically owned large firms. Indeed, the case of Germany is particularly impressive in that their concentration on staying in key areas of manufacturing, despite high national operating costs, has enabled them to preserve both large and small efficient firms in many branches of engineering. Demand for their high-quality competitively priced products also enables them to withstand recessionary periods in circumstances where, rather than complaining about Chinese import penetration, they are a major exporter of manufactured goods to China.

More recently in the United Kingdom, there has been concern for the more specialized needs of the HTSF sub-sector of SMEs (Bank of England 1996; CBI 1997; House of Lords 1997; Bank of England 2001; Oakey 2003a). This concern stemmed from two deep-seated supply shortcomings. The first is 'short termism', where, as noted above, United Kingdom financiers are often unreasonably impatient for returns on their investments. This has caused particular problems for HTSFs, given their frequent need for patient investment to support R&D, in advance of sales (Bank of England 1996; CBI 1997; House of Lords 1997Bank of England 2001). Second, an enduring funding gap persists for early-stage HTSFs, (Oakey 1984b, 1995; Bank of England 2001; Oakey 2003a; Herriot 2005). This gap exists in the £50,000–250,000 range of funding above the normal level of bank lending to SMEs, which venture capitalists often argue is not economic to provide, due to the high administrative costs of equity investment that is, for them, a small amount of capital.

Second, the decline in large manufacturing enterprises in the United States and the United Kingdom, and an inability of the governments of these countries to arrest this decline, has placed greater emphasis on the employment potential of small firms in general, and new HTSFs in particular, to fill the gap left by this large-firm employment contraction. Nonetheless, the key funding environment for these firms remains difficult for the various reasons outlined above, particularly in the United Kingdom. Ironically, since many of these HTSFs are business-to-business subcontractors, the lack of large 'flagship firms' in the United Kingdom economy to buy their products for incorporation into final consumer products further inhibits small-firm growth, an issue returned to in Chapter 8. This problem has recently been noted as particularly severe for United Kingdom motor vehicle component suppliers (*The Guardian* 2011). Moreover, recent world economic uncertainty has placed both banks and venture capitalists in a difficult position, whereby they are encouraged to lend and invest to help small firms grow, in conditions where market demand is flat, prospects for growth are uncertain, and where the memories of past reckless lending remain strong.

7.2 The funding of HTSFs

A common theme that has emerged at several junctures in this book, when considering the problems of HTSFs, is that these firms experience all the usual problems that all small firms face during formation and initial growth, but that these problems are generally far more intense in HTSFs. This is particularly the case when considering the difficulties that HTSFs encounter when seeking to raise finance, mainly to fund R&D. In the late 1970s, set against the background of a growing general concern for the funding problems of SMEs discussed above, the airing on BBC television of the *Horizon* programme 'Now the chips are down' (discussed in Chapter 1), apart from making the point that Europe was losing the race to participate in the burgeoning silicon chip production industry, made the observation that a key triggering resource for the growth of these HTSFs in Silicon Valley had been the availability of local venture capital (Cooper 1970). Individuals, or small groups of investors, had played a major part in the development of a number of new HTSFs by taking equity stakes in these firms, based on a good technical knowledge of various aspects of high technology (in this case, semiconductor) production in the local area.

In the United Kingdom, the then Labour government, in its last days of power, and subsequently the incoming Conservative government of 1979 led by Margaret Thatcher, responded to the perceived lack of adequate equity-based investment institutions in general, and those specializing in HTSFs in particular, by putting pressure on the United Kingdom finance industry to fill this gap in the capital market. By the mid-1980s, a degree of success had been achieved and a number of new venture capital businesses were established, often in the form of subsidiaries of United Kingdom banks (e.g. Barclays; NatWest). Although these new entities were welcome additions to the finance industry, they were not true replications of the Silicon Valley venture capital firms. In particular, these new venture capital firms, since they were often bank subsidiaries or relatively large firms from the outset with their own shareholders, tended to be more bureaucratic than their Silicon Valley predecessors. While individual Silicon Valley venture capitalists could make decisions almost overnight because they were investing their own money, decision making in these new United Kingdom venture capital firms tended to take more time. Indeed, HTSF entrepreneurs often complained that, by the time they had received a decision on whether investment would be made, the nature of the fast-moving high-technology sectors of industry in which they operated meant that the window of opportunity, for which they had sought financial support, had closed (Oakey 1984b). Moreover, another early problem that bedevilled this new United Kingdom venture capital industry, and has continued throughout its existence, was the fact that many of the key people in these firms making investment decisions were from the finance industry (i.e. retired bank managers; accountants) who knew little about the technologies of the high-technology sectors in which they were being asked to invest (Oakey 1984b). This often meant that a decision on whether to invest was based on physical assets (e.g. bricks and mortar) in cases where the only potential assets that new HTSF entrepreneurs had was their technological intellectual property (which could not appear on any balance sheet – this is discussed in more detail below in sub-section 7.3).

Nonetheless, by the end of the 1980s, a rapidly growing venture capital industry in the United Kingdom had been established, while the venture capital industry in the United States showed signs of maturing into the type of larger, more bureaucratic, corporate structure that had existed in the United Kingdom from the outset (Batten Briefings 2011). However, by the mid-1990s, it began to become clear that HTSF investments by United Kingdom venture capitalists in the 1980s had not produced acceptable returns. The alluring stories of fabulous growth that emanated from Silicon Valley in the late 1970s were found to mask a more general tendency for HTSF investment to be highly risky, and even in cases where it did eventually pay off, it took several years to deliver good returns. This reality clearly conflicted with the dictum noted at the beginning of this chapter that investors generally seek high returns over short periods of time at low risk. Moreover, perhaps another ramification of the fact that decision makers in the United Kingdom venture capital industry were not scientists and engineers from high-technology sectors, but accountants and bank staff, was that these service-sector-based people did not have a particular affinity towards high-technology industry. As noted above, this distinguished them from many of the early Silicon Valley venture capitalists who were often previous HTSF entrepreneurs who had 'sold out' to large firms, and used the capital they had received to invest in the local industry they knew. This not only provided knowledgeable investment capital and advice to new Silicon Valley HTSFs; it importantly retained the capital involved within the Silicon Valley cluster. In addition, since the decision makers in the United Kingdom venture capital firms were, in the main, employees of a firm that had its own shareholders to satisfy, who expected a good return on their investment, the lack of any technical knowledge in these individuals naturally made them approach the investment landscape with a view to securing investments conservatively through physical assets with which they were familiar, rather than seeking expert technical advice that they would find difficult to evaluate.

Thus, it was not surprising that by the mid-1990s, the imperative of return maximization began to cause United Kingdom venture capital firms to drift away from investment in new high-technology firms and into sectors that were less technically sophisticated, but had an established 'track record' of success – in the form of management buy-outs (MBOs), management buy-ins (MBIs), and expansions (Murray and Lott 1995). In this context, a key factor was the age of the firm that received their investment. Because many HTSFs seeking investment were 'early stage' and, as will be discussed below, several years away from selling their new product under development (far less making a profit), the risks involved were inevitably large. Consequently, 'early-stage' HTSFs were often avoided on the grounds of high risk. Later Bank of England evidence (Bank of England 1996, 2001) showed that, although the United Kingdom venture capital industry grew rapidly to become the second largest in the world by the mid-1990s, early-stage funding 'trailed along' the bottom of a graph that tracked this generally impressive growth (Bank of England 2001). Thus, the United Kingdom venture capital industry, which had been established following government encouragement of the finance industry to help fund the growth of new HTSFs in the early 1980s, had largely moved away from this sector by the end of the 1990s into established medium- and low-technology investments, save for a few specialist high-technology-oriented venture capital firms.

The reality of this abandonment is clear in the evidence on where venture capital investment went over the period from 2005 to 2010. British Venture Capital Association data (BVCA 2005, 2006, 2007, 2008, 2009, 2010) make it clear that the bulk of venture capital funding over this period was invested in MBOs, amounting to £4,480 million in 2005, rose to a peak of £7,721 million in 2007, and fell back to £4,752 million by 2010, almost certainly as a result of the recession that occurred in 2008. Over the same period, early-stage funding stood at £382 million in 2005, rose to £434 million by 2007, and fell back to £224 million in 2010, which represented only 3 per cent of total BVCA investment in that year. There is strong circumstantial evidence to suggest that the reason for this drift towards the funding of firms that had an existing 'track record' of performance (i.e. MBOs, MBIs and expansions) was that of reduced risk. While there was a great deal of emphasis at the beginning of the United Kingdom venture capital industry in the early 1980s on the massive returns that could be derived from investment in early-stage high-technology firms, venture capitalists began to realize that, for the main part, HTSFs were extremely risky and likely to fail: partly because the technology on which new firms in this sector were based was fragile and revolutionary; and partly because, even in cases where winning products were eventually produced, the long lead times associated with product development (noted in Chapter 4 above) often prevented an 'out' for the investor within a time frame that was efficient from the point of view of timely returns on investment.

Conversely, lower-technology firms in established industries with proven track records and loyal customers represented much less risk. This contrast is indicated graphically in Figure 7.1, where the choice between a new HTSF and an existing going concern is shown. For the new HTSF in position A at the origin, due to a lack of any past history, there is no extrapolation possible. However, for existing MBOs, MBIs and expansions (in position B), a reliable record of achievement was available from which, importantly, future prospects could reasonably reliably be extrapolated in terms of 'best scenario', 'steady continued growth' and 'worst scenario' (see the dashed lines in Figure 7.1).

Nonetheless, even the worst-scenario extrapolation would be more attractive than investment in a new HTSF where no track record existed at all. Moreover, a point made in Chapter 5 (sub-section 5.3.2) on selling HTSF products is worth rehearsing here: not only does a new HTSF have no track record, often due to the novelty of the technology involved, there is often no similar product against which the newly proposed product technology might be benchmarked by venture capitalists to estimate its growth potential. While in rare instances, the novelty of a new HTSF product may prove to be highly disruptive, such that it destroys an industry

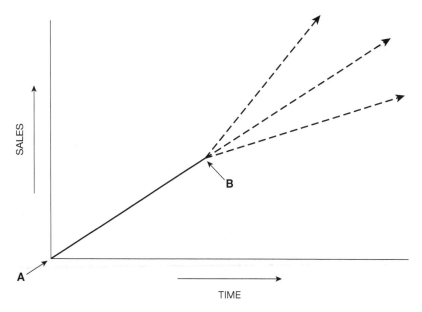

Figure 7.1 The difference in confidence between an early-stage firm and a going concern.

and creates a new way of doing things that is extremely profitable (of which many of the new businesses on the internet are recent examples), there remains much scope for the new idea to be a complete failure, or only a temporary technical success, which would mean that a venture capitalist deciding where to invest would find isolating the HTSF (or HTSFs) most likely to succeed a very difficult process.

In this context, it is worth stating that, although it was an original United Kingdom government intention that the new venture capital industry would fund the formation and growth of new high-technology industries, thus imitating what had occurred in Silicon Valley in the United States, the new venture capital firms that were founded in the early 1980s were no more than investment businesses seeking to make profits acceptable to their shareholders. Thus, it should not be surprising if this desire to be acceptably profitable should lead venture capital firms away from highly risky new HTSFs to areas of business where more reliable returns could be obtained. Here it should be remembered that, even with an increasing focus on firms with an established track record, the average rate of return in the venture capital industry is between 25 per cent and 30 per cent, implying a substantial rate of failure, notwithstanding an avoidance of early-stage HTSFs with no track record. The venture capital industry in recent years has tended to retreat from the title 'venture capital' (possibly in an attempt to distance itself from association with new high-technology ventures) and use the term 'private equity' to describe their industry. Indeed, during the financial boom of the 2000s, some venture capital firms stressed in their advertising literature that they did not invest in early-stage high-technology businesses, clearly because they saw this statement as a sign of greater prudence when seeking to attract investors in their own firms.

There can be no doubt that the funding of a new HTSF is a very risky undertaking in which, not surprisingly, many investors do not wish to become involved. As previously discussed in Chapter 4 on R&D, which is closely related to this chapter on finance due to the importance of R&D spending to the total cost of HTSF operation, there is a 'point of maximum financial stress' in the life of any product-based HTSF (see Figure 4.2). This is a juncture at which, although R&D costs are declining following a long programme of product development, 'red numbers' appear on the firm's accounts due to high R&D spend in the absence of any sales. In addition, production costs have yet to begin and ramp up, while (frequently international) marketing of a product new to the consumer is required in order to make it known to potential customers, often in circumstances where they are wedded to a well-proven existing technology (see also sub-section 5.3.2 in Chapter 5). Clearly, potential venture capital investors in new HTSFs are well aware of this 'point of maximum financial stress' that most

HTSFs will arrive at. However, the length of the R&D process and its outcome (in terms of new product performance), the amount of capital needed for production 'gear up', and the marketing budget needed to sell the new technology effectively, although often predicted in a business plan, are all actually unknown, and likely to take longer (and cost more) to accomplish than forecasted.

7.3 The specific problems of budgeting for HTSF invention and innovation

The above discussion of the impacts of the funding of R&D and marketing in HTSFs makes it clear that, although spending on these two *discretionary* areas of HTSF operation probably will be large, the incidence of these expenditures and the total amount that will be expended cannot be accurately predicted when an HTSF is founded. This uncertainty causes concern for potential venture capitalist investors, who are looking for a predictable 'out' from a company in which they invest in order to gain a good return, in circumstances where, as noted above, the predictions of business plans are often more aspirations than definite 'milestones' that will be adhered to. To these already unattractive key aspects of HTSF operation must be added the unwelcome truth, noted above, that the most valuable asset that an HTSF possesses (i.e. the intellectual property contained in the new product or service under development) cannot be included on the HTSF's balance sheet as an asset. Thus, the control by HTSFs of product development is a very difficult and complex process. This process triggers two major questions to be answered by management.

First, when external capital is required, what type of external capital will be appropriate? The credibility of private sector support in the form of bank loans and/or equity capital will be an important area of concern in that these sources of finance, from both supply and demand perspectives respectively, are often judged too expensive for investors to provide, while not attractive to HTSF managements due to their high 'price', measured broadly in terms of, not only interest rates or the size of equity stakes, but also all the terms and conditions involved (Herriot 2005; Oakey 2007a).

Second, a major question that will determine the success of any HTSF is how, and how effectively, do HTSF firm managements anticipate and deploy capital in order to manage R&D, production and marketing of new products, since these are variable costs that are difficult to predict, and have a strong tendency (particularly R&D) to increase well beyond the levels predicted by HTSF managements. Incompetent management of these key strategic areas, as a result of poor decision making, may result from a lack of the business-management skills that are required of often technically skilled HTSF entrepreneurs. This eventuality might suggest the need for ameliorative action in the form of appropriate management training. Clearly, the efficient management of operating costs within the firm, knowing what they are now and predicting future needs, can be *more important* than obtaining external financial support since an accurate estimate of what is required, which might be reduced by efficient management, determines the extent of such a need.

To achieve this second goal, effective control of the factors that determine the 'net balance of capital' (NBC) in HTSFs is critical, after total costs have been related to total income for a given accountancy period. Clearly, in this context, the NBC does not imply profitability. Figure 4.2 in Chapter 4 has indicated that, for many HTSFs, there are long periods of growing indebtedness that occur before any product sales or profitability can follow. Thus, *negative* NBCs can often occur for protracted periods. Critically, HTSF founders will need to calculate their NBC and, of equal importance, whether the current level of NBC matches that predicted (typically in a previous business plan). Thus, an indebted firm would be deemed *efficient* under this test if the current debt level was in line with that previously predicted. An additional benefit of effective control of capital requirements is the assurance that such efficiency gives existing investors in the HTSF, since this control avoids unnecessary surprises caused by the need for extra financial support at short notice.

Figure 7.2 presents an illustrative 'balance sheet' of assets against costs for a typical HTSF. A major problem for many HTSFs is an inability *accurately to predict, monitor and control* medium-term assets, costs, and

(+) Possible Income/Assets	(−) Possible Costs
Personal savings	Taxes (including corporation tax, employer's NICs, business rates, and VAT)
Equity investments	Operating costs (non-discretionary, rent, wages, materials, etc.)
Assets (buildings; equipment; linventory, etc.)	Discretionary operating costs (e.g. R&D, marketing, etc.)
Loans	Regulatory compliance costs
Government grants	
R&D tax credits claimed when tax is not payable	
Retained profits (if applicable)	
Intellectual property assets (not enterable into company accounts)	

Figure 7.2 The balance of income versus costs in HTSFs

resultant NBC. Such poor control of HTSF performance is a major reason why they have been unattractive to many venture capitalist investors (Bank of England 2001; Oakey 2003a, 2007a).

7.4 Supply and demand capital investment problems

The funding environment for HTSFs has, increasingly since the early 1980s, been characterized by both supply- and demand-side problems. From the perspective of the demand side, as noted above, when HTSF entrepreneurs have sought investment support for their new or established business, there have been instances where apparently deserving firms with viable new product or service ideas do not obtain the capital they need from venture capitalists (Herriot 2005), leading to frequent complaints that impressive applications for support have been rejected after scant consideration (Mason *et al.* 1996; Cruickshank 2000; Fraser 2004). Moreover, the establishment of quasi-public venture capital funds (e.g. Regional Venture Capital Funds in the United Kingdom) charged with the aim of being less risk-averse and seeking to fill the 'possibly fundable' gap in Figure 7.3 (see sub-section 7.5.1 below), has frequently resulted in these funds being underspent in terms of *actual* regional investments (Herriot 2005). Often, failed applicants for support from these regional funds have, again, complained that good proposals for the advancement of funds 'fell on deaf ears'. The two supply and demand sides of the HTSF investment equation are discussed in more detail below.

7.4.1 The demand side

As noted at a number of junctures throughout this book, many HTSF founders are drawn from physical science backgrounds. Often, their first experience of business management is when they found a new HTSF, perhaps when a physical science academic 'spins off' from a university to begin a new academic enterprise. While this type of new-firm formation is now widely encouraged, by both universities and national governments (Select Committee on Science and Technology 1993; DTI 1998; Oakey and Mukhtar 1999; Birley 2001), it has been noted above that some physical scientists can have a rather cavalier approach to business management, viewing management expertise as no more than 'common sense', which can be 'acquired as you go along'. This can lead to imprecision when producing an initial business plan with which to 'pitch' for venture capital support, or when seeking additional funding for a firm that has already been founded and requires further financial investment. Because of the above-mentioned long R&D 'lead times' associated with the funding of a new

HTSF through its early stages, there is a tendency for many founders to be over-optimistic, for example, about the 'time to market' aspects of a new high-technology product development. In particular, there is a tendency to reduce the projected period of 'front-end' development of the firm's first product from a more realistic five to ten years down to three to five years in an attempt to make the project more attractive to investors (Oakey 1995).

This over-optimism may have two negative repercussions: one is short term, while the other will arise in the long run. First, venture capital firms, when evaluating what needs to be achieved in terms of R&D, may decide that the business plan projections for R&D are totally unrealistic, and reject the plan outright without providing support. Second, on a more subtle level, even if the proposal receives support, an inadequate anticipation of required resources will ultimately cause friction with the venture capitalist if R&D costs exceed the cost and the time span predicted in the business plan. At best, this might cause the venture capitalist to withhold second-round funding, or, at worst, totally withdraw support from the firm and cause its failure.

However, these problems may partly stem from a deeper malaise in that many physical scientists, when beginning a new HTSF, do not possess the necessary basic business-management skills that would initially help them to write a more accurate plan and, crucially, subsequently keep their firm on the path they have predicted in terms of deadlines. Simple skills such as understanding management accounting in order that financial data can be interpreted are essential to ensure accurate progress. For example, it is quite possible for a firm's management to believe, on the basis of increasing sales, that they are making strong progress when, in fact, increased sales are driving the firm deeper into debt since each product sold costs more to make than the selling price. While most technical entrepreneurs are rightly praised for their optimism, this attribute can become dangerous if it leads to a 'blind spot' towards bad news and an overemphasis on the positive. Certainly, any venture capitalist considering investment in such a company would be justifiably deterred by a lack of the prudence that comes from a business-management education.

For all these reasons, venture capitalists and bankers often make the point that many applicants for investment capital do not make competent applications for funds. A common complaint by venture capitalists is that applicants for investment from them are 'not investment ready'. Major arguments for unreadiness put forward by venture capitalists investigating proposals for equity investment are that either the project for which capital was sought was untenable (i.e. it was judged that the product or service proposed would not sell profitably); or that, although the proposal might be a viable option, it was poorly presented to the extent that the venture capitalist was unable to be sure whether funding would be advisable. These criticisms are usually the main reasons given for a refusal to offer support.

7.4.2 *The supply side*

The following problems with the supply of external capital to HTSFs mainly relate to whether providers of capital offer an effective service, both in terms of the products they offer, and the level of returns these offerings deliver. In circumstances where both banks and equity investors tend to have worryingly similar approaches to the terms and conditions they offer (that sometimes border on oligopolistic behaviour), it is perhaps not surprising that a significant minority of customers often feel they have very limited choices (Fraser 2004). However, a possible new product that could be offered by banks has been advocated by Herriot (2005), involving a loan with an 'equity kicker'. This proposed offering would involve a combination of a 50 per cent loan with a 50 per cent equity stake, where the bank would provide sums of no more than £100,000 to HTSFs. This approach would ensure a degree of ongoing commitment by the bank, represented by the equity stake, while the size of the total sum advanced would be usefully below the minimum sums usually provided by venture capitalists. However, banks are famously reluctant to offer such radically new products to their customers, especially when loan and equity funding are combined.

These problems of supply encompass a number of issues mentioned above that might be drawn together under a heading entitled 'an unattractive price to the customer'. Here, 'price' does not merely refer to the amount of equity required in return for investment capital, but the whole range of terms that an investor may seek when offering venture capital support to an HTSF (e.g. the amount of equity exchanged; 'hands on' involvement). Thus, if 'price' is used in a wide sense to include not only financial cost, but also the stress caused by onerous terms that favour the investor, it is not surprising that many HTSF owners with reasonable development projects for their businesses, decide to 'soldier on' more slowly on the basis of savings and retained profits, rather than seek equity finance (Mason *et al.* 1996; Cruickshank 2000; Fraser 2004).

The issue of growth potential is particularly critical to HTSFs. A major problem for any firm seeking financial support by raising equity capital is convincing investors that the product under development will sell. In cases where the new product is in a market where there are many current competitors (e.g. satellite navigation systems), as noted above, benchmarking the new product (in terms of specification and price) can be relatively easily achieved, although competition will be strong. However, when the product is 'leading edge', and there is no competitor against which to benchmark, and no sales will be achieved for five years or more, proof of the growth potential of a proposed new HTSF product to a venture capitalist is almost impossible (Reid and Smith 2003; Barber 2006).

However, a further confusing issue relevant to this discussion is the often heard comment by venture capitalists that they 'liked the person' (or people) who were making a pitch for investment support. This type of comment raises the issue of whether support might be refused, not because the application lacked 'investment readiness' in terms of the clarity and force of the proposal, but because the potential investor personally took exception to the applicants. There can be little doubt that instinct plays an important part in the investment decisions of venture capitalists, and that such behaviour, at the end of the day, is an art rather than a science. This instinctual approach leads to the key question as to whether the moderate, often-quoted 25 per cent to 30 per cent return on capital achieved by venture capitalists is caused by the incompetence of the firms that are funded but fail, or the inability of venture capitalists to select *effectively* the correct target for investment by missing good opportunities and selecting bad options due to their lack of objective evaluative rigour, in which it could be argued that instinct should play no part. Clearly, firms that do not receive venture capital funding often fail, but failure might be caused by such a refusal, rather than being a refusal's justification, as venture capitalists often argue (on the basis of hindsight).

Potential funders of a proposed development might also refuse funding, not because they are convinced that the applicant will not moderately or spectacularly succeed, but because they cannot reduce their risk by obtaining good evidence of market potential. However, it is often the products with the greatest potential that have no current market-performance evidence because they are truly ground-breaking, and likely to become highly disruptive, successful and profitable (e.g. Amazon; Google; Facebook). Moreover, as noted above, the inability of HTSFs to value and include 'technology assets' on their balance sheets further reduces, as noted above, their attractiveness to external providers of capital (DTI 1998; Reid and Smith 2003; Barber 2006). Thus, such firms often remain unfunded, not because they do not have growth potential or assets, but because they cannot obtain the 'front-end' funding they need to become viable business ventures by crossing the 'valley of death' caused by high initial R&D costs during product development (see Figure 4.2 in Chapter 4). This is particularly the case for *early-stage* HTSFs (Murray and Lott 1995; Bank of England 1996, 2001; Herriot 2005).

7.5 Closing the funding gap when it occurs

7.5.1 The role of government in ameliorating HTSF funding problems

Clearly, any government development agency seeking to enhance the growth of HTSFs within its sphere of responsibility must seek to increase the attractiveness of private sector capital on offer to HTSF founders. In order to maximize the performance of all HTSFs with growth potential within a national economy, it is clearly essential that no HTSFs with proposals for external funding to support viable programmes of innovation and growth are denied the investment capital they need, and are given the best chance of prosperity. This is an area where national and regional development agencies might seek to take special actions in order to help HTSFs by seeking to repair any failures in the private capital markets for HTSF loan and investment funding, particularly in circumstances where HTSFs with good growth potential are unable to obtain the funding they need for expansion, for which there is substantial anecdotal evidence. In this context, Figure 7.3 assists in our understanding of the problem of extending investment into unfunded, yet viable, HTSFs that seek external financial support.

Clearly, there must always be a percentage of new business ventures that, although keen to raise external capital, would never be eligible for external investment support due to the poor current (and likely future) state of their business. From the perspective of loan and equity funding, these enterprises may be as many as 60 per cent of any given total, as depicted in Figure 7.3, although all the percentages included are necessarily notional, and are only used here in order to make the key point about a potential

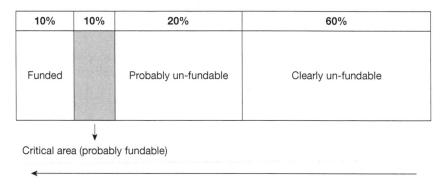

Figure 7.3 Population of firms seeking investment capital support
Source: Oakey 2003a

funding gap. Conversely, a smaller percentage of new business ideas are immediately fundable by the private sector on the basis of the great strength of a new idea (or business plan). Although the 10 per cent of Figure 7.3 might be slightly inaccurate, most studies on this subject suggest that the proportion would not be greater than 20 per cent (Murray and Lott 1995). However, a further 20 per cent of SMEs are termed 'probably unfundable' for a variety of reasons related to management competencies, project viability, market potential and other factors.

The key area of Figure 7.3 is perhaps a small – say, no more than 10 per cent – margin of potential investment capital recipients who currently do not receive help, but are 'probably fundable'. The problem for government agencies, charged with increasing the level of formation of firms, innovation and growth in the national economy over and above that which would otherwise occur through the private sector, is to extend investment into this key area of 'probably fundable' firms. This would be achieved, in the case of Figure 7.3, by doubling the percentage of firms receiving support from 10 per cent to 20 per cent. Funding the 'critical area' of Figure 7.3 involves an essential balancing of the needs for profit with those of national industrial development. Put simply, from a 'hard-headed' business viewpoint, unassisted venture capitalist deal makers would be unlikely to venture into this critical area, in order to preserve their normal required return on investment, which would be likely to decrease if more risk was taken. However, from an 'additionality' perspective, governments might seek to assist these, only marginally more risky, firms and ensure they receive the venture capital or other forms of finance they need in the interests of long-term national industrial growth, given that, as noted above, anecdotal evidence suggests that HTSFs with good business proposals do not currently receive funding (Herriot 2005). These observations lead to some further comments on the way forward.

There has been a growing consensus that public–private partnerships of various kinds are 'the way forward' regarding the financing of HTSFs. In the United Kingdom, the Enterprise Capital Funds (ECF) are one example of how, based on the experiences of agencies in the United States and elsewhere, the UK government seeks to trigger the investment of private capital through public financial support. Specifically, public sector capital is designed to help encourage private sector funding into the 'probably fundable critical area' of Figure 7.3 in order to support currently unfinanced HTSF growth. SMART and SPUR grants have been another possible source of capital for HTSFs, now replaced since 2005 in England by the Grant for Research and Development Scheme.

However, a major problem with any grant funding is that, notwithstanding the fact that many HTSFs will not be successful in obtaining aid, for firms

that do receive funding, it is a lump sum, with no guarantee of medium-
to long-term commitment. While these grants have often triggered further
private sector support (Ross 2002), there is *no certainty* of medium-term
financial security (Smallbone *et al.* 2000; Oakey 2003a). Other more local
public sector initiatives involving grants (e.g. the Proof of Concept Grant
Scheme) are also aimed at encouraging private sector investment beyond
what is currently achieved, into the 10 per cent 'critical area' of Figure
7.3. However, a similar problem with this type of grant is, again, that there
is usually little medium-term commitment by the granter or lender to the
financial stability of the investee firm concerned. Since the financing of
HTSFs is clearly a major policy issue, the funding of HTSFs will be further
considered in the conclusions that follow in Chapter 8.

7.6 Chapter summary

When introducing this chapter, the point was made that capital was the
lifeblood of an industrial firm since it is convertible into a range of assets
important to a firm's survival and growth. However, it was also noted that
converting these assets back into profits was no easy exercise and that, due
to a range of disadvantages, SMEs in general, and HTSFs in particular,
find this process, which is the key to success, more difficult to negotiate
than large firms. This is partly because large firms find the raising of capital
much easier than small firms. In terms of provision of security (i.e.
collateral) and cost of capital, large firms generally find raising capital a
simpler process that costs them less money. It was noted that, to a great
extent, SME funding has been a continuing concern in the United Kingdom
since before the Second World War, and a number of successive
government enquiries have failed to solve this problem.

However, in the late 1970s, there was a revival of interest in the funding
and growth problems of small firms in many Western democracies. This
renewed concern, it was argued, had three major drivers. First, the decline
in the large firms of many previously key manufacturing sectors,
particularly in the United States and the United Kingdom (e.g. motor
vehicles; heavy engineering; electronics) increased the proportionate
employment contribution of small firms to national economies. It was
argued by some academics (e.g. Birch 1979) that SMEs could compensate
for the jobs lost by the large firms of declining sectors. As a consequence,
the study of how to encourage SMEs became a preoccupation of many
academics throughout Europe and the United States. Second, there was a
growing realization that the rise of the multinational firm meant that the
degree of control which national government could exert on these
enterprises in terms of the international location of their investments, even

when they were headquartered in the capital of the government concerned, was very limited.

A third reason for concern over the financial well-being of SMEs was triggered by the realization in the early 1980s that the funding of newly important HTSFs was particularly inadequate. As noted in Chapter 1, awareness of the growth of new high-technology SMEs in the Silicon Valley and Route 128 clusters in the United States further fuelled the already growing debate on how to nurture and grow HTSFs. The previously mentioned problem of small-firm funding was brought into sharp focus by the emergence of new HTSFs in these United States clusters, where a key driver in helping these firms to grow was the venture capital that was available, especially in Silicon Valley. It was realized that no equivalent financial services sub-sector existed in Europe. In the United Kingdom, therefore, there was a conscious effort by government to replicate the venture capital industry observed in Silicon Valley in order to assist the formation of both new SMEs in general and HTSFs in particular, although the venture capital organizations that were formed as a result of this process had a number of deficiencies when compared with their United States counterparts (e.g. lack of technical expertise, bureaucracy caused by being subsidiaries of national banks, and concentration on physical rather than technological assets).

Nonetheless, by the mid-1980s, a large degree of success had been achieved in terms of the growth of the United Kingdom venture capital industry. However, as this new part of the United Kingdom financial sector moved into the 1990s, there was growing concern that HTSFs, a major reason for the establishment of the new venture capital sector, were progressively being avoided by venture capital firms in terms of funding support. It was clear that an initial enthusiasm for HTSF investments, partly fuelled by stories of major success from the United States, was confounded by early actual experience of investing in HTSFs. Generally, HTSFs began to be perceived as highly risky 'front-end-loaded' investments with a low rate of success, and when firms were successful, the payback period was protracted. It was noted that this was not an attractive set of characteristics for investors seeking high rates of return at low risk over short time spans. Clear evidence was provided to indicate that, although the United Kingdom venture capital industry had grown to be the second largest in the world, throughout the 1990s and 2000s, this growth had been mainly achieved through investment in existing lower-technology firms with proven track records of performance. Thus, early-stage businesses, common in the HTSF sub-sector of SMEs, were consistently poorly provided for.

Moving to a more detailed investigation of the funding problems of HTSFs, this chapter discussed the 'net balance of capital' between income and expenditure in HTSFs. It was generally argued that the net balance of capital was difficult to keep track of, initially because the management accounting expertise of HTSF founders (being mainly from a physical science background) was often inadequate. However, it was also noted that a major difficulty in determining the resources needed to bring a high-technology product to market was the very difficult task of determining the future costs of R&D and marketing. Due to the long lead times involved in the development of new HTSF products, which for some biotechnology firms might be more than ten years, predicting the total costs of developing and selling a product a decade in advance would always be likely to be inaccurate. It was noted that such uncertainty is at odds with the type of management regime that venture capital investors would prefer to encounter when considering investment. Moreover, such uncertainly concerning the two major areas of HTSF costs (i.e. R&D and selling) is further exacerbated by the inability of HTSF founders to include a value for technology assets on their balance sheets. This is particularly problematic, since such assets are often the only thing of value possessed by an HTSF. Thus, the net balance of capital in HTSFs is only vindicated when a technology under development becomes a winning product in the market at which it is aimed.

Although success can happen, the number of venture capitalists avoiding HTSF investments indicates that HTSF involvement is not popular, and investment has been increasingly directed at management buy-outs, buy-ins and expansions. In terms of the possible difficulties with the flow of investment funds into HTSFs, this chapter examined this process by dividing it into demand- and supply-side problems. From a demand-side perspective, problems are usually concerned with general 'investment unreadiness', as argued by venture capitalists. There has been much debate on this issue and, in particular, whether the lack of early-stage HTSF investment is a supply- or demand-side problem. It was observed that if venture capitalists are using 'investment unreadiness' as an excuse for not investing in an HTSF to obscure their own supply-side shortcomings (e.g. if they do not understand the technology involved), it is a supply problem. However, valid demand-side problems manifested by HTSF owners were noted often to be focussed on their lack of management expertise, inaccurate estimates of R&D and marketing costs, and an inability to produce convincing due diligence on the sales potential of a new HTSF product, although it was noted that, for totally new HTSF leading-edge products, this is an almost impossible task.

In terms of supply-side problems, much of the criticism made by HTSF founders of the types of funding that are available centre on a poor range of offerings, which tend to be unattractive and limited in scope. Since it is common for HTSF founders to value their independence highly (which is often the main reason for beginning a new HTSF), onerous terms might include not only the amount of equity that must be exchanged for capital, but also the degree of intrusiveness that the venture capitalist would seek. In this sense, equity capital is similar to bank lending in that the high required rates of return and security expected frequently tip the balance heavily in favour of the investor or lender. Venture capitalists, in particular, are frequently criticized for their inflexibility in terms of the way they invest. The tendency not to invest sums of less than £250,000, and the unwillingness of banks to consider, for example, a mix of loan and equity funding for sums less than £100,000 provide evidence of inflexibility, leaving substantial parts of the market for finance unsatisfied. Finally, as noted above, although the general flight of venture capital investment from early-stage HTSFs over the past 20 years confirms that the funding problems of HTSFs in general, and new HTSFs in particular, remain unresolved, a possible solution to this problem was suggested. This would involve using various forms of public capital to leverage private sector funding to expand into the 'probably fundable' area of Figure 7.3, currently not receiving the capital for expansion they need, further explored in the Conclusions that follow.

8 Conclusions

8.1 Introduction

There is now overwhelming evidence, gained over the last 40 years, to confirm that high-technology small enterprises can make a major contribution to manufacturing industry in particular, and technological progress in general. However, the tantalizing problem for both theory and policy alike is that, although we can see in retrospect great advances in technology prompted by HTSFs, predicting the future course of how and when new technologies will be produced is an especially difficult task. To this uncertain picture regarding the conceptual and practical logistics of how high-technology industries emerge must be added the problem that statistical evidence on the performance of these new sectors is often scarce or non-existent. For example, although James Watson and Francis Crick discovered the DNA double helix in the early 1950s that led to the birth of the biotechnology industry – and notwithstanding the existence of substantial biotechnology production in most developed nations – this industry remains unclassified in the government statistics of many developed nations (e.g. the United Kingdom). Because new high-technology industries can emerge on the boundaries between one or more existing industrial sectors, they are often attributed to these existing sectors when, in fact, they are a new sector that has not been statistically acknowledged (e.g. multimedia; nanotechnology) (Scott 1993). This lack of new sectoral data, years after a new industry has been widely acknowledged to exist, renders high-technology sectors difficult for industrial planners and academics to research, understand and promote.

However, HTSFs are destined to play a major role in the development of the new industries that will be of social and economic importance during the next 100 years. Thus, despite periods of neglect, often exacerbated by recessionary episodes in economic performance, national governments throughout the world must continue to focus on the difficult, but rewarding, quest of encouraging HTSFs to establish and grow, in order that they can make major future contributions to national economic performance. It is increasingly clear that the major wealth-creating industries of the twenty-first century will be high-technology, often derived from the leading-edge curiosity-driven basic research of universities (Russell Group 2010).

Most of the following sections of this chapter are based on one or more earlier chapters of this book. These sections comprise 8.2 'Origins' (i.e. Chapters 1 [Introduction] and 2 [The role of the entrepreneur]), 8.3 'Physical and organizational structures to promote HTSF growth' (i.e. Chapter 3 [Clusters, incubators and science parks]), 8.4 'Taking the HTSF products to the market' (i.e. Chapters 4 [Research and development], 5 [Selling HTSF products] and 6 [Strategy]), 8.5 'The funding of HTSFs' (i.e. Chapter 7 [Finance]) and finally, 8.6 'The way forward'.

8.2 Origins

In many ways, the high-technology firm is not new. From the beginning of the Industrial Revolution, technical entrepreneurs, in the growth industries of the day, were employing revolutionary ideas in new high-technology firms either to develop or create novel ways of making industrial products. It was noted in Chapter 2 that, at a time when economists were focussed on capital and labour as the main means by which economic growth could occur, entrepreneurially-led technological improvements in textile machinery, steam engines and transportation methods were reducing the cost of production, and in many cases, negating the need for labour. The common link between these eighteenth- and nineteenth-century technical entrepreneurs and the new HTSFs of today lies in their ability to perform R&D effectively, leading to the production of better results than larger existing firms in established industries. These firms were thus able to revolutionize production through the efficiency and novelty of their new inventions and, in this sense, they were key protectors of the capitalist principle of free and fair competition. This tradition continues today, and the significance of new HTSFs lies not merely in their role in providing significant innovations and inventions within existing industries, but also in their ability radically to change the direction of (often ossifying) large existing industrial sectors, and, perhaps more importantly, begin new industrial activities that through disruption or 'creative destruction' offer new exciting consumer choices. The recent service-sector and manufacturing activities associated with new HTSFs making use of the internet are fully in the above tradition of HTSF technical entrepreneurship.

Thus, since we already know a great deal about how spontaneous technical entrepreneurship occurs, it might be assumed that it should be easy to promote it through enlightened regional policies designed to nurture such developments. However, knowledge of how technical entrepreneurship naturally occurs is often of little help in its replication. This is because much of the manner in which new HTSFs occur is random in terms of the sector, location, and personnel involved, and the innovation and/or inventions produced. For example, while we know something about the process by which high-technology clusters occur, often involving a series of 'spin-offs' as original firms in the cluster grow and fragment, beginning a cluster in a replicated manner is often only partly successful, and rarely to the extent that occurs in a spontaneous cluster.

The example of academic enterprise is instructive in this context. It is clear that universities contain concentrations of curiosity-driven research work that occasionally can form the basis for new HTSFs, and a large number of science parks, incubators and clusters have been promoted with a view to exploiting this knowledge locally (discussed in section 8.3). However, although there have been a number of partial successes, much of this artificially constructed infrastructure has been unimpressive in terms of increasing the level of local high-technology industrial activity in the decades since it was put in place from the early 1970s. Perhaps the reason for this relative lack of success is that the factors that combine to create a successful HTSF are many and very subtle in nature. Although they may come together randomly in a location to produce a conducive environment, the natural rate at which they occur in any region is notoriously resistant to the creation of additional occurrences through well-intended public sector encouragement. In many instances, university science-park occupancy by academic 'spin-off' firms has proven difficult to achieve, while in other instances, firms that would have existed in the area in any case, many of which are not truly high-technology, have moved onto the science park to very little additional advantage. Moreover, as noted in Chapter 2, when considering academic enterprise, there is a moral hazard issue in that artificially encouraging academics to become entrepreneurs could prove detrimental if academic staff, not suited to a business career, are persuaded to become entrepreneurs who then fail.

Thus, this introductory consideration of origins must conclude by making the point that there may be limits to what artificial replication can (or should seek to) achieve in terms of additionality. However, this does not mean that encouragement should not occur, or that the viable entrepreneurs who do come forward should not be supported as much as is possible in order to maximize their success. Indeed, it is because new and gifted technical entrepreneurs are such a 'rare breed' that we should take every opportunity to assist the most gifted of their number to achieve the best success possible, but such encouragement should not be unrealistic in terms of goals that become a negative force if they are not met.

8.3 Physical and organizational structures to promote HTSF growth

Notwithstanding the substantial problems associated with inducing HTSFs into birth, discussed above, regional and national governments charged with industrial development, in both developed and developing countries, have sought to provide conducive environments that could nurture HTSF growth in order to 'fast track' these enterprises to sustainable size, with the potential for creating substantial local long-term high-wage employment. As noted above, universities have featured strongly in these policy initiatives since they are often the only concentration of high-technology expertise in development regions, where industries of the Victorian era have often declined, and high-technology industries are sought to replace them. It was observed in Chapter 3 that, in many instances, new high-technology industries are often agglomerated (or clustered) in order to reap the benefits of concentrated local labour and service advantages (Oakey 1985a), in common with industries of the Victorian period (e.g. textiles; steel production). In particular, it was noted that the clusters of Silicon Valley and Route 128 in the United States (located, respectively, around the major technical universities of Stanford and MIT) were seen by policy makers as 'role models' for replication in other national contexts (especially in Europe).

However, those seeking to replicate this American success in Europe made a number of incorrect assumptions about the causality associated with cluster success, and perhaps the most damaging of these assumptions was that local universities played a major role in the development of the clusters that surrounded them. While, in the case of Silicon Valley, there was a degree of initial stimulation provided by local universities at the beginning of the cluster's formation (e.g. the role of Fred Terman in the development of Silicon Valley in the 1930s), overall, the influence of Stanford University was of limited significance in providing academic 'spin-offs'. Moreover, Stanford University was of yet lower importance in nurturing the 'spin-off' process, by only occasionally providing technical assistance to local HTSFs once they had spun off (Oakey 1984a). Most Silicon Valley 'spin-off' firms, during the major growth period of Silicon Valley in the 1960s and 1970s, were derived from earlier HTSFs that had become large in the 1950s (e.g. Fairchild; Hewlett-Packard). While this point might otherwise be deemed unimportant, the big mistake made by planners in Europe seeking to replicate the success of Silicon Valley was to place universities at the heart of most of their policies aimed at creating HTSF clusters. The 'nested' approach to cluster development, presented in detail in Chapter 3, was often anchored at a local university, where it was believed that either new HTSF founders would originate from constituent academic departments (discussed above) or local non-academic technical entrepreneurs would join this process at the incubator stage, network with academia, and ideally progress as the firms grew, through an adjacent science park, and onward to form part of a growing local high-technology industrial cluster. The problem with this policy approach was that, as noted above, the idea that universities were the driving force for cluster development in the United States was a misconception, and this 'progression through nested stages approach' bore no resemblance to what had made places such as Silicon Valley a success. Put simply, European planners tried to copy a process that they did not understand, and consequently produced an approach that has never delivered the HTSF growth that it promised.

We can all agree that cluster advantage does occur. This phenomenon is a well-established fact, and has taken place on numerous occasions since the Industrial Revolution in, for example, clock making, cotton textiles, steel manufacturing and, latterly, semiconductor production. However, as noted above, merely being able to detect that this phenomenon exists does not mean that we understand how it might be manipulated to human advantage. For example, doctors can understand the characteristics of a disease and how it develops, without knowing how it might be cured. Human beings, when confronted with a problem they do not understand, often over-simplify the causal mechanisms and consequently produce a comfortable, although inaccurate, explanation. In the current context, it might be argued that the 'nested' cluster development model, discussed above, remains too simplistic a means of replicating spontaneously forming clusters.

In particular, a major problem with any type of attempted replication is an inability to reproduce the economic conditions that occurred naturally in the past. This is due to at least four fundamental impediments. First, economic progress is punctuated by randomly occurring windows of opportunity. For example, it might be argued that the window of opportunity for microprocessor-based product development in HTSFs was approximately from 1965 to 1975. While we might argue about the size and temporal positioning of the 'window', it is strongly argued here that the 'window' for HTSF entrants to the desktop computer industry had definitely closed by 1980. Thus, European attempts in the 1980s to copy the success of Silicon Valley, at a time when the conditions that had helped to cause this much sought-after success had dissipated, were largely unsuccessful, certainly when compared with the amount of growth achieved in Silicon Valley in the 1970s.

Second, a major reason why existing clusters cannot be easily replicated is that the factors that create naturally forming clusters are so complex, they defy replication. This problem also explains why economic modelling is rarely accurate. Economists often seek to model the workings of a whole economy by the application of their equations (or models), only to find that their predictions are highly inaccurate. This is because their models derive from only a few variables when, in reality, the economy is driven by thousands (possibly millions) of key factors that remain uncontrolled by their economic modelling. In the case of a successful cluster, local advantage is created by a subtle mix of thousands of random (unintended) and/or planned advantages, from which substantial disadvantages must be subtracted (e.g. local congestion and high wage levels) before overall and substantial cluster advantage can occur. Once a cluster is created, firms that enjoy these advantages tend to prosper, while owners of firms and entrepreneurs from elsewhere who see this locational advantage often relocate into the cluster to share cluster benefits, to the further greater advantage of the cluster in a cumulative and causative manner. However, as noted above, understanding how spontaneous clusters occur is of little help in their replication.

A third reason why the replication policies of (particularly European) governments have been misguided is their overemphasis on high-technology *small* firms, particularly in the United Kingdom. While it would be foolish for this book, arguing for the importance of HTSFs, to decry the value of this type of firm to industrial growth (which in both aggregate and individual cases can be substantial), European attempts to replicate the successful clusters of the United States have been too heavily focussed on a few, in many ways atypical, new HTSFs that were spectacularly successful. Throughout economic history, clusters have become strong through a blend of small and large firms interacting with each other. In the case of Silicon Valley, most of the much vaunted 'spin-off' activity that created large numbers of HTSFs was (often involuntarily) incubated from large firms within this cluster. Well-established firms such as Hewlett-Packard and Fairchild, respectively begun just before and just after the Second World War, have acted as 'nurseries' for hundreds of new small firms based on high technology, often appropriated from the incubating 'parent' either with or without its blessing. Indeed, the founders of Fairchild, who later went on to form Intel, must have taken some intellectual property-based knowledge with them when they left Shockley Semiconductor in the 1950s, knowledge that may have, in turn, benefitted their 'Fairchildren' who spun off from them in the 1960s. These 'spin-off' companies have, in turn, acted as incubators for further 'spin-offs' (Mason 1979).

If governments outside the United States wish to replicate places such as Silicon Valley, they must help to create *both* small *and* large firms.

Without large firms to lead the industrial sectors on which the cluster is based, there will be no 'hub' incubator firms for new HTSFs to spin off from. Moreover, without flagship large firms within the cluster, there will be no industry leaders to compete internationally in the mass-production sectors of high-technology markets, where only large firms can effectively operate (e.g. computers; mobile phones; software); and, as important, there will be no local customer for HTSFs to supply with components and sub-assemblies on a business-to-business basis. In the United Kingdom in particular, over the past 30 years, a substantial number of large domestic electronics firms in computing and high-technology electronics have closed, or been absorbed into other foreign or United Kingdom companies. For example, originally, the General Electric Company (GEC) acquired a number of previously independent large electronics firms (e.g. Plessey; Marconi; Elliott Automation), only to be most recently acquired in turn by BAE Systems, a company that largely is involved in defence contracting for the United Kingdom government. Thus, very few large independent high-technology electronics firms remain that seek to serve civil markets. Therefore, if any cluster policy is to be successful, government must be involved in helping to create large national flagship firms in strategically important high-technology sectors to lead key high-technology industries. These firms might also act as incubators for new HTSFs, which would possibly be a better development model, and certainly more in keeping with the Silicon Valley experience, than relying on universities. While small firms in general, and HTSFs in particular, are an important component of any successful economy, they will find it difficult to survive in competitive national and international markets without the patronage of domestically owned large firms that lead the sector, trade with local firms in business-to-business relationships and provide spin-off opportunities for new local small firms.

A fourth and final reason why it is difficult to replicate high-technology industrial clusters relates to the age of such concentrated areas of production. If the previously mentioned burst of interest in the fortunes of HTSFs in Europe is again recalled, a preoccupation with the new silicon chips emerging in the late 1970s, although undeniably important, tended to imply the Silicon Valley cluster had been developed from the mid-1960s onwards. In fact, the beginnings of this cluster can be traced back to the 1930s. The key series of technical innovations that took the transistor from a single entity to the sophisticated microprocessor we currently enjoy took at least 40 years, and continues today. These important factors are relevant to subsequent cluster replication policies, especially in the United Kingdom; the idea that any government or, even less likely, a series of governments with different ideological approaches, would pursue a consistent industrial development policy over several decades is difficult to contemplate. While clusters that occur naturally, without government intervention, can emerge at their own pace, governments have a tendency to treat industrial policies in an inconsistent manner. For example, an almost 'road to Damascus' conversion to cluster policies was undergone by the United Kingdom Labour government in the mid-2000s when Michael Porter persuaded the Department of Trade and Industry (DTI), and most Regional Development Agencies (RDAs) to adopt cluster strategies (championed by Lord Sainsbury). However, today (in 2012) there is no Department of Trade and Industry, no RDAs and little residual enthusiasm for cluster policies, which the RDAs were intended to deliver. Since this 'cluster policy' enthusiasm emerged and disappeared in less than ten years, any cluster development policy that would take 50 years to achieve in theory would be unlikely to occur in practice.

Any general analysis of attempts to create spatial policies to help the formation and growth of HTSFs over the past 30 years must conclude that, not only in the case of clusters, but also with regard to science parks, incubators and academic enterprise, there has been a tendency for sudden bursts of enthusiasm punctuated by periods of total neglect. This has certainly been the case in the United Kingdom. Overall, there has been a general inability to understand the need for a logical and consistent policy, while changes in political party and personnel have meant that what has been delivered has been often inappropriate, and generally inconsistent. What has always been needed is a consistent long-term national industrial strategy that seeks to target specific industrial sectors, with an emphasis on high technology when the nation concerned has a competitive 'basic science' advantage in many sectors that should be encouraged on the ground by substantial and consistent regional development policies designed to achieve these goals.

8.4 Taking HTSF products to the market

This section, concerned with the journey of an HTSF product to the market, brings together a number of separate chapters from the earlier parts of this book. The reason for this amalgamation is that, in a conceptual sense, separation is somewhat misleading, since they are all parts of an uninterrupted series of actions and iterations that are sequentially linked together, with strong feedback loops (e.g. between R&D and marketing through customer feedback). Moreover, since theoretical and policy considerations likewise cannot be segregated, the whole process of 'bringing the product to market' is discussed below as a single stream of related events. However, because raising capital is probably the most important factor governing HTSF birth, survival and growth, as it is the most difficult to achieve, this topic will be dealt with separately in the last part of this chapter. Detailed consideration of the current theme of the 'journey to market' begins with conclusions on the general topic of HTSF R&D.

8.4.1 Research and development

Although the production costs of HTSF products may be high, often taking the form of batch or one-off production regimes, such high manufacturing costs can be usually offset by the high mark-up in price that sophisticated high-technology products can command, in circumstances where the uniqueness of the technology involved prevents imitation by potential competitors. However, in order to deliver this advantage, HTSF R&D needs to produce world-beating new technology, often at the leading edge of scientific knowledge. Achieving this challenging task is at once both attractive and daunting to potential external investors in HTSFs. For example, on the one hand, the discovery of a new biomedical cure for a major (currently incurable) disease would imply massive profitability and public good, while on the other hand, the difficulty of achieving such a breakthrough is often underestimated and may have unintended damaging side effects, ensuring that the ensuing new product takes more time to bring to market (involving substantial extra costs, or total failure).

Research and development is necessary *but not sufficient* to ensure success. This means that no success can be achieved without (often substantial) expenditure on R&D, although success cannot be assured, suggesting that in many cases, highly expensive R&D spending results in failure. As noted in Chapter 7 on finance, although venture capitalists were initially attracted to HTSF investment in the 1980s, this interest waned as it gradually became clear that HTSFs were highly risky investments, mainly because of the high cost of R&D, its unpredictable duration, and an inability to guarantee successful products at the end of this process. Moreover, we have no robust theory to explain why, when or where success will occur. Essentially, the best that can be said about successful discoveries that emanate from R&D is that they can be nurtured by R&D spending, but not assured by such cost. 'Throwing money at the problem' would seem a rather crude strategy to adopt, but large pharmaceutical firms, for example, do this by adopting a portfolio approach to R&D. This approach usually involves, at any given moment in time, the initiation of perhaps 12 major product development projects, with the expectation that only two or three will be successful. Thus, the small number of successful products in this industry, due to strong patent protection, can more than compensate for the failures.

The problem for new HTSFs, however, is that they often find it difficult to gain R&D funding for *one* product under development. This difficulty can be exacerbated by the manner in which HTSFs emerge as independent entities. As noted in Chapter 1, there are two main ways in which HTSFs are born. First, new HTSFs can emerge as spin-offs from existing large high-technology firms, of which the 'Fairchildren' of Silicon Valley are an excellent example. Second, new HTSFs can also emerge from universities as 'academic spin-offs'. Often, especially in the case of industrial spin-offs, and sometimes in the case of academic spin-offs, these new firms are formed at an earlier stage than would have been ideal from an R&D funding viewpoint. In the case of the industrial spin-off, development within the incubating company would be less costly than spinning off and founding a new company with a yet unproven product technology. In the case of the academic spin-off, keeping the new idea in the public sector for longer would also eventually reduce the costs of R&D when spin-off occurred.

The reason why firms 'spin off' earlier than is otherwise financially desirable is to acquire more easily the intellectual property they have created in the previous organization (Roberts 1991; Oakey1995). Once a new technology of this type passes, for example, the 'proof of concept' stage, it has obvious increased value that was probably not evident when in an embryonic form. However, from the viewpoint of attracting venture capital funding, a product development in its embryonic form is a major drawback that implies a longer period of 'front-end' R&D, the success of which cannot be easily assured at such an early stage. Thus, it is essentially the problems of not having a reliable predictive model to indicate which product developments will succeed when at a nascent stage, and a frequent lack of good HTSF business-management expertise, that have been the root causes of the long-standing problems of funding R&D in HTSFs. Moreover, given such uncertainty, the flight of venture capital investment into lower-technology firms with proven track records of performance, as noted in Chapter 7, seems a sad but logical strategic trend.

While it is clear that the funding of 'front-end-loaded' R&D in advance of any sales is the major reason why many HTSFs struggle to survive, consideration of the policy implications of this problem will be reserved for the discussion of finance in section 8.5.

8.4.2 The selling of HTSF products

The selling behaviour of HTSFs is not well served by existing theory on marketing. As observed in Chapter 5, the popular 'stages' approach to exporting, in which the market area of new firms geographically expands over time from the local area through regional and national sales to exporting, is largely irrelevant to HTSFs. From a conceptual viewpoint, HTSFs are frequently 'born global', not in a strategic sense whereby the decision to sell abroad is chosen from a range of options open to the new firms at formation, but simply because the specialist nature of much high-technology production means that appropriate customers for such output do not exist locally, and *must* be sought on an international basis. Put simply, while a firm making office furniture might readily find customers in its local area, a firm making highly sensitive pressure transducers for high-performance aircraft would need to seek customers on a worldwide basis, implying extra selling costs.

Certainly as far as HTSFs are concerned, the selling of finished products is best seen theoretically in the context of a complete product life-cycle model, in which selling is only the final part of a cycle of production that ranges from conception of the original product idea to obsolescence (as shown in Figure 4.2 in Chapter 4). For a product to be an economic success, all stages in the cycle, from invention, through R&D and production, to final sales, need to be conducted efficiently. Thus, from a conceptual viewpoint, selling should not be seen as a separate activity, but as part of a process where all elements in the product life-cycle process interact with each other, not only in a sequential manner (in the sense that a product cannot be sold until the sales staff know its characteristics), but also in an iterative manner (e.g. when customer feedback helps research engineers to modify or improve a new product). Moreover, viewing the product life cycle as a complete entity reflects the fact that, in HTSFs, the cost of any individual phase in the life cycle influences, and is influenced by, all other costs. Indeed, one of the reasons why the selling of HTSF products is often inadequately performed is that the cost of R&D, and a labour-intensive production process where mass production is rarely possible so financially weakens the HTSF that little capital remains, or can be obtained from external investors, with which to launch the new product effectively in 'expensive to reach' international markets.

Moreover, if after-sales support and servicing are taken into account, the selling of high-technology products in this small-firm area more often involves helping the customer to learn how to use the new product than would be the case for the selling of electronic 'white goods' where the technology is well established, mass production can be adopted and the product is easy to use. What this complexity means financially is that, from conception of a new product idea to the final sales to customers, costs are consistently high. When the product does reach the correct final consumer, such high costs can usually be vindicated by the high profit margin that sophisticated products of this type can command. Nonetheless, as noted frequently above, all these complexities tend to alarm potential investors in HTSFs, and generally, send them in the direction of lower-technology firms with well-established customers.

Regarding the way that HTSF founders seek to reach their potential customers, it has been noted on a number of occasions that the selling behaviour of such firms is less than optimal (Oakey 1984a, 1991). This is partly due to a lack of capital with which to sell effectively (noted above), which may result from an arrogant belief among many engineers that their new product is so good that it will 'sell itself', and that customers will be 'lucky to get it'; and partly due to the real complexities that surround finding out how to reach disparate international customers with different currencies, legal systems, and methods of distribution. The arrival of the internet has provided a major potential new selling tool, especially relevant to the needs of HTSFs. The low cost of reaching customers and the relatively high level of detail that can be included in internet communication with potential international customers mean that there is great potential for selling at very low financial risk. However, recent research has shown that HTSF owners have been slow to exploit effectively this potentially valuable selling tool (Oakey 2007c).

In terms of policy, there is a considerable amount of assistance that could be provided by local and national governments to help HTSFs to sell their products abroad. Although financial support exists in many countries to aid exporting (e.g. UK Trade and Investment [UKTI] in the United Kingdom), the aid given is often not particularly effective, and frequently tends to consist of training courses, in circumstances where face-to-face advice on specific marketing problems (e.g. product liability issues in foreign countries) would be more effective. The tendency for governments to break the innovation process into its constituent parts that reflect the shape of bureaucracy, rather than the needs of the industries they are charged to support, is a major barrier to efficiency. For example, in the case of the United Kingdom, it has been noted that the well-regarded SMART scheme, which provided grants to innovative high-technology small firms for the R&D required to develop new products, did not allow for the funding of marketing costs that are necessary to exploit fully any product produced as a result of their grant, since selling the product is handled separately (Smallbone *et al.* 2000; Oakey 2003a). Further detailed discussion of the funding of selling, as part of the complete product life-cycle process, will be dealt with in section 8.5 on HTSF finance, where funding the total life cycle of a new HTSF product will be dealt with in terms of a seamless enterprise in which the key functions of R&D, production and selling the final product must *all* be performed efficiently to ensure success.

8.4.3 Strategy

It is prudent for this discussion of getting the product to market to conclude with a consideration of strategy since, having elaborated the key tasks involved in R&D and selling, strategy should involve a balanced drawing together of what will happen when, and at what cost. Certainly, when external investors are involved in a new HTSF, the efficient management of the firm will be expected in order that milestones predicted by HTSF management in the business plan are met, or not greatly deviated from. However, for a substantial proportion of HTSFs, the management of the process of invention, production and sales is often a rather ad hoc process, for two reasons. First, many HTSFs are founded through a spin-off process in which frustrated high-technology engineers seek to 'shake off' the bureaucracy they experience working for large firms. This sentiment can breed a tendency for rather autocratic behaviour in which control of the newly created entity is prized almost above the financial success of the firm. Independence for these founders is a key asset: although it might be judged illogical in terms of economic rationality, this is an important variable in explaining HTSF strategic behaviour. Strategy for this type of entrepreneur often amounts to a mere reaction to events, in circumstances where the involvement of external agencies regarding loans or investment capital is avoided. Second, the emergence of many HTSF founders from physical science backgrounds means that they may have very little knowledge of management science, and frequently are disparaging of the merits of management science, which they consider merely 'common sense'. The distaste that many engineers have for their marketing colleagues is a good example of this phenomenon.

At the other extreme from the independent entrepreneur is the individual or group of HTSF founders who have a 'grow to sell' approach to strategy. Clearly, by definition, such individuals do not have any problem with the involvement of external parties. Indeed, the writing of a formal business plan is frequently the first step for this type of HTSF entrepreneur as external venture capital is sought on which the new firm will be based. However, it should not be assumed that individuals with a 'grow to sell' approach have an extensive knowledge of management in general, and strategy in particular. Although the willingness to involve external funders is a good first step, here too there may be a problem with understanding good management practices. A major reason why 'grow to sell' founders of HTSFs do not perform in accordance with the business plan they have written is that they are unable to monitor and control the running of their new firm (as noted in Chapter 7). Although a technology under development might remain promising, venture capitalists are often not only reluctant to become involved in funding HTSFs, but are also wary of continued involvement in firms they have invested in when they discover that the HTSF's management is managerially incompetent. In this sense, 'investment unreadiness' can continue *after* venture capitalists have become involved in HTSFs.

The above observations have a number of implications for both policy and theory. From a theoretical perspective, rigid economic profit-optimizing models do not seem appropriate to the behaviour of many HTSF founders. The behavioural science literature probably offers a better explanation of this independent behaviour and dislike for management science shown by many HTSF entrepreneurs. One of the great (but dangerous) benefits of being 'your own boss' is that this management structure allows total freedom to take any action the founder thinks fit. This might include an avoidance of any external ownership involvement, and/or distaste for management education, on the grounds that management skills cannot be taught and are innate. Judged from the viewport of objective management efficiency, these 'indulgences' can be seen as a form of 'non-financial' income in circumstances where financial gain is sacrificed for non-pecuniary 'value' (Cyert and March 1963). While such an approach to running an HTSF might lead to stagnation or closure, this could be judged evidence of the 'free will' of the capitalist system taken to its illogical extreme.

From a policy viewpoint, however, such sub-optimal behaviour should not go unchallenged. Well-run and efficient new HTSFs, as noted many times in this book, have strong future potential for creating wealth and employment. Since it has been noted above that both 'independent' and 'grow to sell'-oriented firms can suffer from poor management expertise, the development of such skills should be encouraged by government through the provision of (possibly subsidized) management training courses for new HTSF entrepreneurs. It is ironic that, while much of the literature seeking to attract new HTSFs to university-based science parks in the 1980s was focussed on the benefits they could gain through technical linkages with the science departments of universities (which rarely occurred), more value might have been achieved by encouraging new HTSF entrepreneurs to take management courses at university business schools on, for example, financial management. This would render the production of strategic documentation by HTSF founders more digestible by venture capitalists, in particular, and by the finance industry with which these entrepreneurs need to deal, in general. This 'blind spot' regarding management training for HTSFs often largely stems from an over-concentration on the physical science aspects of a new HTSF at the expense of business management.

8.5 The funding of HTSFs

8.5.1 Demand-side problems

Capital is the key resource governing the process of HTSF formation and growth. It is pervasively important since all the main functions of the firm, from R&D through production to sales, require capital investment. However, since this much could be said of any manufacturing firm, the additional importance that capital investment holds for HTSFs is the fact that most HTSFs need to perform extensive R&D after formation, often long before any income from sales is obtained. This means that not only are substantial amounts of investment capital involved in the funding of HTSFs, but that this funding is 'front-end loaded' and investors must have a high degree of patience before any return on their capital can be achieved. While in some famous cases, the returns from HTSF investment can be spectacular, there is also great scope for failure and, overall, it has been noted above that the venture capital funding of HTSFs has not been popular with investors. This is especially the case if the long lead times for product development and the lack of any track record possessed by most HTSFs are taken into account.

However, investment capital has much in common with the functions that it supports in that it is necessary for success (e.g. R&D; selling), but not sufficient. This point is clearly illustrated by the fact that the success of HTSFs does not simply depend on access to loan or investment capital; sufficiency is achieved when this capital is applied *to good effect* by competent management. Thus, if the funding of R&D is taken as an example, it is not only essential that the technical work performed in R&D departments be a success, but also that the funding of such efforts should be prudently applied, carefully monitored, and subject to accurate financial control in order to make sure that maximum efficiency is obtained. Clearly, external investors may be more readily patient regarding a return on their investment if they see that the firm they are supporting is a well-run enterprise. As already noted, this is significant, not only for the internal solvency of the firm, but also in order to attract and retain external investors. Here again, it is important that new HTSF entrepreneurs should not only have the obvious technical skills they need to invent their new products, but also possess efficient business- management skills to exploit them. As noted above, there is often a conceptual gap among physical-science-trained entrepreneurs in that they undervalue management skills when seeking to develop a successful business.

Moreover, there appear to be a number of subtle problems that inhibit the funding of HTSFs, both during the application for funds process and when funds have been advanced. Since it is clear that most technical entrepreneurs will emerge from a physical science background, they often do not have the requisite skills to enter the social science world of economic and business management. Much of the 'investment unreadiness' claimed by venture capitalists stems from an over-concentration on the technology-based parts of the business process, while not enough effort is devoted to economic viability and efficient management practices. Typical of this approach is over-claiming regarding the degree to which the new technology is superior to other products already on the market, and the assertion that the new technology has multiple potential uses. While it has been acknowledged above that benchmarking the potential of completely new high technologies is an almost impossible task, the lack of precision on market potential that is contained in many business plans submitted to venture capitalists by potential HTSF founders reduces potential investor confidence.

An obvious solution to this problem should involve a choice between two options, or a combination of both. First, as discussed above, prospective and actual HTSF founders might receive management training from a university business school to enable them to develop a working knowledge of business management. However, due to the length of time over which formation occurs, it might be beneficial, in addition to the original HTSF founder gaining management skills, that external full-time management skills are brought into the new firm in order to improve business plan applications, and set up efficient management practices such that potential investors would have confidence in the new enterprise's management team. The hiring of full-time executives might also be an option (CBI 1997). Although this solution might compromise the autonomy of the technical entrepreneur founding the new HTSF, it could also increase the likelihood of external investor support, which might be a price worth paying. This issue of improving the 'investment readiness' of new HTSFs will be returned to in the final section of this chapter.

8.5.2 Supply-side problems

The basic conceptual problem with HTSF funding, regarding venture capitalists in particular, is that there is a clash of cultures. While HTSF founders are particularly concerned with finding technical solutions to scientific and engineering problems, the imperative for all members of the finance industry is maximizing returns on their investment in the shortest time possible, and at minimum risk. While there are wider policy issues associated with HTSF formation and growth in terms of manufacturing employment in industries of the future, national economic output and the balance between productive and consumer-based sectors, the venture capitalist's only concern is to achieve the best results possible for his or her shareholders. The undeniably poor returns derived from HTSF investment over the past 30 years support the argument that HTSFs are often not an ideal vehicle for investment. Similarly, the claim by venture capitalists that investment deals of less than £250,000 are precluded by high administration costs that do not decline with the value of the deal is generally hard to question.

However, there are a number of areas where the behaviour of the venture capital industry might be criticized. First and foremost, there is substantial anecdotal evidence that strong new HTSFs, when seeking investment capital from the venture capital sector, often fail to obtain the funds they need for expansion. Indeed, this criticism also applies to the quasi-public sector regional venture capital funds that were established with the main objective of extending funding beyond that which the private sector was ready to support. Many regional venture capital funds have remained poorly accessed. Second, from a scientific viewpoint, it is often not clear on what basis decisions by venture capitalists are made. While economic theory would suggest that decisions on investment should be based on hard objective evidence, venture capitalists are often proud of their instincts and frequently base their investments on the subjective grounds that they 'liked the people involved'. This raises the question as to whether some of the poor success rate regarding HTSF investments by venture capitalists might be due to this somewhat self-indulgent behaviour and, indeed, might also explain why otherwise viable applicants are refused. Third, and relevant to the criticisms made above, it has been argued for some time now (Oakey 1984b, 2003a, 2007a) that venture capitalists in particular often lack the in-house technical knowledge on which to base investment. The people making decisions on HTSF investment are usually drawn from the finance industry, where a reliance on securing physical assets for security is the main way in which risk is reduced. Put simply, the only assets many HTSF founders have is the technology they have developed, which is often not competently valued by such non-technical individuals.

Given the abundance of practical and conceptual problems that confront HTSF finance in both supply- and demand-side terms, it is not surprising that HTSF funding remains an enduring problem. In the final section of this book, some observations on the way forward will be proposed, and a balanced set of improvements will be suggested that seek to ameliorate a weakness in the capital markets that has resisted improvement over many years. It will be argued that a solution must lie in the better application of both public and private resources to this problem for the reasons suggested below.

8.6 The way forward

Experience of the last 20 years in Western developed nations suggests that there is a need for the combination of both public and private sector capital to provide funding for new and existing HTSFs. Various initiatives have been designed over recent years to share the risks of supporting HTSFs, as they develop new technologies towards market application, between public and private sector institutions (e.g. The Small Business Investment Company [SBIC] in the United States; the initial United Kingdom SMART award scheme [replaced in 2005 by the Grant for Research and Development scheme]; and various proof-of-concept schemes). This public–private approach can be justified on a number of different grounds. Public institutions can justify the use of tax payers' money in a 'partnership' with the private sector on the grounds that the public funding of HTSFs is in the national (or regional) interest, since the jobs created through such financial support will be justified by future taxes paid, both by employees and the firms in which they work. Other multiplier effects will also flow from the successful support of new HTSFs, which have the added bonus of being likely to survive well into the future due to their leading-edge high-technology orientation. Such a 'partnership' should also be attractive to private sector investors, since, although HTSFs will always be risky, they can also be spectacularly successful, while the public sector involvement can reduce risk to a manageable level, especially if the further measures recommended below are taken.

However, what has been missing in previous public–private collaborations of this type is an efficient and sufficiently intelligent organizational structure with which to deliver such provision. Put simply, conventional venture capital firms do not see the 'due diligence' required to allow investment in HTSFs as a good use of their time (i.e. that could be justified to their shareholders when compared to other options). But neither do public sector organizations have the necessary business-management skills to broker effectively the link between those HTSF founders seeking capital and actors from the public and private sectors who may be willing to provide such funds, given adequate and effective due diligence. What is needed is a hybrid organization that would exist between the public and private sectors, necessarily staffed by experienced managers from the private sector, who would bring together public and private sector capital to create new funds to support new and early-stage HTSFs.

This new type of hybrid entity would perform two key functions intended to increase the likelihood that investment in HTSFs would be successful, to the satisfaction of both the investor and the HTSF, thus not only increasing the return to fund investors in individual cases, but also, most importantly, increasing with other potential investors the general credibility of HTSF investment from which venture capital firms have been retreating since the early 1990s. These key functions are as follows. First and foremost, any HTSF applicant for funds would be subjected by the new hybrid organization to a rigorous marketing 'due diligence' exercise, in which both the technical quality and the market potential would be tested by consulting key technical experts and potential customers in these important areas. Because much criticism of private and public venture capital organizations in the past has focussed on their lack of technological skills when evaluating HTSF business-plan proposals, this essential function, when carefully performed, will isolate the best projects for investment, which, in the past, have been neglected by conventional venture capital firms and the banks (Herriot 2005).

Second, since it has already been noted in this chapter and Chapter 7 on finance that 'investment unreadiness' can be a major barrier to venture capital investment, the new hybrid body should, prior to any investment, examine the management structure of applicant firms to assess if any additional training and/or staff might be required prior to investment. For example, it might be recommended that the HTSF employ a finance director to work with the founder to provide clearer, more accurate and regular financial information on the performance of an existing, or a proposed, firm. This function would have two major benefits. Initially, such an addition to the management team would reassure investors that the firm's performance was being accurately reported, and, subsequently, it would reduce the likelihood of unwelcome surprises that might damage the confidence of investors regarding how well the firm was progressing. While previously in this book the point has been made that some independent HTSF founders might not welcome such an 'intrusion', they cannot expect to gain external funds without taking into account the legitimate concerns of potential investors. A person with such an introspective attitude would be rightly considered not to be 'investment ready'.

Critically, as a source of funds, this type of new hybrid public–private organization would be likely to fill more effectively the funding gap discussed in relation to Figure 7.3 in Chapter 7, due to the greater due diligence, in terms of both the new product technologies' potential and better management competence. Public sector support could be contingent on the requirement that the new organization specialize in supporting HTSFs. There is a suspicion that venture capital firms, due to the lack of time they have to explore individual applications for funds in great depth, either skim off the obvious best HTSF funding applications for support and/or act on personal hunches as to whether they 'like the people' involved. There is substantial anecdotal evidence, as noted above, that deserving new and established HTSFs do not receive the funding that they need and should receive on merit. Thus, the new proposed hybrid organization would spend a greater amount of time on performing due diligence of applications that, after initial screening, look like they could be good investments. The measures discussed above on assessing the technology and staff of an applicant HTSF should reveal HTSFs that are candidates for support, which the wider venture capital industry may have missed. Put simply, the availability of a proportion of public sector capital in any well-scrutinized investment deal would compensate for the additional scrutiny such an organization would need to perform. Government bodies can often provide capital, but are not able to cater for the commercial needs of HTSFs, while the private venture capital industry possesses these commercial skills, but has been reluctant to provide the financial support due to the high risk of HTSF investment. This new type of hybrid delivery body would be appropriate since it would possess both public sector capital and private sector business skills, with which the problems of HTSF funding can be addressed more effectively.

Finally, to take a broader view of HTSFs in developed economies, it should be reiterated that HTSFs are of critical importance to the manufacturing health of any developed nation. Until recently, the increasing preference that many Western governments have displayed over the last 30 years (especially in the United States and the United Kingdom) for the development of a service-sector-based economy (especially financial services), reflects a general belief that we have moved from agriculture through manufacturing to services. This is a flawed premise. Most of the Gross Domestic Products (GDPs) of the United Kingdom and the United States today are reliant on consumption, fuelled by excessive borrowing and the spending of capital gains obtained from increasing property prices. Such consumption has two negative impacts. First, it encourages the purchase of imported consumer goods manufactured abroad (especially from China) to substitute for previously domestically owned and produced manufactured products that no longer exist (e.g. televisions; motor vehicles; electronic white goods). Second, dependence on these imports reflects the reality that domestically produced goods are no longer available nationally, or are avoided because they are no longer attractive to domestic consumers, which further adds to the decline of their manufacturing bases, such that an ability to sell manufactured goods to the rest of the world is reduced, resulting in an alarmingly low level of manufacturing contribution to GDP. In both the United States and the United Kingdom, concern should move away from a fascination with the level of high-street spending and the price of housing as a measure of prosperity, and return to a concern for the national balance of payments, which provides a measure of how much a nation produces and sells to the world compared with what it buys from abroad, rather than simply what it is buying and consuming from other parts of the world. In the current context, GDP is a misleading term in that it suggests that the productive output of any nation is being measured. Certainly in terms of the United Kingdom, Gross Domestic Consumption (GDC) might be a better title in that most of what is 'produced' is consumption. Presumably, a renewed focus on this type of consumption, based on borrowing rather than on tradeable manufacturing goods, would return Western economies, within a short period, to the brink of another consumption-fuelled recession based on excessive borrowing.

What is needed in many Western nations is a return to national production through manufacturing. The reason why Germany better weathered the recent 2008 recession was that manufacturing had not been abandoned. Not only does Germany manufacture high-technology products, but a range of medium- and low-technology products from kitchen appliances through motor vehicles to garden furniture continue to be produced profitably in Germany, despite their high level of operating costs compared with China. Germany has maintained strong manufacturing industries, while the United Kingdom cannot benefit from a manufacturing-based recovery to the same extent because of the abandonment of much of the United Kingdom's traditional manufacturing base. United Kingdom manufacturing since the Second World War has declined at an alarming rate, and currently represents only 13 per cent of national GDP. Therefore, even a strong increase in manufactured products produced from such a small contribution to GDP would be unable to impact significantly on a residual United Kingdom manufacturing sector.

Successful manufacturing in general, and high-technology manu-facturing in particular, is a major way of balancing the trade performance of nations where services have been dominant. High-technology goods command high prices and protection from early imitation due to their technical sophistication. Thus, the development of new high-technology industries in Western developed nations is critical to future economic success, since this is an area where there is a comparative advantage, given the strong science bases of many Western democracies. The experiment with services as a substitute for manufacturing has proven to be inadequate in the cases of the United States and the United Kingdom. Manufacturing in general, and high-technology manufacturing in particular, are the keys to the future economic prosperity of developed Western economies, and this is why the formation and growth of HTSFs, as a crucial part of a new emphasis on manufacturing, should be a major task for all Western developed economies in the future.

Bibliography

Albert P., Bernasconi M. and Gaynor L. (2002). 'Incubators: the Emergence of a New Industry. A Comparison of Players and their Strategies', CERAM Study Report, Sophia Antipolis.

Arthur W. B. (1994). *Increasing Returns and Path Dependence in the Economy*, Michigan, MI: Michigan University Press.

Bank of England (1996). *The Financing of Technology-Based Small Firms*, London: Bank of England.

Bank of England (2001). *The Financing of Technology-Based Small Firms*, London: Bank of England.

Barber J. (2006). 'Intangible Assets and Competitive Advantage in the Knowledge-Based Economy', DTI Economics and Statistics Papers, April.

Batten Briefings (2011). *Whatever Happened to Venture Capital?*, Charlottesville, VA: Batten Institute, University of Virginia.

Bell J., McNaughton R. and Young S. (2001). 'Born-Again Global Firms – an Extension to the "Born Global" Phenomenon', *Journal of International Management*, 7: 173–89.

Benworth P., Hospers G-J. and Timmerman P. (2009). *'Who Builds 'Science Cities' and Knowledge Parks?'*, in R. P. Oakey, A. Groen, P. van der Sijde and G. Cook (eds) *New Technology-Based Firms in the New Millennium*, Vol. VII, Bingley, Yorks.: Emerald Publishing.

Berlin L. (2005). *The Man behind the Microchip: Robert Noyce and the Invention of Silicon Valley*, New York: Oxford University Press.

Bilkey W. J. and Tesar G. (1977). 'The Export Behaviour of Smaller-Sized Wisconsin Manufacturing Firms', *Journal of International Business Studies*, Spring/Summer: 93–8.

Birch D. L. (1979). 'The Job Generation Process', Working Paper, MIT Program on Neighborhood and Regional Change, Cambridge, Massachusetts.

Birley S. (2001). 'Universities, Academics and Spin Out Companies', *International Journal of Entrepreneurship Education*,1(1): 1–21.

Bolton J. E. (1971). *Committee of Enquiry on Small Firms*, Cmnd. 4811, London: HMSO.

Breheny M., Cheshire P. and Langridge R. J. (1983). 'The Anatomy of Job Creation? Industrial Change in Britain's M4 Corridor', *Built Environment*, 9(1): 61–71.

Bullock M. (1983). *Academic Enterprise, Industrial Innovation and the Development of High Technology Financing in the United States*, London: Brand Brothers and Co.

BVCA (2005, 2006, 2007, 2008, 2009, 2010). Annual Reports on Investment Activity, London: British Venture Capital Association.

Cameron G. C. (1979). 'The National Industrial Strategy and Regional Policy', in D. MacLennan and J. B. Parr (eds) *Regional Policy*, Oxford: Martin Robertson, 297–322.

Cardullo M. W. (1999). *Technological Entrepreneurism*, Baldock, Herts: Research Studies Press.

Chapman K. (1973). 'Agglomeration and Linkage in the UK Petro-Chemical Industry', *Transactions, Institute of British Geographers*, 60: 33–68.

Christensen C. M. (1997). *The Innovator's Dilemma*. Boston, MA: Harvard Business School Press.

Christensen C. M. and Bower J. L. (2004). 'Customer Power, Strategic Investment, and the Failure of Leading Firms', in M. L. Tushman and P. Anderson (eds) *Managing Strategic Innovation and Change*, Oxford: Oxford University Press.

Confederation of British Industry (1997). *Tech Stars*, London: CBI.

Cooper A. C. (1970). 'The Palo Alto Experience', *Industrial Research*, May: 58–84.

Countopoulos-Ioannidis D. G., Alexiou G. A., Gouvias T. C. and Ioannidis P. A. (2008). 'Life Cycle of Translational Research for Medical Interventions', *Science*, 321, 5th September.

Cressy R. (2006). 'Determinants of Small Firm Survival and Growth' in M. Casson, B. Yeung, A. Basu and N. Wadeson (eds) *Oxford Handbook of Entrepreneurship*, Oxford: Oxford University Press.

Cruickshank D. (2000). *Competition in UK Banking: A Report to the Chancellor of the Exchequer*, London: The Stationery Office.

Cyert R. M. and March J. G. (1963). *A Behavioural Theory of the Firm*, Englewood Cliffs, NJ: Prentice Hall.

Dandridge T. and Levenburg N. M. (2000). 'High Tech Potential? An Exploratory Study of Very Small Firms' Usage of the Internet', *International Small Business Journal*, 10(2): 81–91.

Denison E. (1962). *The Sources of Economic Growth in the United States and the Alternatives before Us*. London: Allen & Unwin.

Dosi G. (1993). 'Technological Paradigms and Technological Trajectories: a Suggested Interpretation of the Determinants and Directions of Technical Change', *Research Policy*, 22(2): 102–3.

Drucker P. F. (2007). *Innovation and Entrepreneurship*, London: Butterworth-Heinemann.

DTI (1998). *Our Competitive Future: Building the Knowledge Driven Economy*, Cm. 4176, London: HMSO.

Etzkowitz H. and Leydesdorff L. (1997). *Universities and the Global Knowledge Economy: A Triple Helix of University–Industry–Government Relations*. London: Cassell Academic.

Faems D. (2012). 'Transitional Governance in External Technology Sourcing Trajectories: Connecting Pre-Acquisition Collaboration to Post-Acquisition Integration', in A. Groen, R. P. Oakey, P. van der Sijde and G. Cook (eds) *New Technology-Based Firms in the New Millennium*, Vol. IX, Bingley, Yorks.: Emerald Publishing.

Fothergill S. and Gudgin G. (1979). *The Job Generation Process in Britain*, Centre for Environmental Studies Research Series No. 32, London: Centre for Environmental Studies.

Fraser S. (2004). 'Finance for Small and Medium-Sized Enterprises: A Report on the 2004 UK Survey of SME Finances', Centre for Small and Medium-Sized Enterprises, Warwick Business School.

Freeman C. (1982). *The Economics of Industrial Innovation*, London: Frances Pinter.

Freeman, C. (1986). 'The Role of Technological Change in National Economic Development', in A. Amin and J. Goddard (eds) *Technological Change and Industrial Restructuring*, London: Allen & Unwin.

Ganotakis P. (2007). 'Factors Affecting the Performance and Growth of New High Technology-Based Firms in the United Kingdom', unpublished PhD thesis, University of Aston, Birmingham.

Geer D. E. (2003). 'Monopoly Considered Harmful', *IEEE Security and Policy*, 3(3): 14–17.

Glasmeier A. (1985). 'Innovative Manufacturing Industries: Spatial Incidence in the United States', in M. Castells (ed.) *High Technology, Space and Society*, Beverley Hills, CA and London: Sage, 55–80.

Goddard J. and Chatterton P. (1999). 'Regional Development Agencies and the Knowledge Economy: Harnessing the Potential of Universities', *Environment and Planning C: Government and Policy*, 17: 685–99.

Griliches Z. (1957). 'Hybrid Corn: an Exploration of the Economics of Technological Change', *Econometrica*, 25(4): 501–22.

Gupta A. K., Raj S. P. and Wileman P. (1985). 'The R&D Marketing Interface in High Technology Firms', *Journal of Product Innovation Management*, 2: 12–24.

Hägerstrand T. (1952). 'The Propagation of Innovation Waves', *Lund Studies in Geography*, Series B(4).

Hall P. G. (1963). *The Industries of London*, London: Hutchinson.

Harvey D. (1973). *Explanation in Geography*. London: Edward Arnold.

Herriot W. (2005). 'Improving Early-Stage Financing in the East of England', Report by St John's Innovation Centre, Cambridge.

Hotelling H. (1929). 'Stability in Competition', *Economics Journal*, 39: 41–57.

House of Lords Select Committee on Science and Technology (1997). *The Innovation-Exploitation Barrier*, House of Lords Papers No. 62, London: House of Lords.

Hughes A. (1997). 'Finance for SMEs: A UK Perspective', *Small Business Economics*, 9: 151–66.

Johanson J. and Vahlne J. E. (1977). 'The Internationalisation Process of the Firm – A Model of Knowledge Development and Increasing Foreign Market Commitments', *Journal of International Business Studies*, Spring/Summer: 23–32.

Jones C., Hecker R. and Holland P. (2003). 'Small Firm Internet Adoption: Opportunities For[e]gone, a Journey Not Begun', *Journal of Small Business and Enterprise'*, 10(3): 287–97.

Kamien M. I. and Swartz N. L. (1983). *Market Structure and Innovation*, Cambridge: Cambridge University Press.

Katsikeas C. S., Piercy N. F. and Ioannidis C. (1996). 'Determinants of Export Performance in a European Context', *European Journal of Marketing*, 30(6): 6–35.

Keeble D. E. (1976). *Industrial Location and Planning within the United Kingdom*London: Methuen.

Kelly T. J. C. (1986). 'Location and Spatial Distribution of High Technology in Great Britain: Computer Electronics', unpublished PhD thesis, Department of Geography, University of Cambridge.

Khan M. S. (1975). 'A Study of Success and Failure in the Swedish Export Industry', research report, Department of Business Administration, University of Stockholm.

Klein-Woolhuis R. J. A. (1999). 'Sleeping with the Enemy: Trust, Dependence and Contracts in Inter-Organisational Relationships', doctoral dissertation, University of Twente, The Netherlands.

Klofsten M. and Jones D. (2000). 'Comparing Academic Entrepreneurship in Europe: the Case of Sweden and Ireland', *Small Business Economics*, 14(2): 299–309.

Kondratiev N. (1925). 'The Major Economic Cycles', *Voprosy Konjunktury* [Problems of Economic Fluctuation], 1: 28–79. (English translation, reprinted in *Lloyds Bank Review*, 129, 1978.)

Krugman P. (1991). *Geography and Trade*, Cambridge, MA: The MIT Press.

Kuhn T. S. (1962). *The Structure of Scientific Revolutions*, Chicago, IL: University of Chicago Press.

Lachenmaier S. and Wößmann L. (2006). 'Does Innovation Cause Exports? Evidence from Exogenous Innovation Impulses and Obstacles Using German Micro Data', *Oxford Economic Papers* 58: 317–50.

Lambert R. (2003). *Lambert Review of Business–University Collaboration: Final Report*, London: HM Treasury.

Langlois R. N., Pugel T. A., Haklisch C. S., Nelson R. R. and Egelhoff W. G. (1988). *Microelectronics: an Industry in Transition*, Boston, MA: Unwin-Hyman.

Lefebvre E. and Lefebvre L. A. (2001). 'Innovative Capabilities as Determinants of Export Performance and Behaviour: a Longitudinal Study of Manufacturing SMEs', in A. Kleinknecht and P. Mohnen (eds) *Innovation and Firm Performance. Econometric Explorations of Survey Data*, Hampshire, UK and New York: Palgrave, 281–309.

Lindholm Dahlstrand A. and Klofsten M. (2002). 'Growth and Innovation Support in Swedish Science Parks and Incubators', in R. P. Oakey, W. During and S. Kauser (eds) *New Technology-Based Firms in the New Millennium*, Vol. II, Oxford: Elsevier Science.

Lockett A., Siegel D., Wright M. and Ensley M. (2005). 'The Creation of Spin-Off Firms at Public Research Institutions: Managerial and Policy Implications', *Research Policy*, 34(7): 981–93.

Losch A. (1954). *The Economics of Location*, New Haven, CT: Yale University Press.

Luttrell W. F. (1962). *Factory Location and Industrial Movement*, London: National Institute for Economic and Social Research (NIESR).

McAuley A. (1999). 'Entrepreneurial Instant Exporters in the Scottish Arts and Crafts Sector', *Journal of International Marketing*, 7(4): 67–92.

McCartan-Quinn D. and Carson D. (2003). 'Issues Which Impact upon Marketing in the Small Firm', *Small Business Economics*, 21(2): 201–13.

Macdonald and Lefang (1998). 'Patents and Policy in the Innovation of Small and Medium Sized Firms: Building on Rothwell', in R. P. Oakey and W. During (eds) *New Technology-Based Firms in the 1990s*, Vol. V, London: Paul Chapman Publishing.

Macmillan H. (1931). *Report of the Committee on Finance and Industry*, Cmnd. 3897, London: HMSO.

Magee B. (1973). *Popper*. London: Fontana/Collins.

Manchester City Council (2010). Report to the Economy, Employment and Skills Overview and Scrutiny Committee, 15 December.

Markusen A., Hall P. and Glasmeier A. (1986). *High Tech America*, London: Allen & Unwin.

Marris R. (1964). *Managerial Capitalism*. London: Macmillan.

Marshall A. (1920). *Principles of Economics*, London: Macmillan.

Martin J. E. (1966). *Greater London: an Industrial Geography*, London: Bell.

Martin R. (1999). 'The New Geographical Turn in Economics: Some Critical Reflections', *Cambridge Journal of Economics*, 23(1): 65–91.

Marx K. (1961 [1867]). *Capital* [Transl. S. Moore and E. Aveling], Moscow: Foreign Language Publishing House.

Mason C., McNally K. and Harrison R. (1996). 'Sources of Equity Capital for Small Growing Firms: Acost's "Enterprise Challenge" Revisited', in R. P. Oakey (ed.) *New Technology-Based Firms in the 1990s, Vol. II*, London: Paul Chapman Publishing, 8–24.

Mason C., Cooper S. Y. and Harrison R. (2002). 'The Role of Venture Capital in the Development of High Technology Clusters: the Case of Ottawa', in R. P. Oakey, W. During and S. Kauser (eds) *New Technology-Based Firms in the New Millennium*, Vol. II, Oxford: Elsevier Science, 261–77.

Mason D. (1979). 'Factors Affecting the Successful Development and Marketing of Innovative Semiconductor Devices', unpublished PhD thesis, SPRU, University of Sussex.

Massey D., Quintas P. and Weild D. (1992). *High Tech Fantasies: Science Parks in Society*, London: Routledge.

Moenaert R. K. and Souder W. E. (1990). 'An Analysis of the Use of Extrafunctional Information by R&D and Marketing Personnel', *Journal of Product Innovation Management*, 7: 213–19.

Molla A. and Licker P. S. (2005). 'eCommerce Adoption in Developing Countries: A Model and Instrument', *Information & Management*, 42: 877–99.

Morse R. S. (1976). 'The Role of New Technology Enterprises in the US Economy', Report of the Commerce Technical Advisory Board to the Secretary of Commerce.

Murray G. and Lott J. (1995). 'Have Venture Capital Firms a Bias against Investment in High Technology Companies?', *Research Policy*, 24(1): 283–99.

Nicholls V. (1969). 'Growth Poles: an Evaluation of their Propulsive Effect', *Environment and Planning*, 1: 193–208.

Oakey R. P. (1984a). *High Technology Small Firms: Innovation and Regional Development in Britain and the United States*, London: Frances Pinter.

Oakey R. P. (1984b). 'Finance and Innovation in Small Independent Firms', *Omega, International Journal of Management Science*, 12(2): 113–24.

Oakey R. P. (1985a). 'Agglomeration Economies: their Role in the Concentration of High Technology Industries', in P. Hall (ed.) *Silicon Landscapes*, London: Allen & Unwin, 94–117.

Oakey R. P. (1985b). 'British University Science Parks and High Technology Small Firms: a Comment on the Potential for Sustained Economic Growth', *International Journal of Small Business,* 4(1): 58–67.

Oakey R. P. (1991). 'Innovation and the Management of Marketing in High Technology Small Firms' *Journal of Marketing Management*, 7: 343–56.

Oakey R. P. (1993). 'Predatory Networking: the Role of Small Firms in the Development of the British Biotechnology Industry', *International Small Business Journal*, 11(4): 9–22.

Oakey R. P. (1995). *High Technology New Firms: Variable Barriers to Growth*, London: Paul Chapman Publishing.

Oakey R. P. (2003a). 'Funding Innovation and Growth in UK New Technology-based Firms: Some Observations on Contributions from the Public and Private Sectors', *Venture Capital*, 5(2): 161–79.

Oakey R. P. (2003b). 'Technical Entrepreneurship in High Technology Small Firms: Some Observations on the Implications for Management', *Technovation*, 23: 679–88.

Oakey R. P. (2003c). Cluster Development in the North West of England, Report to the North West Regional Development Agency.

Oakey R. P. (2007a). 'A Commentary on Gaps in Funding for Moderate "Non-Stellar" Growth Small Businesses in the United Kingdom', *Venture Capital*, 9(3): 223–35.

Oakey R. P. (2007b). 'R&D Collaboration between High Technology Small Firms (HTSFs) in Theory and Practice', *R&D Management*, 37(3): 237–48.

Oakey R. P. (2007c). 'An Analysis of the International Trade Performance of New High Technology Firms in and near the Daresbury Innovation Centre', Report to the Daresbury Innovation Centre Director, Cheshire, United Kingdom.

Oakey R. P. and Rothwell R. (1986). 'The Contribution of High Technology Small Firms to Regional Employment Growth', in A. Amin and J. B. Goddard (eds) *Regional Industrial Change*, London: Allen & Unwin, 258–84.

Oakey R. P. and Cooper S. Y. (1989). 'High Technology Industry, Agglomeration, and the Potential for Peripherally Sited Small Firms', *Regional Studies*, 23(4): 347–59.

Oakey R. P. and Mukhtar S-M. (1999). 'United Kingdom High Technology Small Firms in Theory and Practice: a Review of Recent Trends', *International Journal of Small Business*, 17(2): 48–-64.

Oakey R. P., Thwaites A. T. and Nash P. A. (1980). 'The Regional Distribution of Innovative Manufacturing Establishments in Britain', *Regional Studies*, 13(3): 235–53.

Oakey R. P., Rothwell R. and Cooper S. Y. (1988). *The Management of Innovation in High Technology Small Firms*, London: Frances Pinter.

Oakey R. P., Hare P. G. and Balasz K. (1990a). 'The Diffusion of Process Innovations in an East European Economy: Some Conceptual Observations', *Science and Public Policy*, 17(2): 97–104.

Oakey R. P., Kipling M. and Wildgust S. (2001). 'Clustering among High Technology Small Firms: the Anatomy of the Non-Broadcast Visual Communications Sector', *Regional Studies*, 35(5): 401–14.

Oakey R. P., Faulkner W., Cooper S. Y. and Walsh V. (1990b). *New Firms in the Biotechnology Industry: their Contribution to Innovation and Growth*, London: Frances Pinter.

Office for National Statistics (2004). 'The North West Planning Region', *Regional Trends.*Office of Technology Assessment (1984). *Commercial Biotechnology: an International Analysis*, Washington, DC: Government Printing Office.

Olsen R. D. (1975). *Studies in Export Promotion: an Attempt to Evaluate Export Stimulation Measures for the Swedish Textile and Clothing Industries*, Studia Oeconomiae Negotiorum, Uppsala: University of Uppsala.

Pavitt K. L. R. and Soete L. C. G. (1980). 'Innovative Activity and Export Shares', in K. L. R. Pavitt (ed.) *Technical Innovation and British Economic Performance*, London: Macmillan.

Perroux F. (1955). 'Note sur la Notion de Pôle de Croissance', *Economie Appliequé*, 8 [Translated version in D. L. McKee and W. H. Leahy (1970). *Regional Economics*, New York: New York Free Press, 93–103.]

Pittaway L. and Robertson M. (2004). 'Business to Business Networking and its Impact on Innovation; Exploring the UK Evidence', Working Paper 2004/032, Lancaster University Management School.

Popper K. (1965). *The Logic of Scientific Discovery*, New York: Harper Torch Books.

Porter M. (1998). *On Competition*, Boston, MA: The Harvard Business Review Book Series.

Pred A. R. (1965). 'The Concentration of High-Value-Added Manufacturing', *Economic Geography*, 41: 108–32.

Premus R. (1982). *Location of High Technology Firms and Regional Economic Development*, staff study for the sub-committee on monetary and fiscal policy, Joint Economic Committee of Congress, Washington, DC: Government Printing Office.

Reid G. C. and Smith J. A. (2003). 'Venture Capital and Risk in High-Technology Enterprises', *International Journal of Business and Economics*, 2(3): 227–44.

Riley R. C. (1973). *Industrial Geography*, London: Chatto and Windus.

Roberts E. B. (1991). *Entrepreneurs in High Technology*, Oxford: Oxford University Press.

Ross H. (2002). 'Supporting High Technology Start-Ups: the Scottish Experience', in R. P. Oakey, W. E. During and S. Kauser (eds) *New Technology-Based Firms in the New Millennium*, Vol. II, Oxford: Elsevier Science, 7–16.

Rothwell R. (1994). 'The Changing Nature of the Innovation Process: Implications for SMEs', in R. P. Oakey (ed.) *New Technology-Based Firms in the 1990s*, Vol. I, London: Paul Chapman Publishing.

Rothwell R. and Zegveld W. (1981). *Industrial Innovation and Public Policy*, London: Frances Pinter.

Rothwell R. and Zegveld W. (1982). *Innovation in the Small and Medium Sized Firm*, London: Frances Pinter.

Russell Group (2010). *The Economic Impact of Research Conducted in Russell Group Universities*, Russell Group Papers, Issue 1, London: Russell Group.

Saarenketo S. (2004). 'Born Global Approaches to the Internationalisation of High Technology Small Firms – Antecedents and Management Challenges', in W. During, R. P. Oakey and S. Kauser (eds) *New Technology-Based Firms in the New Millennium, Vol. III*, Oxford: Pergamon/Elsevier Science, 278–293.

Sant M. E. (1975). *Industrial Movement and Regional Development: the British Case*, Urban and Regional Planning Series, Vol. II, Oxford: Pergamon Press.

Santarelli E. and D'Altri S. (2003). 'The Diffusion of E-commerce among SMEs: Theoretical Implications and Empirical Evidence', *Small Business Economics*, 21(3): 273–83.

Saxenian A. (1985). 'Silicon Valley and Route 128: Regional Prototypes or Historic Exceptions?', in M. Castells (ed.) *High Technology, Space and Society*, Beverley Hills, CA and London: Sage Publications, 81–105.

Schmookler J. (1966). *Invention and Economic Growth*, Boston, MA: Harvard University Press.

Schumpeter J. (1939). *Business Cycles: A Theoretical, Historical and Statistical Analysis of the Capitalist Process*, 2 Vols., New York: McGraw-Hill.

Schumpeter J. (1942). *Capitalism, Socialism and Democracy*. New York: Harper & Row.

Scott A. (1993). *Technopolis: High Technology Industry and Regional Development in Southern California, Berkeley, and Los Angeles*, Berkeley, CA: University of California Press.

Select Committee on Science and Technology (1993). *Realising our Potential: A Strategy for Science, Engineering and Technology*, Cmnd. 2250, London: HMSO.

Simon H. A. (1955). 'The Role of Expectations in an Adaptive Behaviouralistic Model', in J. Bowman (ed.) *Experimentation, Uncertainty and Business Behaviour*, New York: SSRC.

Smallbone D., North D., Vickers I. and McCarthy I. (2000). 'Policy Support for R&D in SMEs: the UK Government's Smart Award Scheme', Centre for Enterprise & Economic Development Research, Middlesex University Business School, London.

Smith I. J. (1979). 'Some Implications on Inward Investment through Take-Over Activity', *Northern Economic Review*, 2: 1–5.

Snow, C. P. (1959). *The Two Cultures and the Scientific Revolution*, Rede Lecture, New York: Cambridge University Press.

Solow R. (1957). 'Technical Change and the Aggregate Production Function', *Review of Economics and Statistics*, 39: 312–20.

Stockport G. and Kakabadse A. (1994). 'New Technology-Based Firms and Inter-Organisational Networks: Developing a Conceptual Framework', in R. P. Oakey (ed.) *New Technology-Based Firms in the 1990s*, Vol. I, London: Paul Chapman.

Storey D. (1994). *Understanding the Small Firms Sector*, London: Routledge.

Storey D. J. (1982). *Entrepreneurship and the Small Firm*, London: Croom Helm.

Swann P., Prevezer M. and Stout D. (eds) (1998). *The Dynamics of Industrial Clustering: International Comparisons in Computing and Biotechnology*, Oxford: Oxford University Press.

Taylor M. J. (1971). 'Spatial Linkages in the West Midlands' Iron Foundry Industry', unpublished PhD thesis, University of London.

The Guardian (2011). 'British Manufacturing Reality Bites', 25th of April.

Thwaites A. T. (1978). 'Technological Change, Mobile Plants and Regional Development', *Regional Studies*, 12: 445–61.

Townroe P. M. (1971). *Industrial Location Decisions*, Occasional Paper No. 15, Centre for Urban and Regional Studies, University of Birmingham.

Trinity College, Cambridge (1983). *Cambridge Science Park Directory*, Cambridge: Trinity College, University of Cambridge.

Weber A. (1929). *Alfred Weber's Theory of the Location of Industry* [Transl. C. J. Friedrich], Chicago, IL: University of Chicago Press.

Westhead P. and Cowling M. (1995). 'Employment Change in Independent Owner-Managed High Technology Firms in Great Britain', *Small Business Economics*, 7(2): 111–40.

Westhead P., Batstone S. and Martin F. (2000). 'Technology-Based Firms Located on Science Parks: the Applicability of Bullock's Soft-Hard Model', *Enterprise and Innovation Management*, 1(2): 107–39.

Wilson H. (1979). *The Financing of Small Firms*, Report of the Committee to Review the Functioning of Financial Institutions, Cmnd. 7503, London: HMSO.

Wise M. J. (1949). 'On the Evolution of the Gun and Jewellery Quarters in Birmingham', *Transactions of the Institute of British Geographers*, 15: 57–72.

Wood P. (1969). 'Industrial Location and Linkage', *Area* 2: 32–9.

Index